Palgrave Studies on Children and Development

Series Editors
Jo Boyden, Department of International Development, University of Oxford, Oxford, UK
Roy Huijsmans, International Institute of Social Studies, Erasmus University Rotterdam, Den Haag, The Netherlands
Nicola Ansell, Social and Political Sciences, Brunel University London, Uxbridge, Middlesex, UK

The series focuses on the interface between childhood studies and international development. Children and young people often feature as targets of development or are mobilized as representing the future in debates on broader development problems such as climate change. Increased attention to children in international development policy and practice is also fuelled by the near universally ratified United Nations Convention on the Rights of the Child and the recently adopted Sustainable Development Goals.

Nonetheless, relatively little has been written on how the experience of childhood and youth is shaped by development as well as how young people as social actors negotiate, appropriate or even resist development discourses and practices. Equally, the increased emphasis in research on children and young people's voices, lived experiences and participation has yet to impact policy and practice in substantial ways.

This series brings together cutting-edge research presented in a variety of forms, including monographs, edited volumes and the Palgrave Pivot format; and so furthers theoretical, conceptual and policy debates situated on the interface of childhood and international development. The series includes a mini-series from Young Lives, a unique 15-year longitudinal study of child childhood poverty in developing countries. A particular strength of the series is its inter-disciplinary approach and its emphasis on bringing together material that links issues from developed and developing countries, as they affect children and young people. The series will present original and valuable new knowledge for an important and growing field of scholarship.

More information about this series at
https://link.springer.com/bookseries/14569

Neil Howard · Samuel Okyere
Editors

International Child Protection

Towards Politics and Participation

Editors
Neil Howard
Department of Social
and Policy Sciences
University of Bath
Bath, UK

Samuel Okyere
School of Sociology, Politics
and International Studies
University of Bristol
Bristol, UK

Palgrave Studies on Children and Development
ISBN 978-3-030-78762-2   ISBN 978-3-030-78763-9 (eBook)
https://doi.org/10.1007/978-3-030-78763-9

© The Editor(s) (if applicable) and The Author(s), under exclusive license to Springer Nature Switzerland AG 2022
This work is subject to copyright. All rights are solely and exclusively licensed by the Publisher, whether the whole or part of the material is concerned, specifically the rights of translation, reprinting, reuse of illustrations, recitation, broadcasting, reproduction on microfilms or in any other physical way, and transmission or information storage and retrieval, electronic adaptation, computer software, or by similar or dissimilar methodology now known or hereafter developed.
The use of general descriptive names, registered names, trademarks, service marks, etc. in this publication does not imply, even in the absence of a specific statement, that such names are exempt from the relevant protective laws and regulations and therefore free for general use.
The publisher, the authors and the editors are safe to assume that the advice and information in this book are believed to be true and accurate at the date of publication. Neither the publisher nor the authors or the editors give a warranty, expressed or implied, with respect to the material contained herein or for any errors or omissions that may have been made. The publisher remains neutral with regard to jurisdictional claims in published maps and institutional affiliations.

Cover illustration: © DrAfter123/DigitalVision Vectors/Getty Image

This Palgrave Macmillan imprint is published by the registered company Springer Nature Switzerland AG
The registered company address is: Gewerbestrasse 11, 6330 Cham, Switzerland

For our children.

And for the millions around the world who are failed by protection systems that seek to save them, rather than support them.

Acknowledgements

By their nature, books are very collaborative endeavours. In this case, we have collaborated with each other as editors, with all our contributors and reviewers, with the wonderfully supportive (and patient) team at Palgrave, with our employers (the Universities of Bath and Bristol), with our partners, and with our children. We've also collaborated with colleagues across the world whose expertise and insight have taught us so much, and with the children whose difficulties at the hands of the international child protection regime have both saddened and motivated us. Beyond this, given the interwoven nature of life, we collaborate in minute ways every day with the people and services that produce the food we eat, the energy we consume, the public services we rely on, and the tools of our trade. Likewise, despite entrenched attempts to convince us and everyone else of otherwise, we collaborate too with our planet, albeit not in the fully reciprocal way that it merits. All of which is to say that, like any endeavour, editing this book has been supported by countless actions from countless others—to all of whom we are grateful.

Sadly, we live under capitalism. And under capitalism money is king. In the course of producing this book, we received funding from a variety of sources, including our universities, our previous universities (Antwerp and Nottingham), and a variety of grant-giving organisations, namely The Canadian Institute for Advanced Research, the Economic and Social Research Council, and the European Research Council. These have all contributed to making this book possible. As indeed have Routledge and

Springer Nature, for giving us permission to re-print the work featured in Chapters 2 and 8.

These are distressing times for our world and our lives as academics are about trying to make it better. This book is one small attempt in that direction. But being able to make it requires plenty of solidarity from those whose companionship and comradeship bring light to the darkness and put (preferably renewable) fuel in the tank. In our joint case, this includes the Children and Work Network, which is an inspiring collection of colleagues striving to make child protection work for working children and refusing to accept the blank denial of fact. There is also the team at Beyond Trafficking and Slavery, who have collectively built something special that reminds us both regularly that the optimism of the will can be a powerful force; and, indeed, many of our collaborators at Terre des Hommes, who genuinely try so often to do things differently. Without naming any names, all of you will know who you are. Likewise, we are deeply grateful to our respective partners, Asha and Irene.

Lastly, and in anticipation, we'd like to thank our readers. If you have this in your hands then you are likely interested in how to make the world work better for its children, in part by making those institutions that are supposed to work for its children work better than they do. Maybe you even work for one of those institutions—in which case, hat tip to you; and please know that we genuinely offer our critiques without condescension or judgement, but rather in the hope that they may serve as constructive and comradely feedback. If anyone doubts that or wants to discuss this or anything in the book, please do get in touch with us.

In solidarity,
Neil Howard
Samuel Okyere

Brighton and Nottingham
August 2020

Contents

1 Introduction: International Child Protection and Its Discontents   1
  Samuel Okyere

2 Moral Economies and Child Labour in Artisanal Gold Mining in Ghana   29
  Samuel Okyere

3 Intergenerational Activism as an Alternative to Child Saving: The Example of the Peruvian Movement of Working Children   57
  Jessica K. Taft

4 Illusions in the Protection of Working Children   77
  Michael Bourdillon and William Myers

5 Children Born of Wartime Captivity and Abuse: Politics and Practices of Integration in Northern Uganda   101
  Allen Kiconco

6 Protection Versus Reintegration of Child Soldiers: Assistance Trade-Offs Within the Child Protection Regime   121
  Jaremey R. McMullin

7	Children's Rights and Child Prostitution: Critical Reflections on Thailand in the 1990s and Beyond Heather Montgomery	147
8	Why Child Mobility Is Not Always Child Trafficking: The Moral Economy of Children's Movement in Benin and Ethiopia Jo Boyden and Neil Howard	167
9	Child Protection in Palestine and Jordan: From Rights to Principles? Jason Hart	189
10	Conclusion: Towards Politics and Participation Neil Howard	213
11	Postscript: What Is Wrong with International Child Protection and What Changes Are Needed? Jo Boyden	225

Index 241

NOTES ON CONTRIBUTORS

Michael Bourdillon, D.Phil. Oxon., taught as a Social Anthropologist for many years in the Department of Sociology, University of Zimbabwe, where he retains the title of Emeritus Professor. While there he published extensively on Zimbabwean ethnography and the anthropology of religion. His recent research and publications have focussed on children in a variety of difficult circumstances, with special attention to working children.

Jo Boyden is a social anthropologist, Professor Emerita, and former Director of Young Lives, a comparative mixed-methods longitudinal study of childhood poverty based at the University of Oxford's Department of International Development. Her research has centred on children's education and work and the association with aspirations and social mobility, as well as young people's experiences of and responses to poverty, armed conflict and forced migration, specifically the developmental and wellbeing outcomes of risk exposure and the factors that contribute to vulnerability and resilience. She has many years of experience working with diverse stakeholders (governments, IGOs, INGOs, CSOs, research institutes, communities and young people) in the use of research evidence to design appropriate policies and programmes for young people living in situations of adversity.

Jason Hart is a Senior Lecturer in Humanitarianism and International Development at the University of Bath, and a Visiting Lecturer in the

Center for Children's Rights Studies at the University of Geneva. His research has explored the experiences of young people in settings of armed conflict and displacement, and the nature of institutional responses, particularly in the Middle East.

Neil Howard is a Lecturer in International Development at the University of Bath. His research focusses on the governance of exploitative and the so-called 'unfree' labour and in particular the various forms of it targeted for eradication by the Sustainable Development Goals. He conducts ethnographic and participatory action research with people defined as victims of trafficking, slavery, child labour and forced labour, and political anthropological research on the institutions that seek to protect them. Currently, he leads a large-scale pilot trialing both action research and unconditional basic income as potential policy responses to indecent or exploitative work in Hyderabad, India. He is the author of *Child Trafficking, Youth Labour Mobility, and the Politics of Protection*, previously published in this series.

Allen Kiconco received her Ph.D. in African Studies from the Department of African Studies and Anthropology, the University of Birmingham in 2015. Since 2017, she has been a postdoctoral fellow at the University of the Witwatersrand. Allen works on the lived experiences of women and girls in both conflict and post-conflict settings of Africa, including abduction, captivity, sexual slavery, forced marriage and forced pregnancy. This work includes extensive fieldwork with former combatants and sexual violence survivors in northern Uganda and Sierra Leone.

Jaremey R. McMullin is a Senior Lecturer in the School of International Relations at the University of St Andrews. He received his D.Phil. in International Relations from the University of Oxford. He has published research on ex-combatant reintegration in *International Peacekeeping*, *Review of International Studies*, and *Third World Quarterly*. His 2013 monograph, *Ex-combatants and the Post-conflict State: Challenges of Reintegration*, was published by Palgrave Macmillan's Rethinking Political Violence series. He has also produced evaluations and reports on ex-combatant reintegration for the United Nations Department of Peace Operations in Liberia and Burundi.

Heather Montgomery is a Reader in the Anthropology of Childhood at The Open University. She is a social anthropologist interested in ideas of childhood and cross-cultural parenting and also of children's rights. She is the author of *Modern Babylon? Prostituting Children in Thailand* (Berghahn, 2001) and *An Introduction to Childhood: Anthropological Perspectives of Children's Lives* (Blackwell, 2008), the co-author (with Victoria Cooper and Kieron Sheehy) of *Parenting the First Twelve Years: What the Evidence Tells Us* (Pelican, 2018) and the co-editor with Martin Robb of *Children and Young People's Worlds* (Policy Press, 2018), and with Martin Robb and Rachel Thomson of *Critical Practice with Children and Young People* (Policy Press, 2019).

William Myers, MPA, Ed.D. is retired from the United Nations, where he worked for UNICEF and the International Labor Office on child protection issues, especially in regards to working children. He is an independent researcher and author or co-author of various publications, including, co-edited with Michael Bourdillon, *Child Protection in Development*, Routledge, 2013.

Samuel Okyere is a Senior Lecturer at the University of Bristol. He is interested in the use of sociological, anthropological, and policy perspectives to address, especially in African contexts, the interplay between human and child rights, power, class, ethnicity, (un)freedom, inequality, the legacies of slave trade, and colonisation under conditions of globalisation. Over the last decade, he has pursued this overarching interest through studies on child labour and child work, migration, land grabs, mining, prostitution, forced labour, precarious labour, trafficking, 'modern slavery', and contemporary abolitionism.

Jessica K. Taft is an Associate Professor of Latin American & Latino Studies at the University of California, Santa Cruz. She is the author of *The Kids Are in Charge: Activism and Power in Peru's Movement of Working Children* and *Rebel Girls: Youth Activism and Social Change Across the Americas*, as well as numerous articles on the political lives of children and youth in North and South America. Her research focuses on young people as political subjects and bridges the scholarship on childhood, youth, and girlhood, with research on social movements, activism, and political engagement and draws from intersectional feminism to illuminate how age functions as an axis of power and inequality in complex relation with other social differences.

CHAPTER 1

Introduction: International Child Protection and Its Discontents

Samuel Okyere

In social policy, development and humanitarian circles, few social problems elicit condemnation more quickly than those involving children. Consider 'trafficking' or 'labour exploitation', for example. Both are widely regarded as awful, but in each case, the addition of the prefix 'child'—as in 'child trafficking' or 'child labour exploitation'—renders the bad even worse. This is the power of the concepts of 'childhood' and 'child', especially as presented within dominant international child protection discourses underpinned by the United Nations Convention on the Rights of the Child (CRC), the International Labour Organisation's Minimum Age Convention (No.138) and the Worst Forms of Child Labour Convention (No. 182), among others. These UN Conventions

S. Okyere (✉)
School of Sociology, Politics and International Studies, University of Bristol, Bristol, UK
e-mail: sam.okyere@bristol.ac.uk

© The Author(s), under exclusive license to Springer Nature Switzerland AG 2022
N. Howard and S. Okyere (eds.), *International Child Protection*, Palgrave Studies on Children and Development,
https://doi.org/10.1007/978-3-030-78763-9_1

have collectively inspired major global consciousness on the state of childhood and children's rights and also informed the formation and expansion of diverse, influential and vibrant child rights actors and concerns in international development, social work, social policy, and many other fields. As the most widely ratified Convention in the history of the UN, the CRC has been most influential in this regard. Across the globe, national and regional governments, trades unions, academics, individual human rights advocates and innumerable non-governmental organisations (NGOs) have taken on the cause of this Convention. For many, the CRC (and to a lesser extent the International Labour Organisation [ILO] Conventions 138 and 182) is an affirmation by global leaders of children's important place in society and of their entitlement to special protections and rights in their own names. The Convention and other UN childhood-centric instruments have thus provided a 'language structure', as O'Byrne (2012) puts it, through which child rights claims can be made across the globe. Today, almost every country in the world has a form of national or regional legislation and policies driven by the language and political structure provided by the CRC and ILO Conventions 138 and 182.

Yet, behind this immense support lie significant problems. Child rights violations are still a commonplace occurrence across the globe. Children routinely suffer both structural and personal violence that make a mockery of commitments to their protection in rich, powerful and poor, less powerful nations alike. Indeed, despite the near universal ratification of the CRC, no country has successfully fulfilled all of the CRC's principles. Core tenets of the CRC such as non-discrimination have arguably retrogressed rather than progressed over the past decade. This is especially clear when we consider the oppressive and inhumane ways in which child migrants, refugees and asylum seekers are treated by some countries. At the time of writing this chapter, the forced separation of child migrants from their parents or adult companions, alongside the confinement of children in torturous and inhumane immigration detention facilities or refugee camps, are routine aspects of border control in the USA, Europe, Australia and many other places (O'Connell Davidson, 2016). Successive targets and deadlines set by global leaders for meeting children's rights to adequate standards of living, education, healthcare and other provisions have floundered in high-, middle- and low-income countries alike. In the area of children's work—a particular focus of this book—despite increased ratification of Conventions 138 and 182 and the intensification of child labour abolitionist efforts led by the ILO, the number of children estimated by the ILO to be in conditions of illegal or hazardous work fell by only 3% between 2008 and 2012 and 1% between 2012 and 2016 (ILO, 2017, p. 11). Based on this rate of decline, by even the most optimistic assessment, at least 52 million children will still be found in hazardous work in 2025 (ILO, 2017, p. 11), when all such cases should have been 'eradicated', according to Target 8.7 of the Sustainable Development Goals (SDGs).

From the foregoing, it should be clear that there are numerous disjunctures between the promises, potentials and ideals enshrined in the dominant international child rights conventions on one hand and the realities of many children's lived experiences on the other. Two questions therefore come to mind. First, what are the causes or causal factors of these disconnections and, second, how can these be bridged such that the virtuous promises made to children by world leaders can fully be realised? These two questions constitute the main preoccupation of this book. The book argues that more innovative and radical actions are needed to accelerate progress on all child rights issues, to genuinely protect the world's children from the various adversities they face, and more broadly to advance their well-being in the way that the child rights architecture aims to do. This point has been acknowledged by UNICEF, when it declared on the occasion of the 25th anniversary of the CRC, that 'business as usual' will not be enough to make the Convention's vision a reality for all children (UNICEF, 2014). This book argues that departure from business as usual and a move towards more innovative, renewed and radical thinking must start with an evaluation of the structure that has been at the helm of global child rights agendas for the past three decades and will continue driving those agendas for years to come. Indeed, our key objective is to critically interrogate this structure—which we describe as the 'international child protection regime'—through particular focus on its weaknesses and failures and how these can be overcome.

We adopt the phrase 'international child protection regime' to highlight a distinction between extant dominant international child protection practices and ideas on the one hand and 'child rights' more broadly conceived on the other. Recognition of this distinction is important in that we believe that it can help to promote better outcomes for children. To be clear, there are inseparable conceptual and practical relationships between the two. It is often the case that children needing special protection from dire circumstances also tend to be the ones whose rights are being most flagrantly violated, and far fewer children would require special protection measures if their rights were conscientiously honoured (Bissel et al., 2009, p. 5). This book therefore agrees that 'rights and protection concerns are a good marriage and belong together, each perspective illuminating and being illuminated by the other, each contributing to a unity greater than the sum of its parts' (Bissel et al., 2009, p. 5).

Nonetheless, there are also important distinctions between 'child rights' and 'child protection'. Child rights typically refer to (often abstract) sets of idea(l)s, provisions or entitlements intended to benefit children; the most notable articulations of which are the CRC and related international instruments. Child protection, on the other hand, typically denotes the measures or practices aimed at safeguarding children or protecting them against abuse and threats to their lives, well-being, development and other interests. The concept of child protection therefore forms part of child rights, as the four core tenets of the CRC make clear. However, child protection is *narrower* than child rights, in part because it focusses only on advancing children's negative freedoms from specific ills as opposed to their positive freedoms to enjoy worthwhile goods. In addition, its practices, values and standards are rooted in very particular socio-cultural, political and economic principles, idea(l)s and frameworks, even as it makes claims to universality. This means that alternative and arguably better child protection (and child rights) modalities and possibilities can and do exist outside those of the current regime, and—as we discuss later—ethnocentric insistence on the regime's strict parameters can sometimes be inimical to children's best interests.

We consequently apply the suffix 'regime', per Foucault's analysis (1975, p. 30; 1976, p. 30), to signify the *hegemonic* nature of the international child protection architecture and its operations. Thus, we define the 'international child protection regime' as the actors, corpus of knowledge, practices and 'scientific discourses' which presently dominate child rights debates and practices at national and global levels. These mainly include:

1. The dominant ways in which childhood and child rights issues of diverse forms are promoted and understood internationally;
2. The conventions, policies, activities and practices that dominate or have become socio-politically accepted as valid knowledge or truth in international child rights circles;

3. The organisations and individuals formally charged with policy-making on child rights issues, who therefore largely determine and sustain what are usually accepted as 'truths' or valid knowledge about child rights and how to protect or advance them;
4. The actors who by virtue of political, social and economic clout shape or sustain the positions adopted by those formally charged with determining legislation, policies and practices on child rights, child protection and child well-being;
5. The dominant ideas, practices, modalities, policies and interventions that are sanctioned and promoted by the above actors as the main legitimate bases for addressing or advancing child rights and well-being.

From the foregoing, it should be understood that the international child protection regime incorporates all international conventions and instruments relating to childhood and child rights such as the CRC, the ILO Conventions 138 and 182, the Protocol to Prevent, Suppress and Punish Trafficking in Persons, Especially Women and Children (hereafter Palermo Protocol) and the UN agencies behind these conventions. It also includes dominant interpretations and accepted truths around these conventions and how they should be operationalised. Likewise, it includes the accepted conceptions, practices and ideologies of childhood, child rights and child protection derived from them and from the mostly Western-based (or backed) actors whose beliefs, policies and practices presently dominate the international child rights advocacy, humanitarianism, social work and development landscapes. (For sure, these landscapes have recently witnessed changes inspired by the increasing influence of China, Brazil and India, among others with ideologies, attitudes and approaches to childhood, child rights and child protection that diverge from those held by the dominant Western based societies and institutions. However, the reality is that global wealth, political power and influence in the international child protection field and in cognate fields such as international development are still largely driven by the dominant Western-based or derived ideologies, practices, funding and institutions.) A fourth element of the international child protection regime is the broad spectrum of individuals, rights activists, social movements, multinational corporations, NGOs and governments who support, apply and sustain the regime's ideologies, practices and conventions (see Howard, 2017 for further discussion of this point, especially as it relates to children's work and mobility).

An Outline of the Foundations of the International Child Protection Regime

On 20 November 1959, the UN General Assembly adopted the Declaration of the Rights of the Child, marking one of the most significant milestones in the genealogy of the international child protection regime. The premise for the Declaration of the Rights of the Child was simple: society owes children special safeguards and care, including legal protection before and after birth because of their physical and mental immaturity relative to adults. In adopting the Declaration of the Rights of the Child, the UN General Assembly promised to continuously seek the improvement of children's well-being and development over the world. Consequently, on the 30th anniversary of the adoption of the Declaration of the Rights of the Child, concerned that many children across the globe were in perilous situations and that these were worsening due to inadequate social, political and economic conditions, natural disasters, armed conflicts, exploitation, illiteracy, hunger and disability, the General Assembly adopted the Convention on the Rights of the Child as a legally binding instrument to accelerate child protection, development and well-being. The CRC's core remit, akin to its predecessors', was to pursue children's fundamental rights to survival, protection from abuse and exploitation such that they could have a chance to develop to their fullest potential and fully participate in socio-cultural and family life.

The CRC is presently the most widely supported UN Convention and also the most comprehensive international statement of child rights to date. UNICEF is implicitly assigned the role of the Convention's guardian as it is named in Article 45 as a body which can provide expert advice and assistance on children's rights. Additionally, on February 27, 1991, the UN established the Committee on the Rights of the Child as a body of eighteen independent experts to monitor the CRC's progress and implementation by the states that have ratified it.

Concurrent to these wider measures on children's rights, the ILO has focused more exclusively on the elimination of child labour for over a century. This objective was adopted as one of the ILO's core remits at its foundation in 1918. Article 427 of the Treaty of Versailles, which brought the ILO into being, stipulates that one of the ILO's most important functions is to seek the abolition of child labour and the imposition of such limitations on the labour of young persons as shall permit the continuance of their education and ensure their proper physical development. To this end, over the last century the ILO has established a raft of international conventions aimed at regulating and eliminating children's involvement in jobs that the ILO deems unfit for children. Notable among these conventions are the Minimum Age Convention No. 138, through which the ILO banned paid work or formal employment of children under 12 years of age. Convention 138 also limited the employment of those under 14 to a maximum of 14 hours per week and those under 17 to a maximum of 43 hours per week. The second most significant milestone in the ILO's child labour abolitionist mission was the adoption of the Worst Forms of Child Labour (Convention No. 182) and the accompanying Worst Forms of Child Labour Recommendation (No. 190) in 1999. A marked difference between Conventions 138 and 182 is that the latter is mainly interested in the elimination of children's involvement in work deemed especially egregious or harmful to them, rather than the elimination of all forms of work per se. The elimination of child trafficking, which is included in Convention 182, was further reaffirmed by the Palermo Protocol, adopted by the UN on November 15, 2000.

Collectively, the aforementioned international child rights declarations, conventions and protocols, and the UN agencies in charge of them, have inarguably afforded child rights an important place in international human rights considerations and practices. Child rights issues are today are seen both as 'special' and distinct and as part and parcel human rights issues more broadly. Likewise, they are embedded in international development agendas such as those enshrined in United National Sustainable Development Goals (SDGs). As Richardson et al. (2017, p. 8), posit: 'The Resolution adopted by the General Assembly on 25 September 2015—"Transforming Our World: The 2030 Agenda for Sustainable Development"—was unambiguous about the need for investing in all children, and for those children to be provided the safe, protective, and nurturing environments required for them to achieve their full potential, to be heard and to participate in change, and be supported in their roles as "critical agents" in the transformation of societies, and sustainable social and economic progress'.

It is worth stating that the lives of many children the world over have been improved as a result of this push towards children's rights.

At the policy level, innumerable regional and national governments, local and international NGOs, businesses, faith organisations, multinational corporations, academics, trades unions and individuals now belong to the global coalition of children's rights activists and advocates driving through legislation, financial, human and material investment and other transformations in an attempt to ensure that children are protected, provided with good healthcare and education, safeguarded from exploitation and violence, and afforded the resources and opportunities they require to thrive in their societies. Child mortality rates have been halved since 1990; globally, children were twice as likely to reach their fifth birthdays in 2017 as compared to 1990 (UNICEF, 2018). Also, despite recent setbacks in Afghanistan, Somalia and elsewhere, lifelong debilitating conditions such as polio have been virtually eliminated through measures such as the Universal Childhood Immunization Initiative and the Global Polio Eradication Initiative. In the area of education, while the Millennium Development Goal of attaining universal primary school education enrolment by 2015 was not attained, a still impressive 91% of children eligible for primary school were enrolled by 2015.

And yet most evaluations of the state of children's rights today show that we are still very far from fully attaining any of the promises made to the world's children. While there have been successes in areas such as those mentioned above, such progress seems mostly to be concentrated in the affluent countries of the Global North or in emerging economies such as China, India, Russia and Brazil. Progress in regions such as sub-Saharan Africa has been relatively modest, if there has been any at all. UNICEF's first study to quantify the number and depth of multi-dimensional child poverty in sub-Saharan Africa using data on individual children found that two of every three children in 30 countries (247 million children in total) are deprived of at least one of the following basic needs: good health, nutrition, water, housing and social protection (UNICEF, 2015). Likewise, as each of the chapters in this book demonstrates, we now have clear evidence that many interventions designed to protect or advance the rights and well-being of children, particularly in the Global South, not only fail but in fact make lives worse. Understanding the reasons behind these failings requires an urgent critical evaluation of the international child protection regime, its structures, ways of working, and received ideas, and it is on this basis that the book proceeds. The next sections of this chapter briefly trace the main thematic critiques to which it intends to contribute.

THEMATIC CRITIQUES OF THE INTERNATIONAL CHILD PROTECTION REGIME

A Universal Character?

Over the last four decades, scholars have noted that despite its virtuous ideals and claims to empower children, in practice the international child protection regime can be narrow, ethnocentric and disempowering for many children and their communities (Boyden, 1994; Gadda, 2008; Khan, 2010; Kaime, 2011; Liebel, 2012; Pupavac, 2001). The most significant and widely acknowledged aspect of this critique is its reliance on primarily Western-derived (neo)liberal, and romantic norms around childhood and child rearing, and its advocates' tendency to present these as the features of a universal, 'normal' or 'best' type of childhood, which is supposed to be fundamentally different from adulthood and primarily a time of (school-based) learning and play. These critiques therefore centre around how childhood is defined, what an 'ideal' childhood is like, how children should spend their time, as well as on policy and practice considerations over how best to promote children's rights, well-being and protection.

Per Article 1 of the CRC, which largely guides the international child protection regime's definition of childhood, a child is defined as every human below the age of 18, unless majority is attained earlier under the laws applicable to where a person lives. The second half of this definition acknowledges that the age 18 boundary set between childhood and adulthood is not fixed or immutable. Those who framed the Convention inarguably considered the diversity of childhoods and the fact that maturity and legal adulthood are attainable before one's 18th birthday. This is lent further credence by Article 5 which calls for attention to be placed on the child's maturity and evolving capacities instead of rigid adherence to chronological age considerations in some child rights considerations such as consent to medical treatment. Yet, this nuance has been lost in the decades following the CRC's adoption and implementation. The age 18 notion is largely presented as sacrosanct, unchangeable and an unquestionably universal standard for defining or determining childhood. Countries which ratify the CRC are placed under enormous pressure to conform to this supposed universal standard notwithstanding the Convention's definitional nuance as well as the paradox that virtually every country or society which has ratified it had and still maintains different (often lower) ages for most things typically considered to be appropriate for adulthood such as consent for sex, marriage, military service, and liability for criminal or civil proceedings among others.

Thus, rigid insistence on adherence to the age 18 framework overlooks the concern that while one's chronological age can signify one's level of biological development or (im)maturity, focusing exclusively on this criterion also risks reducing human maturity and competence to simple factors of biology and chronological age. In reality, there is nothing unique or special about one's 18th birthday which makes a person better or less suited to adulthood. Nothing changes biologically, physically or mentally on the night of one's 18th birthday that transforms a person into an adult or endows them with the skills, capacity and competences required for adult life. Historically, across many societies, childhood and adulthood represented stages on the ladder of social hierarchy and were not determined by chronological age alone but by other factors such as one's achievements, compliance with virtuous social norms and practices, and other criteria such as marriage or reproduction. In fact, antecedents of the CRC such as the Geneva Declaration on the Rights of the Child (1924) and the Declaration of the Rights of the Child (1959) did not prescribe minimum or maximum ages for childhood. They emphasised the status of children as rights-bearers and articulated some of these rights but left it to each individual state to apply them to the category of people they defined as children.

It is worth noting that efforts to establish an age barrier between adulthood and childhood in the CRC were hotly debated even by its drafters (Vandenhole et al., 2019, p. xxix). As Detrick (2009, pp. 645–657) notes, some members of the CRC Working Group (WG) proposed 18 as the upper age for childhood in order to ensure that 'childhood' be applied to as large an age group as possible and by extension maximise the number of people who could be protected by the CRC. This number was not meant as a definitive judgement on maturity or immaturity per se. Indeed, others in the WG argued that 18 years was quite late and that 14 would be a more appropriate upper limit for childhood because it was the end of compulsory education as well as the legal age for marriage in many countries at the time (Detrick, 2009, p. 58). A third group proposed that the limit be set at 15 in keeping with the position adopted by the UN General Assembly in relation to the International Year of the Child. Those advocating for age 18 prevailed, but only on the understanding that the definition would be qualified with the wording 'unless under the law applicable to the child majority is attained earlier'.

It is also important to stress that the WG's discussion of 'majority' was largely in reference to legal recognition rather than maturity or immaturity (Detrick, 2009, p. 59), for then as now, across many societies, whether one is regarded as 'mature' or competent rests upon a combination of considerations and not simply on chronological age. It is, of course, the case that a 7-year-old is likely to be biologically and physically less developed than an 18-year-old. However, as the literature on adolescence shows (see for example Arain et al., 2013; Jaworska & MacQueen, 2015; Sawyer et al., 2018), maturation boundaries are fluid and influenced by biological *and* environmental or social stimuli. Thus, a 16-year-old can be more biologically, emotionally and socially mature than an 18 or 22-year-old depending on the environmental and social stimuli to which they have been exposed and to which their 'maturation' ultimately represents their adaptation. Likewise, as O'Connell Davidson (2005, p. 3) argues, a drug-addicted, socio-politically disengaged 38-year-old is not necessarily better placed to make informed, competent choices than a 15-year-old non-drug user who is heavily invested in socio-political events in their society. The 'spirit' or intention behind the focus on age 18 by the CRC may have been to protect adolescents as 'children', but (mis)application of this intention and the CRC definition means that in some contexts the CRC is instead used to facilitate the infantilisation of adolescents and to impede their preparation for adulthood. The childhood label typically implies immaturity, incompetence and an inability to exercise meaningful agency and autonomy, a bracket from which this group of children are not allowed to escape until their eighteenth birthdays. As some have argued, the regime's excessive focus on chronological age creates a problem of 'age-normativity' whereby certain rights, responsibilities, and places, as well as the evaluation of the appropriateness of particular activities carried out by young people, are dissociated from life phases with little regard for other equally important social, cultural, historic factors surrounding the child's existence (Huijsmans, 2015, p. 14).

This age-normativity also illegitimises understandings of childhood which are contrary to the globalised middle-class ideas of 'age-appropriate behaviour' enshrined in much child protection practice and often reducible to the formula 'childhood = school + play' (Huijsmans, 2015, p. 15) coupled with dependence on adults rather than interdependence with adults. This is especially true for communities which have traditionally adopted a combination of calendar or chronological age, biological maturity and social experiences instead of chronological age alone to determine the status of minors or adults. Their ideas of childhood and related practices are stigmatised for not conforming to the regime's 'truths', even if these norms and practices are not inimical to their children's rights and best interests (Boyden, 1997; Howard, 2017; Pupavac, 2001). As such, there is an urgent need to rethink the construction and understanding of childhood which guides international child protection. The various ILO conventions on child labour and the CRC were all developed in particular historical, political and social moments which look different to the present era and neither can nor will hold for all times and all places. There is thus an urgent need to reconsider more holistic definitions of maturity and to move away from the fixation on chronological age. Clark-Kazak (2012) suggests that adoption of a 'social age' framework alongside the orthodox calendar or chronological age system may bring the international child protection regime much closer to the spirit of the CRC definition, the reality of the twenty-first century and the diverse natures and ways in which childhood is understood across the world. For sure, social age guidance may ensure greater support for the international child protection regime in contexts where chronological age is unworkable in practice.

Such calls have largely been ignored by the regime because the level and diversity of support it enjoys creates a belief among its advocates that the chronological age approach is unquestionably right. This imperviousness to calls for recognition of more diverse socio-culturally grounded ideas or practices of childhood and human maturation can lead to policy-making that harms both children and their communities. Ample evidence of this has been shown by studies carried out in countries as diverse as Benin (Howard & Morganti, 2015) and Bangladesh (Boyden et al., 1998). Large multi-country studies such as Young Lives and Time to Talk also demonstrate that interventions exclusively driven by the regime's normative ideas about childhood and its age-relatedness can further complicate rather than improve the situation of children facing adversity. Indeed, the wider childhood studies and international development literatures are replete with stories which demonstrate that many of the failures of the regime are because its practices map onto and sustain conservative, paternalistic and moralistic values that are oppressive to children and their societies.

Allen Kiconco's chapter in this book (Chapter 5) is a new addition to this literature. It presents the complex case of girls who were abducted by the Lord's Resistance Army (LRA) during the Ugandan civil war and forced to serve as conjugal partners ('forced wives') to male combatants who were themselves often very young at the time. Her study found that many of these initially forced conjugal associations subsequently developed into 'actual' marriages and resulted in children. Now that the war has ended, NGOs pursuing justice and the rights of children via conventional notions of childhood have complicated efforts by local communities to integrate former child combatants and their families using their own indigenous systems or practices. NGOs applying the international child protection regime's ideas and modalities on preventing 'child marriage' (and an associated view that former male combatants who were forcibly married to abducted girls ought to be punished, despite being forced to do so) have produced enhanced stigma towards those whose marriages still exist and in turn towards the children of such unions. While many of the young people involved in these marriages, their families and their communities wish to put the terrible circumstances underpinning the marriages behind them, their efforts to do so using indigenous systems that aim to safeguard the rights of children are being derailed or stymied by NGO discourses and practices which cast these marriages as illegitimate because of having taken place through force and when the people concerned were minors. The problem of a lack of socio-cultural sensitivity within aspects of the international child protection regime is therefore made abundantly clear by Kiconco's chapter, as is the rigid demarcation around biological age 18 in terms of deciding which reintegration approach is suited to whom.

Jaremey McMullin's chapter (Chapter 6) discusses the related issue of the regime's emphasis on criminalising the recruitment of children for war and conflict as a means to prevent states and non-state actors from doing so, regardless of the fact that such emphasis on criminalisation has had minimal impact on the prevention of child soldiering. Additionally, the chapter shows that the prioritisation of criminalisation produces trade-offs within assistance programmes for former child soldiers who are struggling to integrate economically, socially and politically after war, while in some cases perversely making life worse for former child soldiers by incentivising state actions that actually exclude them from reintegration efforts. Further, just as local communities in Uganda are not adequately consulted on reintegration and justice efforts or find their efforts undermined by the regime's actors, so too are former child soldiers rarely consulted about reintegration efforts after war. The chapter therefore highlights the paradox that while the CRC promises children a say in all matters and decisions directly affecting them (and for their views to be given due weight in accordance with their maturity), many actors within the international child protection regime fail to meaningfully guarantee children this right. Actors within the international child protection regime assume that they possess absolute authority or knowledge over what is best for children regardless of the social context or economic, political and cultural specificities. McMullin's chapter thus demonstrates how the regime's erroneous belief in the existence of a homogenous or universal type of childhood for which an 'à-la-carte' or 'one-size-fits-all' solution can be employed creates profound problems for efforts to address child soldiering and reintegration of child soldiers.

Another challenge confronting the international child protection regime is where attempts are made to merge local and global notions of child rights and protections without careful reflection. Sometimes, the issue is not so much a matter of whether there is a clash between universal and particular realities or local contexts, understandings and experiences of childhood and child rights practices. Instead, as Kiconco's and McMullin's chapters (Chapters 5 and 6 of this book) demonstrate, conflicts often emerge where regime actors fail to understand child rights as a holistic practice which requires flexibility as opposed to strict adherence to policy dictates and stipulations that are evidently unsuitable or unworkable in specified contexts.

The Politics of Children's Rights

All three chapters mentioned in the previous section underscore the critique that childhoods and communities which do not conform to the hegemonic norm advocated by the international child protection regime are discredited or maligned as inappropriate, 'backward' or 'anti-developmental'. The use of practices that are not harmful to children— such as puberty rites to delineate the boundary between adulthood and childhood, for example—has been demonised and policed out of existence in many communities where they were prevalent. The same is true for children's work and children's labour mobility practices. While the international child protection regime acknowledges that not all children's work is harmful, the tenor of campaigns aimed at prohibiting or eliminating harmful forms largely creates a perception that childhoods that are not completely work-free are anomalous or deprived of certain rights. As noted earlier, while the CRC itself is much more nuanced, chronological age as a basis for determining majority nonetheless remains pervasive within the international child protection regime, alongside the notion that anyone under 18 is immature, incapable or unwilling to take up work that may be deemed difficult and dangerous. This is especially true in the context of those who migrate or move to seek income-earning opportunities in spheres regarded as the preserve of adults. Such children are routinely misclassified as 'victims of trafficking' or as 'child slaves', as Chapters 2–4 and 8 in this volume make clear. The Palermo Protocol, for instance, considers the consent of anyone under 18 immaterial in determining whether or not that person is a victim of 'child trafficking'. A very low bar has been set by the Protocol in that the mere fact that a person under the age of 18 has travelled with others to take up work that some might class as 'exploitative' meets the threshold of evidence of child trafficking.

This observation is explicit in Chapter 8 by Neil Howard and Jo Boyden, which challenges policy discourses that frame children's independent movement as 'trafficking' or intrinsically exploitative and threatening to their development. Drawing on research with children and adults in Benin and Ethiopia, two countries that have been caught up in efforts to eradicate child migration and the trafficking with which it is often associated, the chapter critiques assumptions about children's inherent vulnerability and physical dependence and contests the idea that healthy childhoods are always necessarily fixed spatially within nuclear family structures. What is clear from the chapter is that children's migration is located within socio-cultural and economic contexts and forms part of a moral economy that confounds simplistic paradigms conflating migration with trafficking. The chapter also makes clear that so many children move in and out of work out of necessity. Thus, the responses to trafficking pursued by the international child protection regime can be limiting and, in some cases, disastrous to these children's attempts to access education, training, livelihood and developmental opportunities that may be linked to their mobility and work, an argument which Hashim and Thorsen (2011) and Howard (2017) have also made elsewhere.

The tendency is to seek to protect children by preventing their mobility and work, but rarely does the regime ask why children move for work or concern itself with addressing the underlying or direct causal factors of children's insecurities in low and middle-income countries. Consequently, many of the campaigns and interventions it produces target only the symptoms of these insecurities. Research has shown that children's work in agriculture (Berlan, 2009) artisanal gold mining (Okyere, 2013) and child prostitution (O'Connell Davidson, 2005) occur for reasons which include the destitution of their homes and communities, in turn related to unjust, historical and persistent global socio-economic and political-economic inequalities. Questions about these causes are rarely addressed by the regime because they are politically sensitive and potentially embarrassing to some regime funders and key actors. By actively avoiding such difficult questions and conversations, the international child protection regime has itself become partly complicit in entrenching the problems. Okyere's contribution to this volume—Chapter 2—provides more detailed analysis of this problem based on a study of the causal factors of children's involvement in artisanal gold mining work in Ghana. The chapter shows that the participation of Ghanaian children in such precarious work is one of the outcomes of structural adjustment and other draconian economic reforms imposed by the International Monetary Fund (IMF) on Ghana since the early 1980s. Yet, the regime's analysis of children's involvement in precarious labour in the country tends to blame local cultures, unscrupulous parents and other micro factors while keeping silent on the structural conditions identified by the chapter.

Similar problems can be found regarding the questions the regime asks or does not ask in relation to the treatment of child migrants, refugees and asylum seekers, and those caught up in situations of armed conflict or mass displacement in some countries. Much has been written of the treatment and experiences of children and youth fleeing war, socio-political persecution, famine, severe socio-economic hardship, drug cartel violence, forced conscription and other adversities in Syria, Afghanistan, Iraq, Sudan, Myanmar, Guatemala, El Salvador, Honduras, Eritrea and elsewhere. Many of these children and youth endure extreme violence, injuries, threats, malnutrition and other problems (Hart, 2015; Rees et al., 2015) at the hands of states and their agents who should in reality be protecting children's and young people's rights as articulated in the CRC and other international children's rights instruments. To compound this, the last two decades have witnessed a marked intensification in hostile immigration policies by many migrant receiving countries in the Global North. Relatively safe travel options used by children and their families have been shuttered by these countries or agents acting on their behalf, often under the guise of combatting child trafficking, human trafficking and human smuggling.

Many thousands of children and their families seeking refuge and better life chances are today forced to use the most perilous modes of travel via the Sahara Desert, Mediterranean and Aegean Seas (Bhabha, 2014; Human Rights Watch, 2009; Save the Children, 2017), while others run the gauntlet of drugs cartels, violent criminals and immigration officials alike (Cantor, 2016; Carlson & Gallagher, 2015; Clemens, 2017; Kennedy, 2014). For many of these children and their adult companions or families, surviving these perilous ordeals and getting into what are often the most stable and prosperous countries does not guarantee protection or peace (Allsopp & Chase, 2017; Hillmann & Dufner, 2019; Humphris & Sigona, 2017). Across Europe, North America and Australia, child migrants are routinely separated and placed in cold immigration holding cells, squalid facilities or camps where they face prolonged delays while their asylum and entry claims are assessed (Cuéllar, 2017; Johnson, 2015; Linton et al., 2017; Nye, 2018; Stubley, 2018). Indeed, while the international child protection regime is more concerned about safeguarding child migrants, asylum seekers and refugees from smugglers and traffickers, draconian and inhumane immigration systems probably constitute the greatest threat to the rights of such child migrants and their families—yet how often is this mentioned by regime actors?

A key root problem here is that ratification of international conventions such as the CRC is no guarantee that a country will actually implement them in full or even abide by any of their principles. And, while ratification is an important step it is also the case that some states parties ratify international conventions through immense pressure, in return for aid or to look good instead of being committed to the conventions per se. Reservations are also routinely used by countries to opt out of important provisions in international conventions, thereby reducing their efficacy. Even where conventions have been ratified without any reservations, the cost of non-compliance or non-implementation is low or non-existent, for rich and powerful countries especially. In fact, the paradox is that powerful advanced liberal democracies which are more likely to criticise others for non-compliance with international conventions are also most likely to set reservations while ratifying human and child rights conventions (Neumayer, 2007, p. 400). The issue of non-compliance by states parties is exacerbated by the fact that bodies such as the UN Committee on the Rights of the Child, which is responsible for monitoring the implementation of the CRC and overseeing measures against the involvement of children in armed conflict, the sale of children, child prostitution and child pornography, have no authority or power to call errant states to order.

The problems that attend on this lack of authority to hold states parties to account and the regime's associated strategy of pursuing patently political or polemic approaches to child rights in supposedly 'neutral' terms form the core thrust of Jason Hart's contribution to this volume, Chapter 9. This chapter highlights the obstacles surrounding the provision of humanitarian support for Iraqi children displaced to Jordan and for young Palestinians living under Israeli occupation. It underscores how NGOs and UN agencies working in these areas (and elsewhere) have adopted 'neutrality' and 'impartiality' codes which prevent them from criticising actors such as Israel, armed groups and others whose actions and inactions have produced the mass insecurities faced by children living under occupation and in the Jordanian refugee camps.

It is worth acknowledging, as Hart does, that these organisations are merely following the key tenet of humanitarian interventions, which is that they must by definition be neutral. Humanitarian agencies such as the International Red Cross, Save the Children and others would rightly assert that the only reason they are allowed to work in conflict zones with civilian populations is because they have committed to remaining 'neutral' and putting the care of civilian victims in emergencies above the politics and disagreements in the areas where they work. Hart posits however, that this 'apolitical' stance produces an approach to child protection which is primarily about throwing money, human and other resources at the symptoms and effects of harm. It could be argued too that in the Palestinian context, the main issue is not so much the neutrality or apolitical approach by humanitarian organisations but the fact that the protracted crisis is still largely defined and treated as a humanitarian emergency rather than a military occupation.

A linked critique is that the international child protection regime has failed to seek accountability from those states and actors whose actions have historically and persistently induced mass impoverishment, socialpolitical fragility and other root causes of child rights violations across the globe. In place of accountability, solidarity, restorative justice and other measures that may equalise unequal power relations, the regime is today dominated by actors pursing children's rights through 'rescue' and 'saviourism'. Responses to child soldiering, child labour, child prostitution, child trafficking, child domestic work, genital mutilation, child marriage and child homelessness are often driven by actors who rely on sensationalist popular narratives and thus overlook or oversimplify the historical, cultural, economic and other dynamics surrounding such problems and the lives and experiences of affected children and their communities. As O'Connell Davidson (2013, 2016) observes, well-meaning actors cast children as blank suffering bodies emptied of will, society, family and socio-political context who can be 'saved' or 'rescued' by the charitable acts of an individual or NGO. Charitable acts have a part to play in righting child wrongs, but the shift towards saviourism does very little to address the structural determinants of children's suffering.

Saviourism can also be highly imperialist for it largely involves top-down dictates from a relatively rich, influential or powerful actor in the Global North to a Global South actor whose relative socio-economic deprivation, marginalisation and lack of influence compels them to comply even if they do not agree with the proposed measures or consider them to be unworkable. Many child rights NGOs are well-meaning and genuinely committed to child protection, but they also secure funding for their work by staying adherent to the regime's dominant messages and modalities. This sometimes involves taking on the role of 'proper guardians' or agents on a civilising mission to the Global South to teach children and adults alike into conforming with the supposed universal ideals of a 'good childhood' (Valentin & Meinert, 2009, p. 23). Even where consultations are held with children and other stakeholders ostensibly to seek collaborative ways forward, the outcomes can be largely tokenistic and at times a facade for co-opting the less influential or powerful partner in the promotion of pre-determined positions.

The emergence of the 'modern slavery' discourse in the international child rights arena over the last two decades has been a key driver for the rise of saviourism, 'rescue' and 'abolitionism' to the top the international child protection regime's agenda. Omission of critical political economy analysis of how child rights and child protection issues are shaped by both local and global political and economic factors informs a tendency to blame cultural practices, child upbringing norms and values of the local communities (especially in the Global South) for children's suffering. This simplistic and stigmatising emphasis on local cultural norms serves to efface the connections between the local and global conditions within which children live and labour, sell sex, participate in armed conflict, move or are moved. A vivid example of this is offered by Heather Montgomery's chapter, Chapter 7, which is based on a study with a group of children in Thailand involved in selling sex to foreigners.

The chapter demonstrates that nearly two decades after the fieldwork (Montgomery, 2001), the international child protection regime remains stale and in urgent need of vibrancy and radical thinking. Nearly two decades of heartrending campaigns about child 'sexual slavery' and child sex tourism have failed to make a meaningful impact because these messages deploy sensationalism and melodrama instead of careful examination of the complexities surrounding this issue. The lingering ineffectiveness, the chapter concludes, is because the extant responses are made in abstraction from the socio-economic circumstances and lived experiences of the affected children, their families and their communities. Individual solutions are proffered for what are systemic or structural problems.

Accountability Lack

The foregoing underscores the problem that the international child protection regime is itself lacking in accountability to children and their representatives; especially those in marginalised, deprived or disenfranchised communities. Notions and practices of accountability in the regime, and in the international development sector more broadly, mainly flow upwards. Accountability is usually seen as the preserve of donors, institutions and individuals with power and privilege rather than children and 'beneficiaries' of interventions.

This theme is fleshed out powerfully by Michael Bourdillon and William Myers in Chapter 4. Drawing on more than 60 years' combined experience and understanding of the international child protection regime, these two eminent scholars provide an evaluative analysis of why child protection policies, practices and other measures become not only counterproductive but detrimental to children in some cases—for them, especially the case of child labour and children's work. For Bourdillon and Myers, the reason is that the organisations and policymakers at the forefront of international child protection fail or simply refuse to respond to the overwhelming evidence on the weaknesses in the measures or policies they put in place for child rights issues such as the prohibition of child labour. The regime judges the success of these interventions primarily in terms of the number of children who have been prohibited from taking up certain jobs rather than whether and how children's lives have been improved as a result of their removal from work. There have been numerous documented cases of how measures intended to counter child labour turned out to be against working children's best interests; mainly because such measures were more adherent to the views and interests of governments, businesses and other powerful stakeholders than those of children and their families. Far too often, the 'success' of child rights interventions is judged on the basis of whether influential stakeholders are satisfied with the outcomes, rather than whether children's social, economic, welfare needs and best interests (as co-determined with the children concerned) have been met (see Rahman et al., 1999; O'Neill, 2003, among others).

This accountability deficit is perhaps most evident in the ILO's persistent refusal to include organised groups of working children in deliberations on child labour and working children's rights—blatantly contravening the CRC's directive that children have a right to be consulted on matters which affect them. Working children and youth unions such as UNATSBO in Bolivia have amply demonstrated their capacity to advocate for their own rights with the due support from relevant authorities. In 2014, they successfully convinced the Bolivian government and parliament to amend the country's laws to permit children aged 10 years and older to carry out independent work and other income-earning activities, in a complete departure from the ILO Minimum Age Convention that permits formal work or paid employment only for those aged 14 and over. One of their main arguments, which is further advanced by Bourdillon and Myers' chapter, is that children's work would not be problematic if children were offered the same wages and protections as adults instead of being prevented from working even when they wish to or need to.

From their perspective, their cultural and socio-economic circumstances are not sufficiently weighed-up by the ILO and other regime actors whose sole focus is on the prohibition of their work instead of on addressing the factors necessitating their work. In a more just and accountable system, such groups of children who are so profoundly affected by the regime's protection measures, and who have managed to organise and are actively engaged in self-representation, would be held up as model for child participation rights and the exhibition of children's relative agency and capacity. Yet it is not just that the ILO and other leading organisations in the international child protection regime fail to include them in consultation and decision-making; it is also that these children are presented as deviants or threats. Because the disparities in their positions undermine the basis on which the ILO and other regime actors claim to be representing working children or advocating on their behalves.

This question of legitimacy and accountability is forcefully picked up in Jessica Taft's chapter (Chapter 3), which draws on the author's research with the Movimiento Nacional de Niños, Niñas y Adolescentes Organizados del Perú (MNNATSOP) and other organisations which form part of the Peruvian movement of working children. The chapter elaborates on these working children's advocacy and social movement organisation, showing how Peruvian working children and youth seek a model of protection which challenges the sometimes arbitrary barriers and limitations placed on their economic, social, and political participation by the international child protection regime. Thus, they challenge what Pupavac (2001) has described as the 'misanthropic vision of child rights', the emphasis on individual rights over collective rights, and the regime's patriarchal controls which exclude working children from crucial decision-making about their lives, contrary to its own dictates. In place of these, the Peruvian working children advocate for an intergenerational social movement in which children and adults work together in the pursuit of an explicitly political vision for progressive social change. A century after the ILO's formation and its vow to eliminate all forms of child labour, such radical changes may offer a more accelerated pathway to protecting working children's rights in light of the mixed successes and sometimes harmful outcomes of extant dominant measures. The inclusion of working children's unions and their representatives in policymaking and other deliberations on child labour will represent a true departure from 'business as usual'.

This theme among others in the earlier sections of the book is reprised by Jo Boyden's Postscript, which draws on Boyden's many decades of experience as a leading child protection researcher who has studied a range of child rights issues in a number of countries. The chapter also reflects findings from Young Lives, a multidisciplinary mixed-methods longitudinal study of thousands of boys and girls in poverty in Ethiopia, India, Peru and Vietnam for over 15 years. Boyden's contribution offers a timely assessment of the status of child rights and the protection regime built around them, as well as how this may be improved, three decades after her seminal warning around its trajectory in the immediate aftermath of the adoption of the CRC. It too concludes that a departure from business as usual is essential. Indeed, accelerating improvements in children's lives requires genuine commitments to making children agents of their own lives, empowering families and communities as the first line of child protection by providing them with a supportive economic and social environment, and ensuring that all child protection interventions are evidence-led. These points are echoed in this book's Conclusion (Chapter 10) by Neil Howard.

Conclusion

Three decades ago, the adoption of the CRC by the UN General Assembly marked a watershed moment in the history of international child protection. A vast and diverse range of actors have today coalesced around the implementation or application of the principles of the CRC and other UN child rights conventions. Immense financial, political, human and other resources have been devoted to this agenda, leading to some important successes in the areas of children's health and reduction in mortality rates. However, even the most optimistic observers agree on the need for a more focused and accelerated progress for attainment of all the promises international leaders have made to the world's children. Also, the era in which the CRC was adopted was substantially different than the present global political order where popular authoritarianism and an apparent retreat from internationalism are on the rise, the world of work is rapidly changing with robotics and other technology increasingly taking jobs, and the climate emergency is ever more likely to have a debilitating effect on us all, unless we see radical changes. Children's rights urgently require an international child protection regime that is adaptive to these shifting sands and inclusive of all diverse virtuous child protection ideologies instead of adhering to business as usual or twentieth-century rationalities.

Through rich empirical, historical and theoretical materials produced by some of the leading scholars and researchers of childhood, child rights, child protection and international development, this book provides examples coupled with critical evaluative analysis of these weaknesses within the international child protection regime and offers solutions for how both the problems and weaknesses identified may be addressed. The authors' collective conclusion is that it is time for genuinely bottom-up, non-dogmatic programming, for real political engagement with the politics of exploitation and injustice, for reflexivity, and for accountability.

References

Allsopp, J., & Chase, E. (2017). Best interests, durable solutions and belonging: Policy discourses shaping the futures of unaccompanied migrant and refugee minors coming of age in Europe. *Journal of Ethnic and Migration Studies*, 45(2), 293–311. https://doi.org/10.1080/1369183X.2017.1404265

Arain, M., Haque, M., Johal, L., Mathur, P., Nel, W., & Rais, A. (2013). Maturation of the adolescent brain. *Neuropsychiatric Disease and Treatment*, 9, 449–461. https://doi.org/10.2147/NDT.S39776

Berlan, A. (2009). Child labour and cocoa: Whose voices prevail? *International Journal of Sociology and Social Policy*, 29(3/4), 141–151.

Bhabha, J. (2014). *Child migration and human rights in a global age*. Princeton University Press.

Bissell, S, Boyden, J., Myers, W., & Cook, P. (2009). *Rethinking child protection from a rights perspective: Some observations for discussion International Institute for Child Rights and Development* (A White Paper).

Boyden, J. (1994). *The relationship between education and child work* (Innocenti Occasional Papers Child Right Series 9). UNICEF, Florence.

Boyden, J. (1997). Childhood and the policy makers: A comparative perspective on the globalisation of childhood. In A. James & A. Prout (Eds.), *Constructing and reconstructing childhood: Contemporary issues in the sociological study of childhood* (pp. 190–216). Falmer Press.

Boyden, J., Ling, B. & Myers, W. (1998). *What Works For Working Children*. Rädda Barnen & UNICEF.

Cantor, D. (2016). Gang violence as a cause of forced migration in the Northern Triangle of Central America. In D. J. Cantor & N. Rodríguez Serna (Eds.), *The new refugees: Crime and forced displacement in Latin America* (pp. 27–45). University of London.

Carlson, E., & Gallagher, A. M. (2015). Humanitarian protection for children fleeing gang-based violence in the Americas. *Journal on Migration and Human Security*, 3(2), 129–158.

Clark-Kazak, C. (2012). Challenging some assumptions about 'refugee youth.' *Forced Migration Review*, 40, 13–14.

Clemens, M. A. (2017). *Violence, development, and migration waves: Evidence from Central American child migrant apprehensions* (Working Paper 459). Center for Global Development, Washington, DC.

Cuéllar, G. (2017). Deportation as a sacrament of the state: The religious instruction of contracted chaplains in U.S. detention facilities. *Journal of Ethnic and Migration Studies*, 45(2), 253–272.

Detrick, S. L. (2009). *A commentary on the United Nations convention on the rights of the child*. Martinus Nijhoff Publishers.

Foucault, M. (1975). *Discipline and punish: The birth of the prisons* (A. Sheridan, Trans. from the French). Vintage Books.

Foucault, M. (1976). *"Society must be defended" lectures at the College De France, 1975–76* (D. Macey, Trans. from the French). Picador.
Gadda, A. (2008). *Rights, Foucault and power: A critical analysis of the United Nation Convention on the Rights of the Child* (Edinburgh Working Papers in Sociology). University of Edinburgh.
Hart, J. (2015). The (anti-)politics of child protection. *Open Democracy*. https://www.opendemocracy.net/en/beyond-trafficking-and-slavery/antipolitics-of-child-protection/. Accessed 13 June 2019.
Hashim, I., & Thorsen, D. (2011). *Child migration in Africa*. Zed Books.
Hillmann, L., & Dufner, A. (2019). Better off without parents? Legal and ethical questions concerning refugee children in Germany. *Journal of Ethnic and Migration Studies, 45*(2), 331–348. https://doi.org/10.1080/1369183X.2017.1404268
Howard, N. (2017). *Child trafficking, youth labour mobility and the politics of protection*. Palgrave.
Howard, N., & Morganti, S. (2015). (Not!) child trafficking in Benin. In M. Dragiewicz (Ed.), *Global human trafficking: Critical issues and contexts* (pp. 91–104). Routledge.
Huijsmans, R. (2015). Generationing development: An introduction. In R. Huijsmans (Ed.), *Generationing development: A relational approach to children, youth and development* (pp. 1–31). Palgrave.
Human Rights Watch. (2009). *Pushed back, pushed around Italy's forced return of boat migrants and asylum seekers, Libya's mistreatment of migrants and asylum seekers*. Human Rights Watch.
Humphris, R., & Sigona, N. (2017). Outsourcing the 'best interests' of unaccompanied asylum seeking children in the era of austerity. *Journal of Ethnic and Migration Studies* (Special Issue). https://doi.org/10.1080/1369183X.2017.1404266
ILO. (2017). *Global estimate of child labour alliance 8.7: Results and trends 2012–2016*. ILO.
Johnson, N. (2015). *Deterrence, detention, & deportation: Child migrants in the United States & the European Union*. Heinrich Böll Stiftung.
Jaworska, N., & MacQueen, G. (2015). Adolescence as a unique developmental period. *Journal of Psychiatry & Neuroscience: JPN, 40*(5), 291–293. https://doi.org/10.1503/jpn.150268
Kaime, T. (2011). *The convention on the rights of the child: A cultural legitimacy critique*. Europa Law Publishing.
Kennedy, E. (2014). *No childhood here: Why Central American children are fleeing their homes*. The American Immigration Council.
Khan, A. (2010). Discourses on childhood: Policy-making with regard to child labour in the context of competing cultural and economic perceptions. *History and Anthropology, 21*(2), 101–119.

Liebel, M. (2012). Do children have a right to work? Working children's movements in the struggle for social justice. In K. Hanson & O. Nieuwenhuys (Eds.), *Reconceptualizing children's rights in international development: Living rights, social justice, translations* (pp. 225–249). Cambridge University Press.

Linton, J. M., Griffin, M., & Shapiro, A. J. (2017). Detention of immigrant children. *Pediatrics, 139*(4), 1–13.

Miljeteig-Olssen, P. (1990). Advocacy of children's rights—The convention as more than a legal document. *Human Rights Quarterly, 12*(1), 148–155.

Montgomery, H. (2001). *Modern Babylon? Prostituting children in Thailand.* Berghahn Books.

Neumayer, E. (2007). Qualified ratification: Explaining reservations to international human rights treaties. *Journal of Legal Studies, 36*(2), 397–429.

Nye, C. (2018). *Children 'attempting suicide' at Greek refugee camp* [online]. https://www.bbc.co.uk/news/world-europe-45271194. Accessed 24 November 2018.

O'Byrne, D. (2012). On the sociology of human rights: Theorising the language-structure of rights. *Sociology, 46*(5), 829–843.

O'Connell Davidson, J. (2005). *Children in the global sex trade.* Polity Press.

O'Connell Davidson, J. N. (2013). Telling tales: Child migration and child trafficking. *Child Abuse & Neglect, 37,* 1069–1079.

O'Connell Davidson, J. N. (2016). De-canting 'trafficking in human beings', Re-centring the state. *International Spectator, 51*(1), 58–73. https://doi.org/10.1080/03932729.2016.1121685

O'Neill, T. (2003). Anti-child labour rhetoric, child protection and young carpet weavers in Kathmandu, Nepal. *Journal of Youth Studies, 6*(4), 413–431.

Okyere, S. (2013). Are working children's rights and child labour abolition complementary or opposing realms? *International Social Work, 56*(1), 80–91.

Pupavac, V. (2001). Misanthropy without borders: The international children's rights regime. *Disasters, 25*(2), 95–112.

Rahman, M. M., Khanam, R., & Nur-Uddin, A. (1999). Child labour in Bangladesh: A critical appraisal of Harkin's bill and the MOU-type schooling program. *Journal of Economic Issues, 33*(4), 985–1003.

Rees, S., Thorpe, R., Tol, W., Fonseca, M., & Silove, D. (2015). Testing a cycle of family violence model in conflict-affected, low-income countries: A qualitative study from Timor-Leste. *Social Science & Medicine, 130,* 284–291.

Richardson, D., Brukauf, Z., Toczydlowska, E., & Chzhen, Y. (2017). *Comparing child-focused sustainable development goals (SDGs) in high-income countries: Indicator development and overview* (Office of Research—Innocenti Working Paper WP-2017-08).

Save the Children. (2017). *Keeping children at the centre: Time for EU solidarity in protecting migrant and refugee children's rights.* Save the Children.

Sawyer, S. M., Azzopardi, P. S., Wickremarathne, D., & Patton, G. C. (2018). The age of adolescence. *The Lancet: Child and Adolescent Health, 2*(3), 223–228. https://doi.org/10.1016/S2352-4642(18)30022-1

Stubley, P. (2018). *Greece's Moria refugee camp faces closure over 'uncontrollable amounts of waste'* [online]. https://www.independent.co.uk/news/world/europe/moria-refugee-camp-closure-greece-lesbos-deadline-waste-dangerous-public-health-a8531746.html. Accessed 24 November 2018.

UNICEF. (2014). *CRC 25th anniversary event* [online]. https://www.childrightsconnect.org/unicef-call-for-speakers-for-25th-anniversary-of-the-crc/#TravelVisa. Accessed 19 June 2019.

UNICEF. (2015). *Multidimensional child poverty in sub-Saharan Africa.* https://blogs.unicef.org/blog/multidimensional-child-poverty-in-sub-saharan-africa/. Accessed 12 June 2019.

UNICEF. (2018). *Under five mortality.* https://data.unicef.org/topic/child-survival/under-five-mortality/. Accessed 12 June 2019.

Valentin, K., & Meinert, L. (2009). The adult North and the young South: Reflections on the civilizing mission of children's rights. *Anthropology Today, 25*(3), 23–28.

Vandenhole, W., Gamze, E. T., & Lembrechts, S. (2019). *Children's rights: A commentary on the convention on the rights of the child and its protocols.* Edward Elgar.

CHAPTER 2

Moral Economies and Child Labour in Artisanal Gold Mining in Ghana

Samuel Okyere

INTRODUCTION: 'MODERN (CHILD) SLAVERY'

To what extent do institutions and social movements reproduce or entrench the problems they set out to challenge? During his debate with Noam Chomsky on human nature, Foucault observed:

> It seems to me that the real political task in a society such as ours is to criticise the working of institutions which appear to be both neutral and independent; to criticise them in such a manner that the political violence which has always exercised itself obscurely through them will be unmasked, so that one can fight them. (1974, p. 171)

S. Okyere (✉)
School of Sociology, Politics and International Studies, University of Bristol, Bristol, UK
e-mail: sam.okyere@bristol.ac.uk

© The Author(s), under exclusive license to Springer Nature Switzerland AG 2022
N. Howard and S. Okyere (eds.), *International Child Protection*, Palgrave Studies on Children and Development,
https://doi.org/10.1007/978-3-030-78763-9_2

Foucault's statement invites us to consider the paradox and bring into focus 'the ruptural effects of conflict and struggle that the order imposed by functionalist or systematizing thought is designed to mask' (Foucault, 1980, p. 82). In his opinion, no ideas, institutions or conventions should be deemed beyond critique; especially those that are presented as benign, apolitical, natural or indispensable to social order. Anatomising the politics, ideologies and practises of normative institutions is not only essential to democratic debate and the practise of freedom itself but it is also indispensable to our understanding of the social world and the production of alternative (and perhaps more credible) ways of conceptualising social phenomena (Foucault, 1980).

Application of this critique to international children's rights conventions and discourses on child labour has revealed their oppressive, superficial and normalising qualities (Myers, 2001; Pupavac, 2001), which became evident again in a conversation with a fellow participant at a recent African Studies conference in Paris. My fellow conference participant worked for an international human rights NGO that had produced a documentary film on human rights violations in gold and cassiterite mining in the Democratic Republic of Congo. The involvement of children in this activity, an issue of mutual interest, was the main topic of our conversation. He intimated that many of the children in the film had been orphaned by the country's civil war and had therefore taken on mining work to fend for themselves in the absence of support from the Congolese government and dwindling humanitarian aid from the UN now that war had ended. Other children, he said, were working alongside 'irresponsible' parents and carers who 'looked on unconcerned while their children as young as 5 slaved away'. He was especially critical of these parents and adults, questioning their conscience and morals for allowing children to work in that sort of environment. He concluded that in response his organisation was lobbying stakeholders against the exportation and sale of 'dirty minerals' produced by children in Congo. They were also in talks with the Congolese government to apprehend and punish parents and adults working with children in the country's mines, to serve as a deterrent to others. Palpably missing was a social welfare strategy or response.

I had no doubt about his organisation's commitment to children's rights and about their conviction that the actions they were promoting were in the best interests of the children featured in their film. However, as I told him, given that the major causal factors he had himself identified for children's involvement in Congolese small-scale mining were the civil war, dwindling humanitarian assistance and non-existent social welfare support, I was dubious of his NGO's responses. They were representative of the ineffective and oppressive responses which have been promoted by the International Labour Organisation (ILO) for nearly a century. Supported by national governments, trade unions, human rights activists, NGOs and myriad other actors, the ILO has been at the forefront of efforts to abolish children's participation in the Worst Forms of Child Labour (WFCL), notably through creation of the Worst Forms of Child Labour Convention (Convention 182) in 1999. The abolitionist campaign has been galvanised in the last two decades by NGOs which have emerged as part of the modern slavery abolishment movement. Notable among these 'neo-abolitionists' are the Global Alliance against Child Labour, the Walk Free Foundation and Free the Slaves (FTS). For neo-abolitionists, children's involvement in artisanal mining and other WFCL is consonant with child slavery, for the two occur in tandem, as FTS has argued (2014, p. 8). The term is therefore employed by neo-abolitionists as shorthand for virtually any scenario deemed to constitute a WFCL.

This observation is most evident in FTS' campaigns in Ghana over the last ten years. Following a study of children's involvement in the country's artisanal gold mining sector between 2012 and 2013, the NGO declared that it had found evidence of 'child enslavement'. On its web pages and other publicity materials, FTS claimed that 12-year- old boys were found working with dangerous chemicals without rest and unable to escape,[1] while girls aged 10 were found working as 'sexual slaves' at the mining sites where the studies were carried out (FTS, 2014, p. 6). Paradoxically, in contrast to these sensational headlines, a more detailed project report makes clear that the study did not actually find any child whose involvement in artisanal mining work was due to violence, force, trickery or coercion (FTS, 2014, p. 8). The 'child slavery' headlines appear all the more astonishing as the report again indicates that the research fieldworkers neither visited nor collected data at the artisanal gold mining sites where FTS publicity materials indicate that children had been 'found' in conditions of abuse and 'sexual slavery'. Citing ethical concerns, the

---

[1] http://www.freetheslaves.net/where-we-work/ghana/.

report further indicates that none of the child research participants were asked questions that could serve as a basis for determining whether their work could be defined as child slavery. The mere fact of their involvement in artisanal gold mining work seemed to have been taken at face value by FTS as evidence of child slavery, ignoring findings in their own research report. Such sensational (mis)representations of children's participation in what are without doubt difficult working conditions reflects the primary strategy employed by FTS and other neo-abolitionist groups in their child and human rights advocacy.

In what follows, this chapter subjects such characterisations and the wider WFCL abolitionist discourse to critical interrogation using evidence from a study I conducted of children's income-seeking activities in the Ghanaian artisanal gold mining sector. I argue that the 'child slavery' and WFCL abolitionist discourses on this activity largely ignore the narratives of affected children and communities. They draw on melodrama, sensationalism and problematic assumptions about children's involvement in WFCL to proffer responses which suture, but do not actually take on the factors underpinning and necessitating children's entry into artisanal mining work in Ghana and elsewhere. The originality of this work is that it is one of the first known ethnographic studies focussed principally on using working children's own narratives as a basis for understanding their work and lived experiences and for critiquing both the nascent neo-abolitionist 'child slavery' and mainstream WFCL discourses on children's involvement in artisanal mining work. It is a distinct and crucial intervention in international child and human rights debates and agendas such as efforts to eliminate WFCL as articulated in Target 8.7 of the United Nations Sustainable Development Goals.

Definition of Key Terms: 'Modern Slavery', 'Child Slavery' and 'WFCL'

A major criticism levelled against neo-abolitionist groups relates to their attempts to distinguish what they class as 'modern slavery' from other statuses or conditions with similar features that are not typically imagined as slavery (Clarke, 2003; Lott, 1998; McGary & Lawson, 1992). Given that there are no slave societies or places in the modern world where the status of slavery still exists as a distinct category as was the case in eighteenth-century American and Caribbean colonies, it is actually very difficult to agree on a distinct or precise measure with which 'slaves' can be separated from 'non-slaves' (O'Connell Davidson, 2015; Salafia, 2013). Thus, in seeking to define 'modern slavery' or 'modern child slavery', abolitionists point to a range of international instruments including, but not limited to, the 1926 Slavery Convention; the 1957 Supplementary Convention on the Abolition of Slavery, the Slave Trade and Institutions and Practises Similar to Slavery; the ILO Forced Labour Convention (No. 29); and the United Nations' Protocol to Prevent, Suppress and Punish Trafficking in Persons, Especially Women and Children 2000.

For some, the 1926 Slavery Convention definition, 'the status or condition of a person over whom any or all of the powers attaching to the right of ownership are exercised' does not fully capture the 'essence' of child slavery in modern times (Kooijmans & van de Glind, 2010). Thus, the term 'slavery-like practices' is also employed to describe conditions deemed to violate various articles of the United Nations Convention on the Rights of the Child (UNCRC). In this context, neo-abolitionists suggest that child slavery is where children's rights under Article 32, the right for children (defined as anyone under age 18 by the UNCRC) to be shielded from economic exploitation; Article 33, the right for children to be protected from drug trafficking and other illicit activities; Article 34, which prohibits child sexual exploitation; and Articles 35 and 38, which call for children to be protected against trafficking and involvement in armed conflict, respectively, are violated. Reference is also made to Optional Protocols of the UNCRC, such as the Optional Protocol on the Sale of Children, Child Prostitution and Child Pornography in attempts to classify various phenomena as modern cases of child enslavement (Buck & Nicholson, 2010; Craig, 2010; Kooijmans & van de Glind, 2010).

Reference is also made to the UN Trafficking Protocol, 2000 in attempting to define 'child slavery'. Under the Palermo Protocol, as it is commonly called, the movement of a child 'for purposes of exploitation' counts as 'child trafficking'. A very low threshold has been set for the identification of child trafficking primarily because policymakers do not accept that a person under the age of 18 is capable of consenting to his or her movement for work and other activities that may be considered 'exploitative', as Hashim (2005) and Bastia (2005) have both identified. The ILO Convention No. 182, commonly referred to as the Worst Forms of Child Labour Convention, is yet another notable source to which abolitionists have frequently turned in attempting to define child slavery. Article 3 of Convention 182 defines WFCL as:

> (a) all forms of slavery or practises similar to slavery, such as the sale and trafficking of children, debt bondage and serfdom and forced or compulsory labour, including forced or compulsory recruitment of children for use in armed conflict; (b) the use, procuring or offering of a child for prostitution, for the production of pornography or for pornographic performances; (c) the use, procuring or offering of a child for illicit activities, in particular for the production and trafficking of drugs as defined in the relevant international treaties; and (d) work which, by its nature or the circumstances in which it is carried out, is likely to harm the health, safety or morals of children. (Article 3, ILO Convention No. 182)

Noting the potential for confusion about what constitutes work likely to harm a child's health, safety or morals', the ILO passed Recommendation No. 190 to specify such jobs as: (a) work which exposes children to physical, psychological or sexual abuse; (b) work underground, under water, at dangerous heights or in confined spaces; (c) work with dangerous machinery, equipment and tools, or which involves the manual handling or transport of heavy loads; (d) work in an unhealthy environment which may, for example, expose children to hazardous substances, agents or processes or to temperatures, noise levels or vibrations damaging to their health and (e) work under particularly difficult conditions such as work for long hours or during the night or work where the child is unreasonably confined to the premises of the employer. The WFCL Convention itself thus amalgamates elements of what is elsewhere defined in international law as both 'slavery' and 'slavery-like' conditions.

Despite this panoply of sources and definitions, some neo-abolitionists have formulated proprietary ideas for identifying a 'child slave' or 'modern slave'. Notable among these is FTS, which primarily relies on a definition provided by Kevin Bales, one of its founders. For Bales (1999), the historic understanding of slavery as ownership or property rights over another person is inadequate in contemporary times. As he argues, instead of owning people outright as the case has been historically, 'slave owners' today simply appropriate 'the economic value of individuals while keeping them under complete coercive control' (Bales, 1999, p. 25). Bales and FTS, therefore, define 'modern slavery' as the situation where a person (a child in this case) is held through force, fraud, violence or coercion to provide services that enable the slaveholder to extract profit or some form of benefit (Bales, 1999, 2005; FTS, 2014[2]).

Critics have described this definition as deficient for deviating from the international legally recognised definition of slavery (Allain & Hickey, 2012) and for promiscuously conflating virtually any form of human suffering with slavery (Patterson, 2012, p. 1). Indeed, using FTS' definition, thousands of migrant workers on sponsorship visas around the world, such as those on overseas domestic worker visas in the UK, could be classed as 'modern slaves'. Their visas legally tie them to their employers; many are subjected to potential and actual wholesale coercive control, violence and various forms of exploitation by their employers or employers' associates and many are unpaid or subjected to wage theft with virtually no means of walking away. Yet, neo-abolitionists discount such cases from their accounts of modern slavery.

Putting its definitional deficiencies aside, Bales' (1999, 2005) definition of 'modern slavery' is also discordant with FTS' classification of children's work in the Ghanaian artisanal mining sector as a form of 'child slavery'. The essential ingredients of Bales' slavery definition – force, fraud or coercive control – are non-existent in the circumstances surrounding the children's work, as the FTS report concedes (2014). As the next section demonstrates using the narratives of children working in this sector, the situation is far more complex than the sensational claims of child slavery and child exploitation presented by neo-abolitionists and within the mainstream WFCL discourse. Hearing these complexities may bring us closer to lasting responses to the problem.

The Research

My study of children's involvement in the Ghanaian artisanal gold mining sector aimed to critically examine the extent to which the narratives of children in this sector squared with dominant discourse and policy directives on occupations deemed to be WFCL. The study was guided by an interpretivist framework focussed on understanding the reality of children's work in this sector from the vantage position of children working in it rather than relying on NGO and ILO accounts which dominated the field at the time of the research. The ethnographic fieldwork

---

[2] http://www.freetheslaves.net/about-slavery/faqs-glossary/.

was carried out at an artisanal gold mining site at Kenyasi, Ghana, for 15 weeks between June and September 2010. A total of 57 children (30 girls and 27 boys aged 14–17) generously provided information for the research. Information was also collected from adult miners, community leaders, officials of Newmont Ghana Gold Limited, government officials, parents and guardians of the children and other actors. Data were collected through the use of unstructured and structured interviews, participant observation and photo-elicitation at the artisanal gold mining site, participants' homes and other spaces in the community.

Understanding the history of the Kenyasi artisanal gold mining site is crucial for understanding the narratives of the children and adults who work there, for circumstances behind the site's creation encapsulate the wider socio-economic and political circumstances within which the research participants' accounts and lived experiences are embedded. In the early 1980s, facing economic ruin, Ghana sought financial assistance from the International Monetary Fund (IMF) and World Bank. IMF structural adjustment conditionalities and other economic reforms imposed on the country since then have compelled Ghana to open up sectors such as energy, mining, water and telecommunications to the private market (Brune et al., 2004; Hutchful, 2002). It is within this context that 10,000 residents of Kenyasi and surrounding areas were dispossessed of their lands, houses and farms in 2005 to make way for the establishment of a gold mine owned by Newmont Ghana Gold Limited (NGGL), a subsidiary of the Newmont Mining Corporation, one of the world's largest gold mining companies.

Previous to the land dispossession, farming had been the mainstay in Kenyasi for generations. Residents faced socio-economic challenges, as some of the adults acknowledged, but, until they lost their lands, most were self-sufficient living off the land. With the loss of their lands, the community was thrust into severe hardship overnight. The elderly found it especially hard to cope, given that subsistence farming was the only livelihood activity they had known all their lives. Their hardships were further compounded when the derisory compensation packages paid for their lands ran out (Armstrong, 2008; Okyere, 2013). The situation eventually reached a crisis point when the youth realised that the jobs promised to them by NGGL were not going to materialise. Now aware that their lands were rich with gold, some started small-scale gold mining activities on family lands which were now legally owned by NGGL. The company was dissatisfied with this encroachment on its property and sought to put a stop to it with the support of the Ghanaian military and police. For almost a year, there were clashes between the town's youth and NGGL security personnel supported by Ghanaian security agents. Some Kenyasi youth were arrested, beaten or harassed, with their rudimentary mining equipment seized and destroyed. For their part, the youth also led demonstrations against the company, some of which turned violent and resulted in destruction of the company's property and sabotage of its operations.

Eventually, in a truce that largely helped to settle the matter, NGGL decided to turn a blind eye to small-scale mining activities on an area of its concession about three acres in size, as long as the small-scale miners did not extend their activities beyond this territory. This space thus became the Kenyasi artisanal gold mining site, which was the source of livelihood for an estimated 4000 people at the time of the fieldwork. Many of these men, women and children were from Kenyasi, neighbouring villages and the country at large, but others were migrants from Burkina Faso and other neighbouring West African countries. Geographically, in addition to the numerous pits dotted across the site, the site was also populated by huts and wooden shacks used as sleeping areas, restaurants and machine repair spaces. Some of these shacks were also used as shops of various sorts including a 'cinema' cum entertainment centre; a space with a generator-powered TV and DVD player where films were screened at night.

The Kenyasi artisanal gold mining site was, during the fieldwork, a largely self-sufficient space. Many of the workers, particularly migrants, lived within the site for months on end without need to visit the main Kenyasi town for supplies or services. Nonetheless, as it was located in a forest area that was previously used for farming, it was generally bushy. Scorpions, rats and other rodents were not uncommon at night. The site's environmental hazards were worsened by the huge volume of stones, sharp rocks, soil and debris scattered across the place following pit excavations and mining operations. Again, as the fieldwork was carried out towards the end of the rainy season, there were stagnant pools of water at various locations which served as breeding grounds for mosquitoes and other insects. The site's generally unhygienic and hazardous environment was one of numerous observations which deeply troubled me during the fieldwork. It was clear to see why the ILO and international children's rights policymakers reason that an artisanal gold mining site is no place for a child to work. However, as the chapter discusses later, the child research participants in whose interests these claims are made reject it because it showed superficial understanding of their circumstances and the range of 'hazards' they were confronted with. Also, the site's harsh physical appearance belied the fact that *socially*, it was very orderly, peaceful and well-organised. Given the circumstances under which NGGL had allowed them to use the land, the workers were wary that antisocial conduct or behaviour might cause the company to rescind its decision. This concern led to the formation of a site governing committee to enforce rules and guidelines for behaviour. Notable among these standards of conduct was a zero-tolerance stance on all forms of violence; all disputes had to be brought before the site committee for arbitration. Those who resorted to violence or took matters into their own hands were banished from the site. Given that there were no lands for farming or other notable employment opportunities and artisanal gold mining work was the town's mainstay, hardly anyone violated this code of conduct. Reflecting on my own situation as an outsider asking sensitive questions in the community, I did not feel at risk or threatened at any point during my three month stay at the site.

The site's very organised, friendly and disciplined nature was one of many observations which challenged the popular assertion that artisanal gold mining sites are violence-prone, lawless domains teeming with criminals and social misfits who have no qualms about abusing children or corrupting their morals. This was one of a number of normative assumptions informing dominant representations of children's involvement in artisanal mining work, which the study sought to scrutinise. Among these widely held assumptions are the following:

a. *Age:* International children's rights policymakers' and neo-abolitionists' attempts to prohibit the involvement of children in jobs they class as WFCL or 'child slavery' are primarily premised on the assumption that anyone under 18 years is incompetent or lacks the capacity to take up such work. Abolitionist literature reviewed around the period of the fieldwork argued that a 'typical child mine worker' was aged 12 (ILO, 2005, p. 8; Jennings, 1999). Indeed, some texts asserted that it was not uncommon to find toddlers, 3- and 4-year-old children, labouring at small-scale mining sites (ILO, 2011, p. 33). The belief is that children are unlikely to take up such dirty, difficult and dangerous work unless compelled by an adult third party through coercion, force or trickery (Amin et al., 2007, p. 18; Hentschel et al., 2002).

b. *Unquestionable victimisation and exploitation:* Another normative abolitionist assumption which the study aimed to subject to critical interrogation was a widely held belief that children in artisanal gold mining work are necessarily victimised or exploited. Policymakers and abolitionists reason that because of children's relative immaturity, they are unlikely to protest against maltreatment or challenge adults at mining sites (ILO, 1999, 2001, 2002, 2011). They are also said to be regarded as disposable and thus exposed to the most hazardous or dangerous jobs which adults cannot or may not want to perform:

> Some of the most dangerous extraction tasks are set aside for children, whose smaller, more nimble bodies enable them to go down into mining shafts to extract minerals that are difficult to access. Young, numerous, cheap (if not free) and often without a parent or guardian to look out for them, these children are seen as expendable. (FTS, 2010, p. 1)

Linked to this is the assumption that children working in artisanal mining are either not paid or given paltry rewards, if it all:

> Many children in mining and quarrying do not get any remuneration for their work; they only receive basic sustenance (in-kind payment). Besides, when they do receive payment for their work, the wages of children are normally inferior to the wages of adults. (ILO, 2005, p. 16)

c. A third normative assumption in the WFCL abolitionist discourse which the study sought to examine is a suggestion that participation in work at artisanal gold mining sites corrupts or risks corrupting children's morals. The discourse places special emphasis on girls' safety and morals, with the argument that they are at risk of sexual violence or of being called upon to provide sexual services to men and boys in mining communities. In fact, this largely unquestioned belief that moral turpitude and 'sexual slavery' of girls, as FTS puts it (2014, p. 8), is a dominant feature of discourse around children's involvement in artisanal mining and forms the basis for the ILO's argument that small-scale mining involves 'unconditional' WFCL:

> Some children are engaged in prostitution and they are also confronted by problems related to alcohol and drug abuse, and violence. So small-scale mining also involves aspects of the unconditional worst forms of child labour. (ILO, 2005, p. 8)

Two key questions which guided the study's aim of scrutinising these dominant abolitionist assumptions were whether these widely held claims were representative of children's work at all artisanal mining sites and, related to this, whether the reality at one artisanal mining site could reliably serve as a basis for a blanket policy on children's involvement everywhere. I was concerned that policymakers and WFCL abolitionists were extrapolating from evidence at individual artisanal gold mining sites (often the worst examples) and also drawing on particular assumptions and definitions of childhood, harm, development, exploitation and 'slavery' for policies and interventions on children's involvement at all other sites. What perspectives and potential solutions were foreclosed by this strategy? As discussed in the next section, the evidence from Kenyasi lends credence to these concerns.

CHILDREN'S LABOUR AND WORKING CONDITIONS AT THE KENYASI ARTISANAL GOLD MINING SITE: A CASE OF FORCE, COERCION, EXPLOITATION AND SLAVERY?

Children's work at the site took two forms. They were either self-employed in roles such as hawking, head porterage, fetching of water and other supplies for the processing of gold ore, or they sold their labour on a day-by-day basis to 'buyers'. Buyers were often adults, and occasionally children or groups of children, who had purchased gold ore and needed assistance to process it. I have avoided describing the relationship between the children and buyers as that of 'employee' and 'employer' because this characterisation would be a misnomer. Everyone who was seeking income-earning opportunities at the Kenyasi artisanal gold mining site could best be described as a hustler in an 'economy of makeshifts' (Brace, 2004; Williams, 2005). The site was populated by adults and children collaborating in an attempt to scrape out a living on the margins of society in the face of mutual hardships arising locally from the loss of lands and nationally from decades of enforced austere socio-economic reforms. Social relations at the site were therefore characterised primarily by mutual dependence in recognition of their limited or non-existent opportunities and livelihood alternatives.

Another notable factor guiding children's work avenues and roles at the site was superstition or spirituality. There was strict adherence to a superstitious belief that if women were allowed direct involvement in gold extraction or the gold processing chain, yields would be low, or worse still, serious accidents may occur. Consequently, roles that were directly linked to the extraction and processing of gold were reserved for boys and men, while women and girls were permitted jobs traditionally regarded as females' work; kitchen work in restaurants or serving customers, hawking of various wares at the site, head porterage, fetching water and other supplies for the processing of gold ore, but not directly participating in that activity itself.

To find work, those who were not self-employed relied on a system outlined by Ayesha during the fieldwork:

> ...we turn up in the morning and go 'door knocking'..., we move from one spot to the other to find out the sorts of work available and who the owner [buyer] is. If we are interested, we ask the owner if they want to work with us for the day. When we finish, he pays us and we go our way.

There was no third-party involvement in the entry of children into work at this site. Self-employed children went around the site by themselves soliciting for work, while those who preferred to work with others went to look for such work on their own, as Ayesha's quote shows. Her account, which was repeated by her friends and further corroborated through prolonged observation during the research cast doubt on the abolitionist assumption that children's participation in work at such spaces was necessarily the product of force, trickery, coercion or other 'unfree' actions by adult third parties. Indeed, the evidence also raised questions about views that no child would choose this sort of work because it is exploitative, dirty and dangerous.

Further evidence on the mechanisms through which children entered into work at site and the conditions surrounding their work also raised questions about FTS' (2010) claims of widespread 'child slavery' in the Ghanaian gold mining sector. Besides the lack of third-party involvement in their entry into work, the child research participants were neither kept in employment nor compelled to work with anybody at the site. The working day typically began at 8 a.m., with an hour break at noon, and ended by 4 or 5 p.m., whereupon workers were paid. However, this was applicable to adults only, for if a child decided to withdraw his or her labour before 4 p.m. for whatever reason, as part of exclusive protections for children instituted by the site governing committee, the 'buyer' or person who had contracted the child's labour for the day was still obliged to pay him or her for the period worked. This and other measures discussed elsewhere (Okyere, 2013) ensured that contrary to WFCL abolitionists' claims of wholesale victimisation and exploitation of children at artisanal mining sites, those at Kenyasi were not only shielded from the most hazardous jobs at the site but also they were not cheated or exploited in terms of remuneration. Although abolitionists insist that child labour is cheap labour, the principle of equal payment for equal work enforced by the site governing committee ensured that as long children performed the same roles as adults, their age and maturity was immaterial to their earning potential.

The gendered nature of work and experiences at artisanal gold mining sites was an abolitionist claim supported by the research findings. Work at the site was indeed highly gendered due to the community's superstitious beliefs about the work that men and women can and cannot do in artisanal mining. However, the assertion that such gendered roles fuel sexual exploitation of girls and women (see ILO, 2011; ILO/IPEC, 2004; Mwami et al., 2002) or 'sexual slavery' as FTS (2014) calls it, could not be substantiated. There was no evidence whatsoever of girls trading sexual favours for money at or near the site, as the literature would lead one to expect. The site's superstitions included the belief that a 'gold goddess' and other spirits who kept workers safe abhorred sexual activity of any kind in their presence. Consequently, there was a strong taboo against prostitution and any sexual activity of any sort at or near the site. These were among a number of activities that were believed to lead to dire consequences for all if practised at the site and were therefore strongly prohibited and policed as part of the site's code of conduct. In fact, instead of prostitution or sexual abuse of girls, the most telling impact of the site's gendered division of work for both adults and children was that boys earned more than women; another research finding that raised questions about abolitionists' claims that children working at mining sites are unconditionally paid less than adults due their relative immaturity.

On the whole, the research findings contradict key assumptions which inform FTS' 'child slavery' and WFCL abolitionists' claims about children's involvement in artisanal mining. For sure, the environment and aspects of the children's work exposed them to severe hazards. But, as discussed in the next section, the child research participants in whose interests abolitionists claim to be working strongly rejected the argument that banning them from accessing earning opportunities at the mining site was the best way to safeguard their rights or best interests.

Why Had Children Taken up Artisanal Gold Mining Work at Kenyasi?

A range of motivational factors informed the child research participants' decisions to seek income-earning opportunities at the Kenyasi artisanal gold mining site. Their work formed part of their attempts to feed themselves and their loved ones. It was also a means of purchasing other basic life necessities, accessing healthcare and pursuing development opportunities such as education, apprenticeships and skills training. I am mainly going to address the education-child labour nexus in this section not only because education was the reason most cited by the children as motivation for taking up work at the site but also because this finding sheds new light on how we think of the connections between child labour and education. This finding forms part of the significant original contributions the study makes to international children's rights debates. The commonly held view is that children in WFCL are mostly illiterate or school dropouts (ILO, 2005; Jennings, 1999). The ILO's designation of jobs such as artisanal gold mining as WFCL is not only due to concern about harm and exploitation, but it is also premised on the belief that such work denies children education and other development opportunities. More broadly, child labour is said to 'allow no room for dreams' as Wahba (1998, p. 1) has argued, and children working at places such as artisanal gold mining sites are described as having no educational or future perspective and therefore condemned 'to a harrowing present and hopeless future' (UNICEF, 2001, p. 11).

So pervasive are these assumptions that prior to undertaking fieldwork, I translated copies of the consent form, participant information sheet and other ethics documents into the local language in anticipation of reading and explaining this information to illiterate children. It was therefore a surprise to discover that 50 of the 57 child research participants were in full-time education and could all speak, read and write in English (which is the language of instruction in Ghanaian schools) very well. Of the 50,

40 had taken up work at the site principally in an attempt to secure funds for their education, as exemplified by these excerpts:

> My father cannot give us money for school and my elder sister has stopped school because of this. I came here with some girls to see if I can get some money for myself and continue school next term; (Adams, aged 14)

> I have been coming here for 3 vacations now. There is nobody to help me [with money to attend school] and that is why I do this; (Rocky, aged 16)

> Sometimes I need money urgently and my mother cannot afford [to give me money]. That day I don't go to school or maybe I don't do extra classes and I come here to work and find the money to go back to school the next day or when I can afford to do so. (Albert, aged 17)

These child participants' predicaments underline a wider problem faced by many poor families in the space where this study was carried out. Government officials interviewed during the fieldwork insisted that all Ghanaian children have free access to education as a result of schemes such as the Free Compulsory Universal Basic Education (FCUBE) and the Capitation Grant (CP). Under these schemes, education is, in theory, free until Junior High School level (JHS), the level that most of the child participants were at. Despite the absence of school fees, Eugene's comments below show that many children are still unable to attend due to household financial constraints:

> It is true that we don't pay fees, but that is not the only problem. There is no money at home; there is even nothing to eat. That is also a problem; you can't go [to school] if you can't eat. (Eugene, aged 17)

Osei et al. (2009) have examined this problem in more detail and similarly concluded that the fee component is just one of many financial burdens that schooling in Ghana imposes on parents: school fee abolition is not just about tuition fees (which do not necessarily constitute the main bulk of fees). School fee abolition must take into consideration the wide range of costs of schooling to families and households. This means any direct and indirect costs/charges (tuition fees, costs of textbooks, supplies and uniforms, PTA contributions, costs related to sports and other school activities, costs related to transportation, contributions to teachers' salaries, etc.) (Osei et al., 2009, p. 4).

In a country with a deprivation score of nearly 50% and 28.6% of the population living below the poverty line, according to the statistics captured in the Human Development Report published around the time of fieldwork, many families are simply unable to meet these additional costs. Thus, although attendance is 'free' as officials insisted, school remains inaccessible to children from poor families or communities. Many drop out as a result, but other children try to support their parents' efforts to fund their education and, in many cases, do so entirely by themselves through work and other income-earning activities. This was the story of many children working at Kenyasi. They mostly worked at the site after school or during vacations, which was the period during which the fieldwork was carried out.

Their educational ambitions coupled with how work was organised and remunerated at the site served to shield them from the most hazardous jobs, contrary to the popular abolitionist assumption that children working in such places are unquestionably lumped with the most hazardous jobs because of their relative immaturity or because they are seen as 'disposable'. The hardest and most dangerous jobs, such as underground work, require long-term commitment, months in most cases, because workers are not paid until they have started hauling gold ore from below the pits. As the longest school holidays lasted for just about six weeks, the child participants were in a race against time to earn as much money as possible to tide them over for the next three-month school term. Waged labour in the 'fringe' and comparatively easier roles which required no long-term commitment assured them of daily payments. Jobs on the fringes of the core mining work provided the security that the child participants could end their stay at the site at any point the need arose, without the risk of going back home empty-handed. These considerations coupled with the fact that work in artisanal mining gave them the best chance of earning a decent amount of money in the short vacation period were the key reasons for their preference of artisanal gold mining work over others such as agricultural labour and head porterage at market centres; jobs which are also targeted for elimination by abolitionists anyway.

In discussing what they saw as the relative advantages of working in artisanal gold mining compared to other options open to them, it was evident that the child research participants were not entirely bereft of agency and choice. For sure, their decisions to undertake paid work at the site were driven by the harsh socio-economic conditions they and their families were facing. Nonetheless, even within this constrained set of circumstances, they were making rational decisions about the sort of work they preferred to do, where they wanted to do such work, who they wanted to work with and the hours they wanted to work. They were essentially making decisions about their own lives under conditions Klocker (2007) describes as 'thin agency': 'decisions and everyday actions that are carried out within highly restrictive contexts, characterised by few viable alternatives' (p. 85).

On the substantive matter of the education-WFCL nexus, the findings firstly call into question the idea that engagement in WFCL automatically deprives children of education. While the study was unable to go into the impact of their work on their school results, attendance or performance, what was without doubt was that the participants' access to schooling was made possible by their earnings from their work at the site. Secondly, and linked to the first point, the findings trouble the notion that schooling is of itself a panacea for disengaging children from dangerous or hazardous work. The paradox in this example is that the children's desire to access education and the challenges they faced in achieving this objective had become a direct causal factor for their entry into work classed by the ILO as a WFCL. Their educational and developmental opportunities were not being threatened or denied to them by their work. Rather, whatever limited access they had was by virtue of it. The barriers they faced in accessing education and other developmental opportunities, much like their participation in work at the artisanal mining site, were the result of socio-economic hardships and structural insecurities facing the country as a whole rather than the actions of uncaring parents or callous adults seeking to exploit children's labour, as abolitionists tend to argue.

All in all, the children's accounts and other evidence from the research showed a clear divergence between how they, their families and the wider community visualised their involvement in artisanal gold mining work and how policymakers and abolitionists also perceive the same situation. For policymakers and abolitionists, there can be no question about it, WFCL must be banned because it is hazardous to children. It threatens them with physical and psychological harms and also deprives them of their childhood. In neo-abolitionist rhetoric, children's participation is without doubt exploitative and evidence of child slavery, because children are tricked, forced or coerced into such work by adults who pay them a pittance, if at all, for their hard labour. And yet, the accounts of this group of children involved in the phenomenon show a far more complex situation than these popular narratives suggest. The child participants agreed with some abolitionist claims about the difficulties and hazards surrounding their work:

> This is very dirty work. The sand and dust gets in your face, your mouth and everywhere, even your eyes. (Jude, aged 15)

> Sometimes after work, it feels like somebody has beaten you up. Your whole body pains you, but you know everyone is feeling the same and so you only think of the reason why you came here and forget about the pains. (Esi, aged 15)

> If you are not careful, you can get injured at any time. I have not been injured before, but I have seen a man who smashed his hand with a hammer when he was working. (Ebo, aged 16)

And yet, pressed on why they still kept coming back to the site to find work each day, particularly when during discussions many of them told me that they knew (from media reports, advocacy campaigns and abolitionist literature I had shown them during the fieldwork), that their work was forbidden by international children's rights policymakers and the Ghanaian government (through the country's Child Rights Act and its ratification of ILO Conventions 138 and 182), a very different narrative often emerged:

> People say this work is bad and so we should stop and go to school...but if I can't buy books, shoes and other things I need, how can I go to school? ... I will go to school but I can't eat school if I am hungry; (James, aged 15)

> I don't need anybody [those calling for a ban on their work] to come and tell me about this work and why I should stop, because I do it myself and know everything. I know that it is difficult and dangerous but if anyone wants me to stop just like that, then the person must give me school money before. (Cynthia, aged 16)

Children's voices, much like those of adults, must be considered critically in research. It is crucial to understand the complexity in their narratives instead of taking them at face value or uncritically presenting everything they say as truth. To this end, careful, repeated and extensive interactions coupled with data triangulation strategies were employed to corroborate their assertions. Their claims were challenged where necessary and at the end critical discourse and thematic analyses were used reflexively to extract and decode both superficial and latent messages in their narratives. Application of these techniques revealed that in the children's own eyes and in that of the community in which they lived and worked, the hazards described by policymakers and neo-abolitionists were of lesser significance than the hazards of humiliating poverty, hunger, lack of clothing, shoes and other personal effects. They considered the potential physical, medical or physiological injuries and hazards associated with their work to be no less hazardous and injurious than the social and economic hazards or harms linked to being unable to access education, healthcare, skills training, apprenticeships and other reasons for which they were toiling at the site. The moral judgements and understandings of deviance, exploitation and harm on the basis of which WFCL abolitionists make pronouncements about the children's work were very different from those held by the children themselves.

This discord between the two assessments brings into focus the fact that while the UNCRC guarantees children the right for their views to be elicited and taken into account in the formulation of policies that affect them, in reality, children's rights policymakers are themselves only willing to take children's views on board if these views are in consonance with theirs. The long-standing refusal by the ILO to engage with organised groups of working children from Peru, Bolivia, Senegal, Burkina Faso, India and elsewhere stems from the fact that these working children's unions insist on their right to take up any form of work necessitated by their socio-economic, political and cultural circumstances; the same arguments made by their peers at Kenyasi. This view directly contradicts the ILO's perspectives on children's work as enshrined in Conventions 138 and 182. A crucial question thrown up by this dilemma concerns the lack of accountability to children by key actors in the international child protection regime. Are the ILO and neo-abolitionists legitimately representing working children and their best interests, as they claim, when they side-line working children and deny them a meaningful role in deliberations about the rights of working children and children's work? This question has become especially poignant in the last decade following statements by organised unions of working children and youth (such as UNATSBO, MANTHOC, and AMCWC) that they now speak for themselves and represent their own best interests after years of having their voices, much like those expressed by their peers at Kenyasi, paternalistically marginalised or ignored by the ILO.

Discussion and Conclusion

This chapter set out to question the depiction of children's involvement in the Ghanaian artisanal gold mining sector as a form of child slavery by FTS and to scrutinise the wider abolitionist discourse on this phenomenon using the accounts of children involved in income-seeking activities in the sector. The children's narratives and other evidence presented by the chapter problematise the characterisation of this phenomenon as a form of 'modern slavery' or 'child slavery' and also undermine key normative assumptions that underpin the wider WFCL abolitionist discourse spearheaded by the ILO. Judged even by Bales' (1999) definition of modern slavery, which has been adopted by FTS, the chapter has demonstrated that the neo-abolitionist NGO's portrayal of such scenarios as child slavery is misguided. Far from being compelled through force or other coercive means to work in this sector, children at the study site take up work without any third-party involvement or compulsion and similarly face no obstacles in withdrawing their labour whenever they wish to. Far from being denied payment or cheated out of their wages, as the abolitionist discourses suggests is the norm, the children's wages were the same as adults', and boys could actually earn more than women in some instances because of the gendered nature of labour at the site. Their wages are also mainly used for their own education and benefit instead of being used by a third-party 'exploiter' or beneficiary. The work done by children and the conditions of their labour were the safest and most secure within the precarious setting in which adults and children alike were compelled to toil; a finding that also troubles the assumption that children in artisanal mining are forced to undertake the most hazardous tasks because of their relative immaturity. Without seeking to idealise their work, the chapter contends that the reality of children's work in artisanal mining at Kenyasi, similar to findings in Northern Ghana by Hilson (2010), bear no resemblance whatsoever to chattel slavery, or any form of slavery. Thus, FTS' (2010) suggestion that about 10,000 Ghanaian children are forced to work in hazardous conditions, and child slavery in the form of debt bondage and forced prostitution also occur in the country's mining communities, without evidence of how this number was obtained or names of specific communities in which such enslavement occurs, is at best a wild exaggeration. It follows the tropes of neo-abolitionist advocacy which harnesses the language of slavery, melodrama and sensationalism to draw attention to its work.

The problem, however, is that such sensationalism and allegations of 'child slavery' or 'modern slavery' can draw public attention to the problem without doing much in practical terms to support the purported slaves and their communities. In the case of children in the Ghanaian artisanal gold mining sector, the solution proposed by FTS, policymakers and WFCL abolitionists to such assertions of slavery is the extraction of individual children from work and a blanket ban on all children's participation in the sector. Such solutions are not only rejected by the children themselves but they also highlight a number of problems that attend on global efforts to eliminate WFCL.

The first is whether informed judgements can be made about children's work without adequate knowledge or consideration of the social, economic and political specificities surrounding the work. The decision by international children's rights policymakers to enforce a blanket ban on jobs deemed to be WFCL may be well-intentioned. However, this sweeping approach misses the variation and nuance of children's experiences in such jobs. Children working in artisanal gold mining work in Ghana, for example, may have patently different motivations, conditions of work and other experiences from their peers undertaking similar work in India or Senegal or even at different sites in the same country. WFCL abolitionists' totalising discourse and children's rights policymakers' tendency to formulate policy for all forms of children's work based on evidence from specific places or instances is therefore inherently problematic. The default abolitionist position to view children's work at places such as Kenyasi only in terms of harm and exploitation obscures the equally important fact presented by this chapter: that in some cases these jobs are also the only available means through which working children attempt to access schooling and other development opportunities or eke out the most basic survival.

To be clear, this chapter is not arguing in favour of the children's continued involvement in hazardous work. Rather its main concern is with those in the international child protection regime, including child rights and neo-abolitionist activists, whose diagnosis of the problem and the solution they proffer is so limited. Ignoring the complexity of the issue and presenting it only in terms of exploitation, harm or slavery, in order to support abolitionist or rescue agendas largely omits from the equation the deficits this particular group of children will suffer if they are deprived access from their work while the underlying issue of individual, household and communal socio-economic deprivation remain untouched. The entry of FTS, the Walk Free Foundation and other neo-abolitionist groups into the WFCL advocacy arena and more broadly into the child protection regime has further deflected attention from the crucial need to address the structural factors at the heart of the problem as an alternative to the abolitionist model the ILO has been pursuing for nearly a century. Neo-abolitionist reformulation of the problem in terms of child slavery or modern slavery produces the false narrative that extracting or 'rescuing' children from their alleged 'slave masters' is all that is required to address the problem. Consequently, the need to take on local and global forces which have created and continue to shape the adverse socio-economic conditions that necessitate the entry of children into precarious and hazardous work largely remains unexamined.

To call on Wright Mills (1959) then, the approach adopted by neo-abolitionists and the international child protection regime for addressing this phenomena is characterised by a rupture of the connections between the biographies or circumstances of the child research participants and their histories, which are in turn enmeshed with the history of their communities and the country at large. As discussed earlier in the chapter, creation of the Kenyasi site where the entire community was attempting to secure their livelihoods was a direct outcome of obligations placed on Ghana to open up its mining sector to the private market as part of IMF structural adjustment conditionalities imposed on the country in the 1980s. These conditionalities and other forced market liberalisation measures have exposed millions of Ghanaians to abject socio-economic deprivation. The child slavery discourse obfuscates understanding of the fact that for decades, to be able to access aid, loans, debt relief and other assistance from the IMF, World Bank and richer nations, poorer countries such as Ghana have been compelled to pursue economic policies and socio-economic reforms that are patently deleterious to the social welfare and other interests of their own citizens. As the NGO Action Aid (2010) argues in a report on the impact of IMF economic reforms in Ghana, while there have been improvements in macro-economic stability in successive years:

> Stability has been achieved against the backdrop of high unemployment, poverty and increased inequality. IMF policies have thus not contributed to shared growth and income redistribution in Ghana. The IMF required the Government of Ghana to reduce spending on health, education and development. In effect, the IMF demands the poor in Ghana to have lower standard of living. (p. 45)

Ghana's underdevelopment and her inability to provide an accessible, viable and sustainable welfare safety net for children and families are also largely due to her colonised past and current weak position on the global economic and political stage. Faced with the lack of a state welfare safety net such as those available in Britain and elsewhere, residents of Kenyasi, like millions of other Ghanaians, are left with no option than to seek out jobs they themselves readily recognise as undignified, dirty, difficult and dangerous. Martin Verlet (2000) echoes this point, when he argues that the worsening of living conditions in Ghana and children's uptake of precarious work can be attributed to 'domestic deregulation in the country':

> the break-up of family units combined with the increasing fragility and destabilisation of households which has been gathering pace and becoming more serious under the impact of the polices of liberalisation through structural adjustment. A connection exists between the deregulation of the labour market and what we call domestic deregulation. Clearer still is the correlation between both these processes and the general spread of child labour. (p. 67)

I conclude by reasserting Foucault's (1974, p. 171) point on the urgency of holding up to scrutiny the practises, discourses and work of institutions which appear to be both neutral and independent, in such a manner that the political violence which they perpetuate can be unmasked and challenged. FTS and WFCL abolitionists' calls to eliminate children's work at Kenyasi and similar spaces appear uncontroversial. Who can argue, after all, that they are in support of children's work in artisanal mining, child slavery or child exploitation? The 'child saving' rhetoric is largely unquestioned, for it is presumed to be wholly in children's best interests. But it is precisely this kind of discourse which Foucault argues we ought to critically scrutinise. This undertaking by the chapter shows that the 'child saving' or emancipatory goals FTS and WFCL abolitionists envisage are undermined by their failure to question global economic forces which prioritise profits over human need and shape systems of inequality affecting many over the world. The conceptualisation of children's work in artisanal mining exclusively in terms of harm and exploitation (which they also mainly attribute to children's own parents and communities) forecloses understanding of the nuances surrounding it as well as the structural causes underpinning it.

By attributing the problem to individual 'slave masters' or 'exploiters' instead of bringing into focus the need for socio-economic and political structural reforms and action against the deleterious aspects of global capitalism, many children and their families may remain trapped in the precarious work and existence conditioned by these factors. By localising or individualising the causes, neo-abolitionist and mainstream rhetoric unwittingly or deliberately depoliticises and avoids the intrinsically political task of campaigning for fairer trade deals, debt relief, reparations for historic wrongs and a more equal playing field on the global economic stage so that poorer countries like Ghana can meet their welfare obligations to their citizens, improve their livelihoods and ultimately reduce the need for children to take on hazardous work. It is this paradox which Foucault's philosophy of normativity, highlighted at the start of this chapter, invites us to consider.

References

ActionAid Ghana. (2010). *Implications of IMF loans and conditionalities on the poor and vulnerable in Ghana*. ActionAid. http://bit.ly/28Slcqi. Accessed 23 June 2016.

Allain, J., & Hickey, R. (2012). Property and the definition of slavery. *International and Comparative Law Quarterly, 61*(4), 915–938.

Amin, S., Quayes, S., & Rives, M. (2007). Are children and parents substitutes or complements in the family labor supply decision in Bangladesh? *The Journal of Developing Areas, 40*(1), 15–37.

Armstrong, A. T. (2008). *Gold strike in the breadbasket: Indigenous livelihoods, the World Bank and territorial restructuring in Western Ghana* (A Report for the Institute for Food and Development Policy Development [IFDPD]). http://goo.gl/VXqEZ. Accessed 1 June 2010.

Bales, K. (1999). *Disposable people: New slavery in the global economy* (2nd ed.). University of California Press.

Bales, K. (2005). *Understanding global slavery: A reader*. University of California Press.

Bastia, T. (2005). Child trafficking or teenage migration? Bolivian migrants in Argentina. *International Migration, 43*(4), 57–89.
Brace, L. (2004). *The politics of property: Labour, freedom and belonging*. Edinburgh University Press.
Brune, N., Garrett, G., & Kogut, B. (2004). The international monetary fund and the global spread of privatization. *IMF Staff Papers, 51*(2), 195–219.
Buck, T., & Nicholson, A. (2010). Constructing the international legal framework. In G. Craig (Ed.), *Child slavery now: A contemporary reader* (pp. 43–60). Policy Press.
Clarke, S. (2003). Slaves, servility and noble deeds. *Philosophical Inquiry, 25*(5–4), 165–176.
Craig, G. (Ed.). (2010). *Child slavery now: A contemporary reader*. Policy Press.
Foucault, M. (1974). Human nature: Justice versus power. In E. Fons (Ed.), *Reflexive water: The basic concerns of mankind* (pp. 135–197). Souvenir Press.
Foucault, M. (1980). Two lectures. In C. Gordon (Ed.), *Power/knowledge: Selected interviews and other writings by Michel Foucault* (pp. 1972–1977). Pantheon Books.
Free the Slaves. (2010). *Findings of slavery linked with mineral extraction in Eastern DRC* (Free the Slaves Research Brief). https://bit.ly/2IHDkzO. Accessed 1 May 2016.
Free the Slaves. (2014). *Child rights in mining pilot project results & lessons learned*. https://www.freetheslaves.net/wp-content/uploads/2015/03/ChildRightsinMiningPilotProjectOverview.pdf. Accessed 1 November 2016.
Hashim, I. (2005). *Exploring the linkages between children's independent migration and education: Evidence from Ghana* (Migration DRC Working Paper WP-T12). http://bit.ly/28QSktn. Accessed 23 June 2016.
Hentschel, T., Hruschka, F., & Priester, M. (2002). *Global report on artisanal and small-scale mining* (Report Commissioned by the MMSD project of IIED). http://goo.gl/A3KNC. Accessed 3 January 2017.
Hilson, G. (2010). Child labour in African artisanal mining communities: Experiences from Northern Ghana. *Development and Change, 41*(5), 445–473.
Hutchful, E. (2002). *Ghana's adjustment experience: The paradox of reform*. Oxford University Press.
ILO. (1999). *Social and labour issues in small-scale mines* (Report for the Tripartite Meeting on Social and Labour Issues in Small-Scale Mines). ILO.
ILO. (2001). *Anatomy of a prohibition: ILO standards in relation to night work of women in industry*. ILO.
ILO. (2002). *A future without child labour*. ILO.
ILO. (2005). *A load too heavy: Children in mining and quarrying*. ILO.
ILO. (2011). *Children in hazardous work: What we know what we need to do*. ILO.
ILO/IPEC. (2004). *Action against child labour and quarrying: A thematic evaluation*. International Labour Organization.

Jennings, N. S. (1999). *Small-scale gold mining: Examples from Bolivia, Philippines and Zimbabwe. Sectoral Activities Programme* (Working Paper, SAP 2.76/WP.130). ILO.
Klocker, N. (2007). An example of 'thin' agency: Child domestic workers in Tanzania. In R. Panelli, S. Punch, & E. Robson (Eds.), *Global perspectives on rural childhood and youth: Young rural lives* (pp. 83–94). Routledge.
Kooijmans, J., & van de Glind, H. (2010). Concept of child slavery: Historical background. In G. Craig (Ed.), *Child slavery now: A contemporary reader* (pp. 21–41). Policy Press.
Lott, T. (1998). *Subjugation and bondage: Critical essays on slavery and social philosophy*. Rowman & Littlefield.
McGary, H., & Lawson, B. E. (1992). *Between slavery and freedom: Philosophy and American slavery*. Indiana University Press.
Mwami, J. A., Sanga, A. J., & Nyoni, J. (2002). *Investigating the worst forms of child labour No. 15. Tanzania children labour in mining: A rapid assessment*. ILO.
Myers, W. E. (2001). The right rights? Child labour in a globalising world. *Annals of the American Academy of Political and Social Science, 575*, 38–55.
O'Connell Davidson, J. (2015). *Modern slavery: The margins of freedom*. Palgrave Macmillan.
Okyere, S. (2013). Are working children's rights and child labour abolition complementary or opposing realms? *International Social Work, 56*(1), 80–91.
Osei, R. D., Owusu, G. A., Asem, E. E., & Afutu-Kotey, R. L. (2009). *Effects of capitation on education outcomes in Ghana*. Institute of Statistical, Social and Economic Research.
Patterson, O. (2012). Trafficking, gender and slavery: Past and present. In J. Allain (Ed.), *The legal understanding of slavery: From the historical to the contemporary* (pp. 322–359). Oxford University Press.
Pupavac, V. (2001). Misanthropy without borders: The international children's rights regime. *Disasters, 25*(2), 95–112.
Salafia, M. (2013). *Slavery's borderland: Freedom and bondage along the Ohio River*. University of Pennsylvania Press.
UNICEF. (2001). *Beyond child labour, affirming rights*. UNICEF.
Verlet, M. (2000). Growing up in Ghana: Deregulation and the employment of children. In B. Schlemmer (Ed.), *The exploited child* (pp. 67–82). Zed Books.
Wahba, J. (1998). *Child labour and poverty transmission: No room for dreams* (ERF Working Papers Series, No. 0108). http://goo.gl/neBLi. Accessed 1 January 2016.
Williams, S. (2005). Earnings poor relief and the economy of makeshifts: Bedfordshire in the early years of the new poor law. *Rural History, 16*, 21–52.
Wright Mills, C. (1959). *The sociological imagination*. Oxford University Press.

CHAPTER 3

Intergenerational Activism as an Alternative to Child Saving: The Example of the Peruvian Movement of Working Children

Jessica K. Taft

"We are a social movement," Mari reiterated to the roomful of children, adolescents, and adults. "This means we don't just do activities and support each other as individuals, but we have political campaigns and initiatives," the tiny fourteen-year-old continued. A few minutes later, one of the adults in the crowded room spoke up to suggest that their organisation had recently focused too much on the political aspect of the movement, trying to lobby and influence decision-makers, but not enough on mobilising, engaging, and educating new participants, or, as he put it, "on the social part of the movement." A few young

J. K. Taft (✉)
University of California, Santa Cruz, CA, USA
e-mail: jtaft@ucsc.edu

© The Author(s), under exclusive license to Springer Nature Switzerland AG 2022
N. Howard and S. Okyere (eds.), *International Child Protection*, Palgrave Studies on Children and Development, https://doi.org/10.1007/978-3-030-78763-9_3

57

people nodded, but Mari and a handful of others shook their heads to signal their disagreement with this position. As part of the bi-annual strategic planning process of MNNATSOP, the Movimiento Nacional de Niños, Niñas y Adolescentes Organizados del Perú, the group was having a wide-ranging debate on the future of the organisation. As the conversation continued, it became clear that everyone agreed on the same organisational goals. They wanted to support working children, to change intergenerational relationships and improve children's place in society, and to create a more just and equitable world. Their disagreements were largely about how to accomplish these goals, and how much organisational time and energy should be devoted to each aspect of this work.

In this chapter, I'll outline how MNNATSOP and the other organisations involved in the Peruvian movement of working children articulate and enact a multi-scale vision for improving working children's lives. This movement's goals and programmes operate to increase the wellbeing of working children at three inter-related but distinct levels. First, at the micro-level, they seek to improve the current and future lives of the individual working children who are part of the movement. Second, at the meso-level, the movement aims to develop more egalitarian and non-hierarchical relationships between children and adults, prefiguring and modelling a version of community in which children are included as capable participants in economic, social, and political life. Third, at the macro-level, the movement seeks to create a more just, sustainable, and equitable society for people of all ages, challenging larger structures of global inequality, poverty, and exclusion. The movement's approach has some overlap with that of other children's rights institutions and children's organisations, including those that form part of the child protection regime, but it also significantly challenges those institutions and pushes beyond their frameworks of children's rights, children's participation, and the provision of care for children by building an intergenerational social movement in which children and adults work together in the pursuit of an explicitly political vision for progressive social change. The empirical example of the Peruvian movement of working children provides a clear alternative to the dominant models of children's rights and child protection documented and critiqued in this book. In presenting and analysing this case, this chapter emphasises the value of intergenerational solidarity over and against paternalism and calls for a politicised, rather than abstractly humanitarian approach to childhood and the task of improving children's lives around the world. Further, it highlights children's own active contributions to this task, showing how they can be engaged political actors and play an important role in the pursuit of social justice and children's rights.

THE PERUVIAN MOVEMENT OF WORKING CHILDREN: A BRIEF INTRODUCTION

Founded in 1976, the Peruvian movement of working children has a long history of advocating for the rights, well-being, and dignity of working children. The movement's goals and agenda have shifted somewhat over time, but many of the elements of their approach have been worked on and carefully developed over the course of decades. Rooted initially in liberation theology, Freirean pedagogy, and the popular and workingclass movements of the 1970s, the movement has a long political history and connection to other struggles for social and economic justice in Latin America (Cussianovich, 2000; Swift, 2000). Over the past forty years, the movement has grown from a single organisation (MANTHOC: El Movimiento de Adolescentes y Niños Trabajadores Hijos de Obreros Cristianos or the Movement of Working Children and Adolescents, Children of Christian Workers) into a complex multi-institutional and multi-organisational field that involves close to 10,000 working children or NATs (*Niños y Adolescentes Trabajadores*) from around the country, as well as a few hundred adult supporters, called *colaboradores*. Much of the work of the movement is done in base groups—small, localised groups of working children that meet weekly, bi-weekly, or monthly. These base groups are most heavily concentrated in Peru's cities, including Lima, Ica, Arequipa, Cajamarca, Cusco, Ayacucho, Puno, Juliaca, Pucallpa, and Iquitos, but there are also bases in rural areas of the Amazon basin and the Andes mountains. Some base groups operate from within schools, churches, or neighbourhoods, while others are attached to movement-run centres for integrated support that have their own space and provide multiple services to participating NATs. Children are recruited into the bases informally via the social networks of each group and may participate for only a short period of time or may become long-term organisational members, continuing their involvement into adulthood by becoming *colaboradores* after they age out of participation as children. Each base elects delegates who participate in regional meetings and each regional coordinating group elects delegates to national coordinating committees. In addition to regular meetings of the members of the regional and national committees, there are regional and national assemblies for all of the NATs. At each of these levels of organisation, one or two adults serve as supporting *colaboradores*, providing structure, guidance and encouragement to the youth, but striving to leave the organisational decision-making power in the hands of the NATs (Taft, 2015). Some of the *colaboradores* are former child participants, while others have been involved in the movement only as adults. In all of these groups, participating children develop their skills for social movement activism and community organisation and build their collective knowledge about children's rights and child labour politics. They launch educational and awareness-building campaigns on a variety of subjects related to working children's lives, engage in advocacy work at the local, national, and international levels, plan and implement cultural events and group activities, raise funds for their projects and participate in wider networks of children's organisations, as well as in occasional political events and gatherings organised by governments, NGOs, or allied social movements. They also receive and give each other support on schoolwork, family issues and problems in their workplaces.

The working children and adolescents in the movement range from ages 8–17, with the largest concentration of participants being between the ages of 11 and 15. They are generally poor and working class, but their work varies a great deal. Most work alongside their families in small enterprises, including on family farms, in restaurants, market stalls and shops, or as street vendors. Some of the girls in the movement primarily do work in the context of the household, helping care for younger siblings and conducting other forms of reproductive labour for immediate and extended family. Others work for employers outside of the family, but in very similar contexts. Some run their own small businesses, funded partly through a movement micro-lending and entrepreneurship programme.

The movement seeks to decriminalise and destigmatise children's work and directly challenges the abolitionist 'end child labour' approach of the International Labour Organisation (ILO) and its partners within the child protection regime. It argues instead for a more nuanced policy perspective that would protect working children from exploitation and harmful working conditions, but allow for and value children's work when it is done in conditions that do not interfere with their well-being, learning, and development (Liebel, 2004; Liebel et al., 2001). Beyond the concrete policy objective of protecting children's right to dignified work, the movement of working children also offers a model for non-hierarchical intergenerational collaboration and seeks to create communities where children are deeply respected and are valued as equal and full participants in economic, social and political life (Cussianovich, 2010).

The analysis offered here is based on extensive ethnographic field research conducted from 2012 to 2015 with movement organisations in and around Peru's capital city of Lima. In addition to attending countless hours of meetings, workshops, social gatherings, assemblies and other movement events, I spent time with a few children outside of the movement context in their neighbourhoods and with their families. I also conducted in-depth interviews with ten adult and fourteen child participants in the movement. Finally, I draw upon a variety of movement-produced documents, publications and materials, including proclamations, pamphlets and other public articulations of their perspective and approach. These different types of data and sources are put in conversation with one another to provide a holistic picture of the movement's activities and approach.

Supporting Working Children as Individuals

Graciela started working in her mother's market stall when she was six years old. She remembers that she used to walk by one of MANTHOC's centres for integrated support every day on her way to the market from her house and often wondered what was happening there with all the children. One day when she was eight, she was given a flier about an event at the house and, curious, she decided to attend. From that point on, in addition to her time spent at school and helping at the market, she began spending several hours a day at MANTHOC. Run with funds from international organisations and individual donations, the MANTHOC centre in Graciela's neighbourhood is a brightly painted multi-level house that sits just off a busy street near several major markets and at the base of a few steep-sided, dusty hills covered in small houses. On a typical weekday, a few dozen children like Graciela pass through the house to hang out, play games, be tutored and assisted with their schoolwork by both Peruvian and international volunteers, and to participate in ongoing workshops on topics ranging from nutrition and mental health to participatory budgeting and local governance, as well as economic activities, like making greeting cards to sell. The house is most crowded right around lunch time, when children who attend both afternoon and morning school line up and pay a few *soles* to get a healthy and filling meal.

The MANTHOC Yerbateros centre is one of a handful of such centres around the country where working children self-organise and participate in building a social movement for their rights and receive holistic and individualised support from dedicated and caring adults. The adult *colaboradores* and shorter-term volunteers at the Yerbateros centre and in other base groups provide significant individualised attention to working children. They give advice and help the NATs to strategise about how to deal with family conflict, relationships with friends or romantic interests, problems at school, or issues in their workplaces. This support, guidance, and care helps children to deal with stress, anxiety, violence, depression, and other personal struggles. As Graciela describes it, "*colaboradores* are our friends, our confidants – we can tell them anything, including the most personal.... They can give us advice when we ask them questions that we might not want to ask our parents.... They help us make our own decisions." MANTHOC also provides workshops for parents on topics like positive discipline, communication styles, and gender bias in families. By working with both children and parents, the organisation tries to improve family dynamics and to facilitate better understanding between children and parents in order to further the participating children's best interests.

Much of what happens in movement base groups like the Yerbateros centre is also occurring at a number of organisations that support marginalised children around the world. However, MANTHOC's work with individual children is distinguished by the fact that, in addition to helping children deal with their most immediate problems, whether it be hunger, a tough maths assignment, or a conflict with a parent, the movement's activities and practices also give working children the skills, knowledge, and attitudes needed to be engaged and confident community leaders and empowered individuals who can advocate for their rights. Graciela entered MANTHOC thinking it would be a place where she would get support with homework and have fun with her peers. And, while this was true, she also quickly learned that MANTHOC was different because "I learned to organise." This process begins in the weekly assemblies, held Saturday mornings at the Yerbateros house. At the assemblies, NATs develop and practice their skills of facilitation, political discussion, organisation, and mobilisation. They have important discussions about issues of children's rights and child labour politics, and they decide on and plan public education campaigns, including recent campaigns to raise awareness of gender-based discrimination, violence against children, and environmentalism. They negotiate and make collective democratic decisions about everything from changes in house rules and behavioural expectations to the topics for upcoming workshops and the content of a public proclamation. Over the years of attending weekly assemblies, Graciela learned a great deal of political information about a range of topics and learned how to plan a meeting agenda, facilitate a discussion, and organise a rally. Then in 2011, at age fourteen, she was elected by the other NATs in Lima to be one of the national delegates of the organisation. In this new role, she began to interact with key decision-makers in the country including national legislators, high-level officials within the ministry that addresses children's issues, and the mayor of Lima. As she took on these responsibilities, she was supported by another set of *colaboradores* who helped her develop her ability to make clear and convincing political arguments, to speak in front of large audiences, and to maintain communication and encourage organisation across the different base groups around the nation.

Over the past forty years, hundreds of NATs have taken on similar responsibilities and have developed their political leadership skills through participation in the movement of working children. Tania Pariona, elected to the Peruvian National Congress in 2016 as part of the Frente Amplio, is the most obvious example of the movement's influence on these young people. An indigenous thirty-two-year-old woman from Ayacucho, Pariona began her community work as an active member and then national leader of MNNATSOP, an overarching umbrella organisation for many working children's groups. She went on to get a degree as a social worker and then spent many years working for the Centro de Culturas Indígenas del Perú (Chirapaq), organising programmes for youth and promoting indigenous rights ("Los Desafios de Tania Pariona, Congresista Indígena Electa," 2016). In Congress, Tania Pariona continued to emphasise her pride in her indigenous heritage by being sworn in in Quechua in addition to Spanish and by wearing traditional clothing ("Congresista Tania Pariona Juramentó En Quechua Y Por Los Pueblos Indígenas," 2016). She also continued to speak out for the rights of children as workers and against an abolitionist approach to child labour (Ruiz, 2016). While Tania Pariona is the most visible example of the political leadership of former organised NATs, she is not the only example. *Colaboradores* with many years of experience in the movement have a variety of anecdotal tales of former national and regional delegates who have gone on to become important figures in their communities, either through participation in government, social movements, or community organisations. And, as Norma, one of the *colaboradores* told me, even former participants who do not have these kinds of roles are confident in themselves and in their ability to speak out about issues that matter to them. She said, "they tell me, thanks to MANTHOC, I can go out and speak in public. I am not embarrassed.... I can say what I think." My own ethnographic observations also suggest that the children who participate in the movement are vocal, direct, proud of their identities as workers, and more than willing to share their thoughts and ideas with adults. They are willing to say what they believe and to challenge injustices when they see them. The movement has been a significant source of political learning, socialisation, and empowerment for many working children.

Unfortunately, there is no systematic social scientific data on the impacts of the movement of working children on the individuals who have participated. However, both my interactions with children in the movement today and the stories told about former participants suggest that the movement encourages them to become vocal and empowered members of their communities. And, in addition to developing their skills and confidence for organisation and community participation, the movement has helped working children to stay in school and go on to develop professional careers. Numerous former working children who were once part of the movement are now social workers, teachers, lawyers, sociologists, or other professionals. The movement helps children think beyond the confines of their immediate surroundings and imagine other futures for themselves, and it gives them the support to get there. Joaquín, a young man from a very poor farming family in a rural area outside Piura, came to Lima when he was fifteen to serve as a national delegate for MNNATSOP. In Lima, he attended a better school than he would have had access to in his hometown, improved many of his academic skills through his role as a leader of the movement, and then went on to attend an international school and eventually was given a scholarship to study at a small liberal arts college in the United States. While the evidence remains anecdotal at this point, there is a clear indication of a trend towards upward mobility for at least a sizable number of former child workers who were actively involved in the movement. In contrast to the claims that child labour inevitably leads to low human capital and ongoing individual and national poverty (Fyfe, 2007; International Labour Organisation, 2010), these examples make clear that working children, when given appropriate support and encouragement, can grow up to become highly successful individuals who contribute economically and politically to their communities, their nation, and the world.

The movement of working children substantially improves children's experiences in the present by giving them warm meals, relationships with caring adults, knowledge about their rights, and valuable tools for addressing problems in their lives. And, while further research would be necessary for more definitive statements, there is a strong indication that participation in the movement improves working children's lives over the long term. These signs of positive individual impacts are also notably consistent with the social scientific research on the effects of participation in youth activism, which has found that such participation improves young people's civic skills and knowledge, psychosocial well-being, sense of efficacy, and academic achievement (Ginwright, 2010; Kirshner & Ginwright, 2012; Taines, 2012).

Transforming Intergenerational Relationships

The movement of working children is distinct from many other programmes for marginalised children in that it supports the development of individual NATs in a politicised way that explicitly seeks to transform dominant ideas about childhood and to create more egalitarian modes of interaction between children and adults. According to MNNATSOP's official Declaration of Principles, the organisation "at every level, wants to be an experience of a new relationship between generations as a concrete sign of our vision for a world in which children and adults can all exercise our rights to be protagonists, with no one excluded." The participants in the movement are thus trying to create a model for a new intergenerational culture that respects children as equals, that values children's perspectives, and that includes children as active agents in economic, social, and political life. This new approach to intergenerational community is best captured through two core concepts in the movement: children's *protagonismo* and adults' *colaboración*.

Multi-layered and complex, the concept of children's *protagonismo* is practically impossible to translate into a single English word (Cussianovich, 2001), but refers to the enactment of both individual and collective agency and power (Taft, 2017). The idea of children's *protagonismo* was initially constructed in relationship to *protagonismo popular*, a term used by social commentators in the late 1960s and 1970s in

Latin America to describe how poor people, neighbourhood groups, women's groups, unions, indigenous groups, and others were claiming space as protagonists, or central actors, on the national political scene (Cussianovich, 2000; Montoya, 2003). It described the activism and political agency of these groups, their collective power, and their sense of collective identity as a political bloc. From this lineage, *protagonismo* refers to a social group, especially a marginalised social group, coming to see its own significance and claiming space in the political field. For the movement of working children, this has meant discussing how children are an oppressed social group that has been excluded from power, often with paternalistic justifications, *and* that such exclusion is unjust and not inevitable if children mobilise as a collective force.

The movement's view on childhood also describes children as being fundamentally equal to adults. It argues that children should be seen as social and political subjects with inalienable rights and with their own distinctive knowledge based on lived experiences as children. Chronological age, they suggest, does not define an individual's worthiness of respect, their contributions to knowledge, or their political skills and capabilities. Everyone, including children, can learn new skills and so can become critical agents of social change. In interviews, children talked about *protagonismo* as "being able to be part of the construction of a better world," and "being a social actor." Children's *protagonismo* thus signifies a vision of childhood as a politically salient collective identity and of children as capable and knowledgeable actors and decision-makers.

Protagonismo emphasises children's equal capabilities, knowledge, and potential for contributions to the world around them, but it does not mean that the movement thinks adults have no responsibilities for supporting children's development, growth, or well-being. Instead, adults are *colaboradores,* working alongside children in the movement. Article 18 of the MNNATSOP Declaration of Principles states that "adults are part of MNNATSOP as *colaboradores*. They are not representatives of the movement; they are not directors of the movement; they are not teachers or managers. To collaborate means to co-accept responsibility, to co-promote, to co-accompany, to co-act, to co-decide, to co-participate without substituting for or supplanting the NATs. To collaborate is to exercise and develop one's own *protagonismo* alongside the permanent development of the *protagonismo* of the NATs." *Colaboración* is an active practice of working alongside children in which adults try to amplify children's power, agency, and *protagonismo*. *Colaboradores* do not do things for children, nor act on children' behalf, but instead act in egalitarian partnership with children, building relationships based on solidarity rather than paternalism.

In order to create meaningful collaborations with genuinely shared decision-making power, both children and adults in the movement have to challenge their own internalised assumptions about childhood and adulthood. They have to question the common beliefs that adults know best, that children do not really understand the issues, and that adults should be "in charge." As one *colaboradora* explained to me, "in order to change how adults treat children, you have to change how they think about children." I would add that you also have to change how children think about themselves. This transformation of ideas is well underway within the movement, with both NATs and *colaboradores* articulating strong commitments to horizontal relationships, intergenerational equality, and children's leadership within the movement. However, a transformation of ideas is not enough to transform intergenerational power relationships (Taft, 2015). Enacting horizontalism is quite difficult given the larger social context (in Peru and beyond) of children's marginalisation, age-based inequalities, and adult privilege.

Despite the very real difficulties of creating egalitarian intergenerational relationships, the movement of working children has developed a variety of strategies and practices that further this goal. Children call the adults by their first names, without any titles or honorifics. Adults use a variety of pedagogical tactics that amplify children's voices and draw out their contributions. They listen deeply to children's ideas and perspectives, regularly reiterating their desire for children to "be protagonists." The NATs also elect the *colaboradores* who will work with them in the regional and national delegations and have regular opportunities to provide feedback to the *colaboradores,* encouraging *colaboradores* to be responsive to children's desires for these relationships. The children articulate a strong sense of their ownership and power in the movement, and express that they feel like they are treated as equals by the *colaboradores*. Graciela stated, "in society there isn't equality between adults and children because the adult is seen as being above, seen as knowing more, and the kid is seen as below, as not being able to make his or her own decisions – the kid should just think and do what the adult says. But when you are in the movement all this changes, it goes away." Or, as Enrique, a former NAT and now *colaborador* explained, in wider society the discourse is "because you are a kid you don't know anything, and you don't get to give your opinion, your ideas don't matter, you don't have a voice or a vote. But, in the movement, we have the opposite, we have a will to listen to [the kids], to follow their lead, to raise up and support them. What they think, what they propose, what they imagine – we work together to make it happen." While far from perfect, the movement has created a collaborative intergenerational culture in which children and adults work together to try to reduce adultism and age-based hierarchies; these organisations can therefore serve as a model and inspiration for families, schools, social movements, government programmes for children's participation, and other sites of intergenerational interaction.

Tracing the effects of the movement on the broader culture of childhood or on intergenerational relationships in Peru is, from a social scientific standpoint, nearly impossible. All we can do is speculate about these diffuse and nearly invisible lines of influence. Children and adults who participate in the movement certainly come to see childhood in a new light, but the ripple effects of these transformations are hard to know. My ethnographic research suggests that these ideas have had some influence on the families and schools that interact with the movement, but beyond these specific cases, any conclusions would be speculative. One place where the impacts *are* more visible is in the many adults who work in a variety of children's rights organisations and institutions in Peru and whose vision of childhood has been deeply informed by the ideas of the movement, either via their own direct participation in the movement or through the movement's broader intellectual influence via Alejandro Cussianovich, a key movement figure who is also a prolific writer and teaches university courses on childhood. The idea of children's *protagonismo* appears in a variety of other spaces in Lima now, including local and national government projects for children's participation. This suggests that the movement has had at least some success in encouraging a re-imagining of childhood.

Activism for a Better World

Many of the international organisations and institutions that focus on children and childhood and comprise the international child protection regime under discussion in this book do not address the political and economic agendas that produce poverty, inequality, and marginalisation. As the introduction to this volume makes clear, they avoid serious engagement with the histories of colonialism, imperialism, resource extraction, and neoliberal capitalism in favour of supposedly more "safe" or "neutral" concerns like children's health and protection from harm. But, by not discussing the *causes* of problems in children's lives, they fail to situate children's issues in context and may even imply that these problems are the fault of poor children, their families, or abstracted notions of "culture" rather than the result of centuries of exploitation and oppression (Bent, 2013; Hoffman, 2012; Sensoy & Marshall, 2010). In contrast to this abstracted and a-historical humanitarianism, with its tendencies towards naturalisation and victim-blaming, the movement of working children is explicit about its politics.

The movement of working children's social change goals expand beyond the micro- and meso-level changes I have described to include the pursuit of a much larger vision of social and economic justice. MANTHOC's statement of their objectives, for example, includes "to promote and defend the rights of children and adolescents in the exercise of our citizenship and, through our transformative and intercultural actions and proposals, to contribute to creating a more just, humane and caring world." In addition to transforming ideas about children and including children as full and equal members of communities, they seek to "create a culture that rejects all forms of inequality and promotes the care of our biodiversity," to facilitate a solidarity economy that is "an economy of sharing that is at the service of people" and to "change situations of exploitation and marginalisation, developing values like equity, solidarity, justice, and *protagonismo*." These goals, while somewhat abstract, suggest some of the contours of the movement's larger political perspective, which is rooted in liberation theology, Leftist and anti-capitalist critique, and indigenous theories of communalism and interdependence. Movement materials have challenged the debt regime and neoliberal economic policy, and speak explicitly against free trade agreements like the Free Trade Area of the Americas, which degrade labour conditions and reduce environmental regulations. They denounce not only the exploitation of child workers, but also the "prevailing economic system that creates conditions of exclusion and exploitation" (MOLACNATs, 2010). *Colaboradores* frequently argue that collaborative, mutually supportive, community-based work done by people of all ages is part of Peru's indigenous heritage, and that hierarchical and authoritarian approaches to both children and workers are the products of colonialism and Western thinking.

The movement's politicised perspectives on labour, exploitation, global capitalism, and children's rights are not just ideas that circulate in movement conversations, educational workshops, or public proclamations. They are instantiated in social movement activism aimed at changing laws and policies at the local, national, and international level. For example, on July 28 2015, Peru's independence day, NATs and *colaboradores* from MNNATSOP took to the streets in a march, hoping to garner attention for a set of policies that various organisations within the movement had proposed to President Ollanta Humala, but which had largely been ignored. This included a list of 10 policies and programmes to protect and support street children, modifications to the law on domestic workers, and a set of changes to the national law on childhood and adolescence. A couple of hundred participants, mostly children and adolescents, marched through the busy centre of Lima, chanting for their rights to be heard and increasing the public visibility of the movement.

MANTHOC and MNNATSOP have marched in solidarity with other working class and labour organisations in the annual May Day marches in Lima, advocated for women's and girls' rights in the #niunamenos march in 2016, held regular rallies and public events against violence against children, and been part of environmental and anti-mining protests in Lima and Cajamarca. The NATs and *colaboradores* also regularly interact with Peru's national legislature as they attempt to influence the laws on childhood and adolescence. They meet with legislators and speak at public forums in order to pursue a national policy agenda for children's rights. They have also worked with other working children's organisations globally to advocate for the inclusion of working children's perspectives in ILO discussions of child labour policy and against minimum age laws that criminalise children's work (Liebel, 2004; Taft, 2013).

As social movement organisations, MANTHOC and MNNATSOP make no pretence at being "apolitical" nor of "protecting" children from the complex and messy world of politics. Instead, children and adults work together to develop their critical perspectives and then act on those perspectives in the pursuit of a more just world. The movement identifies systems of inequality that need to be challenged and suggests that they *can* be challenged by children and adults working together. However, the movement's achievements in these areas have been fairly limited. The movement and others like it have struggled to halt or reduce the criminalisation of children's work despite it being their primary concrete policy agenda.[1] Of course, social movements' success should not be judged by their ability to achieve their most lofty goals. Ending poverty, creating sustainable communities, and dismantling global inequality are not straightforward tasks that can just be checked off an organisational to-do list. Rather than dismiss social movement activism and children's attempts to create macro-level change on the grounds of this difficulty, we could instead ask what might be possible if more children's organisations took up this approach. Or, on the flip side, what might happen if "adult" social movements were more engaged with children and children's issues and if more movements were intentionally intergenerational? In short, we should not give up on macro-level political change just because it is difficult. People who are interested in supporting children's rights and children's well-being would benefit from thinking about these issues as part of political, social movement struggles, rather than as neutral humanitarian concerns and children's rights advocates could learn a great deal from other social movements for rights, justice, liberation, and equality.

Expanding Intergenerational Activism

The Peruvian movement of working children suggests a vibrant and viable alternative to the models of children's rights and child protection that constitute the dominant approach of the international child protection regime. Intergenerational activism empowers individual children, improving their lives in concrete and tangible ways as it seeks to influence the cultural, social, and political conditions that shape children's lives. But, shifting towards such an approach is not easy and requires a much more politicised interpretation of the causes of global poverty, inequality, and children's suffering. Doing intergenerational activism for global social and economic justice also requires a vision of what such justice entails, and such visions are inevitably sites of contestation and disagreement. Many children's rights and child protection institutions are able to gain leverage and funding on the basis of a supposedly neutral and universal version of humanitarian concern for children's safety and

---

[1] The obvious exception here is in Bolivia, where UNATsBO, the working children's union in Bolivia had a key role in the passage of a new law that allowed children to work but sought to protect them from exploitation, long hours, and dangerous conditions. While this law has since been revoked, it was a striking example of children's potential to influence policy.

well-being. Intergenerational activism makes no such claim of political neutrality and thus could create major challenges for organisations that have historically tried to position themselves as outside or beyond politics. However, we should remember that such claims of neutrality are not actually outside politics, but instead are usually rooted in the politics of maintaining the status quo or making minor reforms. As the radical historian Howard Zinn (2010) reminds us, "you can't be neutral on a moving train."

Shifting some child protection organisations and programmes towards becoming intergenerational social movements is certainly a difficult endeavour, but it is not entirely without precedent. The field of youth development provides a valuable and highly relevant example for this kind of programmatic change. In the United States in the mid-1990s, a growing number of youth service providers and funders began to discuss the potential value of youth activism and youth organising as a youth development model. These programmes were a response to public concerns about youth disengagement from politics in general and anxieties about the supposedly "delinquent" and "risky" behaviour of low-income youth of colour in particular (Kwon, 2013; Taft & Gordon, 2013). But rather than simply keeping youth off the streets or focusing on individual youth support, the youth organising approach built opportunities for young people to work together to address community problems (Checkoway & Gutierrez, 2006; Clay, 2012). It marked a "paradigmatic shift in youth services, from a 'kid-fixing' model to 'positive youth development'" (Kwon, 2013, p. 52) and was the result of a "deliberate investment made by a select group of philanthropic foundations to promote alternative youth development programmes that incorporated political activism" (Kwon, 2013, p. 54). In addition to the explicit promotion of youth activism by a set of funders and youth advocates, this approach also flourished thanks to the work of juvenile justice organisers, hip hop activists, environmental racism organisations, queer youth movements and Gay-Straight Alliances, and feminist discussions about the "third wave" (Ginwright, 2002; Gordon, 2010; Hosang, 2003; Taft, 2010; Weiss, 2003). While youth activism is still only a very small portion of youth-serving organisations, these programmes became fundable and were generally accepted within this larger landscape (Kirshner & Ginwright, 2012; Kwon, 2013). There are certainly limits, challenges, and problems that have emerged with the instutionalisation of youth activism within the youth development landscape, but the substantial growth of this programmatic model over the past 20 years suggests some of the possibilities for a similar shift in the international child protection field. Acknowledging youth as capable political subjects and agents of social change and identifying the ways that youth activism supported youth development outcomes helped to create a flourishing set of organisations devoted to supporting youth activism; acknowledging children's political agency and the value of intergenerational activism for children could have similar effects. There are also, as this chapter suggests, already models for doing intergenerational activist work to further children's rights. The movement of working children offers one example, but it is not the only one. Other working children's movements around the world (Liebel et al., 2001) and intergenerational feminist groups (Bent, 2016; Brown, 2016; Edell et al., 2016) are just a few of the many spaces currently practicing adult–child political collaboration in the pursuit of social justice. These already existing intergenerational social movements provide a crucial foundation upon which new approaches to child protection can be built.

References

Bent, E. (2013). A different girl effect: Producing political girlhoods in the 'Invest in girls' Climate. In J.K Taft & S. Kawecka Nenga (Eds.), *Youth Engagement: The Civic-Political Lives of Children and Youth, Sociological Studies of Children and Youth, 16*, 3–20.

Bent, E. (2016). Making it up: Intergenerational activism and the ethics of empowering girls. *Girlhood Studies, 9*(3), 105–121.

Brown, L. M. (2016). *Powered by girl: A field guide for supporting youth activists*. Beacon Press.

Checkoway, B. N., & Gutierrez, L. M. (Eds.). (2006). *Youth participation and community change*. Haworth Press.

Clay, A. (2012). *The hip-hop generation fights back: Youth, activism and post-civil rights politics*. NYU Press.

"Congresista Tania Pariona Juramentó En Quechua Y Por Los Pueblos Indígenas". (2016, July 22). *Diario Correo*. http://diariocorreo.pe/politica/congresista-tania-pariona-juramento-en-quechua-y-pueblos-indigenas-video-686628/

Cussianovich, A. (2000). Participación Y Ciudadanía de Los NATs. In *Niños, Niñas Y Adolescentes Trabajadores: Derechos, Ciudadanía Y Protagonismo* (pp. 39–57). MANTHOC.

Cussianovich, A. (2001). What does protagonism mean?. In M. Liebel, B. Overwein, & A. Recknage (Eds.), *Working children's protagonism: Social movements and empowerment in Latin America, Africa, and India* (pp. 157–169).
Cussianovich, A. (2010). *Paradigma Del Protagonismo.* INFANT.
Edell, D., Brown, L. M., & Montano, C. (2016). Bridges, ladders, sparks, and glue: Celebrating and problematizing 'girl-driven' intergenerational feminist activism. *Feminist Media Studies, 16*(4), 693–709.
Fyfe, A. (2007). *The worldwide movement against child labour: Progress and future directions.* International Labor Organisation.
Ginwright, S. (2002). New terrain in youth development: The promise of a social justice approach. *Social Justice, 29*(4), 82–95.
Ginwright, S. (2010). *Black youth rising: Activism and radical healing in Urban America.* Teachers College Press.
Gordon, H. (2010). *We fight to win: Inequality and the politics of youth activism.* New Brunswick. Rutgers University Press.
Hoffman, D. M. (2012). Saving children, saving Haiti: Child vulnerability and narratives of the nation. *Childhood, 19*(2), 155–168.
Hosang, D. (2003). *Youth and community organizing today.* Funders' Collaborative on Youth Organizing.
International Labor Organisation. (2010). *The Hague global child labor conference: Towards a world without child labor: Mapping the road to 2016.* International Labor Organisation.
Kirshner, B., & Ginwright, S. (2012). Youth organizing as a developmental context for African American and Latino Adolescents. *Child Development Perspectives, 6*(3), 288–294.
Kwon, S. A. (2013). *Uncivil youth: Race, activism, and affirmative governmentality.* Duke University Press Books.
Liebel, M. (2004). *A will of their own: Cross-cultural perspectives on working children.* Zed Books.
Liebel, M., Overwien B., & Recknagel, A. (Eds.) (2001). *Working children's protagonism: Social movements and empowerment in Latin America, Africa, and India.* IKO.
"Los Desafíos de Tania Pariona, Congresista Indígena Electa". (2016, May 31). *Chirapaq.* http://www.chirapaq.org.pe/noticias/los-desafios-de-tania-pariona-congresista-indigena-electa
MOLACNATs. (2010). Pronunciamiento Por El Día Mundial Del La Dignidad Del Niño Trabajador. *Revista NATs, 20,* 157–160.
Montoya, L. W. (2003). Poder, Jóvenes Y Ciencias Sociales En El Perú. *Ultima Década., 11*(18), 21–68.
Ruiz, P. (2016, September 29). La Defensora de Los Derechos de Los Niños Que Apoya El Trabajo Infantil. *Eldiario.es.* http://www.eldiario.es/desalambre/entrevista-Tania-Pariona-infantil-positivo_0_562044142.html

Sensoy, Ö., & Marshall, E. (2010). Missionary girl power: Saving the 'third world' one girl at a time. *Gender & Education, 22*(3), 295–311.

Swift, A. (2000). El Movimiento Nacional de Niños, Niñas Y Adolescentes Trabajadores de Peru. *Revista NATs, 5/6*, 99–174.

Taft, J. K. (2010). Girlhood in action: Contemporary U.S. girls' organisations and the public sphere. *Girlhood Studies, 3*(2), 11–29.

Taft, J. K. (Ed.). (2013). *Nothing about us, without us: Critiques of the international labor Ooganisation's approach to child labor from the movements of working children.* IFEJANT.

Taft, J. K. (2015). 'Adults talk too much': Intergenerational dialogue and power in the Peruvian movement of working children. *Childhood, 22*(4), 460–473.

Taft, J. K. (2017). Continually redefining protagonismo: The Peruvian movement of working children and political change, 1976–2015. *Latin American Perspectives, 46*(5): 90–110. [Online First]. https://doi.org/10.1177/009 458X17736037

Taft, J. K., & Gordon, H. R. (2013). Youth activists, youth councils, and constrained democracy. *Education, Citizenship and Social Justice, 8*(1), 87–100.

Taines, C. (2012). Intervening in alienation: The outcomes for Urban youth of participating in school activism. *American Educational Research Journal, 49*(1), 53–86.

Weiss, M. (2003). *Youth rising.* Applied Research Center.

Zinn, H. (2010). *You can't be neutral on a moving train: A personal history of our times.* Beacon Press.

Illusions in the Protection of Working Children

Michael Bourdillon and William Myers

Introduction

Over the past 20 years, and as exemplified by the previous two chapters, a growing body of research and experience has provided evidence that national and international policy on child labour hurts many of the children it is supposed to help—especially true of policies intended to prohibit children below mid-adolescence from working (Bourdillon et al., 2009). Interventions to remove children from work are usually assessed in terms of reduced numbers of children working, and rarely in terms of holistic outcomes in children's lives; when such outcomes are considered, they frequently show that some children are damaged (for some examples see Bourdillon et al., 2011, pp. 1–6, 181–192, and see the two cases below).

M. Bourdillon (✉)
Mount Pleasant, Harare, Zimbabwe

W. Myers
Elk Grove, CA, USA

Yet responsible organisations have failed to respond to this evidence by making their policies safer for children. How can that be? Why would an otherwise responsible agency intended to protect children persist in counterproductive policies and practises detrimental to them?

To convey a sense of what we are talking about, we open this chapter with two cases, on which we have recent information, and in which the supposed protection of children clearly contravened their long-term best interests. We then offer an explanation in terms of five illusions (some would say delusions): about how to protect children, about the competence of agencies within the child protection regime supposedly protecting them, about the competence of children, about childhood, and about morality. We discuss each illusion separately in the light of our decades of experience as academics and practitioners in the field, indicating historically why practise towards working children has failed them. Finally, we propose an approach that could be more fruitful, and which echoes the calls of the two previous chapters in this volume.

Case 1: Stopping Education by Stopping Work

Journalist Ngoni Shumba, recently posted a report: "Zimbabwe: when ending child labour does not end child exploitation".[1] He argued that although "rights groups scored a victory" when a tea company in the Chipinge District ended its "earn-and-learn" scheme in 2013, the situation facing former child workers did not improve. Nearly two years later, many children in Chipinge were looking for any means of survival and some pointed out that the tea estates at least gave them access to education and hope for a way out of poverty. Onai Muzeya, a 14-year-old street vendor, said "I certainly would have been better off working for my fees than what I am currently doing".

The "earn-and-learn" schools had provided schooling for pupils who contracted to work on the estates. Author Michael Bourdillon (1999) spent several weeks at one of the schools, speaking with pupils, their teachers, their families, management and workers on the estate, and others living and working in the area. Life for the pupils was hard. In the peak season, they arose early for a full morning's work picking tea before school in the afternoon (in the off-season it was easier: school in the morning

---

[1] http://africanarguments.org/2015/09/10/zimbabwe-when-ending-child-labour-does-not-end-child-exploitation/ (accessed 9 June 2018).

followed by perhaps three hours in the fields). Work and school in peak season left little time for play or even sleep. Pupils complained of dangers and injuries in the fields. Not a few dropped out; those who remained wanted improvements, but not an end to the system. Indeed, subsequent to Bourdillon's research there were some improvements: school moved to the morning, prior to work; working hours were cut; and there was some attention to working conditions.

Payment was on a piece-work basis; children were paid the same rates as adults and received subsidised schooling as well, so it was not cheaper for the company than adult labour. Management regarded the school as a service to the community. One top manager commented that in an ideal world, such schools should not exist, but in the current Zimbabwean situation the schools served a useful purpose.

All the children interviewed had chosen to be there—some from far away had to persuade their parents to allow them to attend this school. For most, it was the only available chance of secondary schooling: several commented that previously they had been sitting at home doing nothing. A few chose this school because they noticed that the teachers were more committed and examination results were better than in the surrounding government schools.

All kinds of people in the area asserted that the schools served a useful function, and many in the neighbourhood asked for more such schools to be established. Past pupils commented that they did not mind the hard life because they had a purpose. At the local offices of the Ministry of Education, one official asserted that he got to where he was through one of these schools. A clerk on the estate pointed out that his attendance at the school resulted in his current relatively well-paid employment; now he could afford to send his younger sister to the easier life of a mission boarding school.

How can the removal of this kind of chance for disadvantaged children be regarded as a victory for children's rights? Did the advocates for child rights really know better than the children and the local communities what would help them? Why did the children's efforts to improve their lives receive no respect?

Case 2: Missing the Rehabilitative Function of Work

Eighteen years ago, anthropologist Rachel Burr studied street children in Vietnam and wrote about a reform school to which several of them were committed. Staff at the school came to understand that most of the committed boys were not malevolent or particularly delinquent; the offences they committed in the eyes of the authorities resulted from their need to sustain themselves and their families. Unless something were done to change their situation, on release the boys would have had no alternative but to return to the activities that had brought them to the reformatory. With the help of Butterfly Trust, a humanitarian NG), and at the request of the boys, the school introduced programmes for training in various skills—motorcycle mechanics, computer services, carpentry, and crafts—to enable the boys to earn an honest living when they left. To be sustainable with limited funding available, and to give the boys experience of the economics of their new trades, these programmes were funded from sales of goods and services. Butterfly Trust continued such training for the most vulnerable boys leaving the reformatory, with boys as young as 12 involved in their workshops. Years later, the young adults spoke of this training as having changed their lives and they remained in touch with Butterfly Trust. However, when members of UNICEF visited the reformatory and saw the boys at work, they accused the school and the NGO of "colluding in child labour" and wanted the programme stopped (Burr, 2006, p. 163).[2]

How could members of an organisation at the very heart of the international child protection regime, which aims to protect children and their rights, demand something that was clearly damaging to the future prospects of these disadvantaged boys?

The Illusions

These two cases illustrate the problematic nature of the assumption that stopping 'child labour' protects children and their chances, which rests on a number of illusions that we consider in this chapter:

1. **The illusion of protection**: If we do not stop children from working, we cannot protect them.
2. **The illusion of expertise**: Child protection agencies and experts know best what is good for children.

---

[2] Information from the book was supplemented by private correspondence with Rachel Burr, who has kept in touch with some of the persons involved. The programme was eventually stopped by the Government of Vietnam, which closed the school and instead committed boys to labour camps.

3. **The illusion of incompetent children**: Children are unable to decide what is in their best interests.
4. **The illusion of a universal childhood**: Productive work below a certain age is bad for children.
5. **The illusion of moral superiority**: It is moral to stop as many children as possible from working.

The Illusion of Protection

A widespread assumption in child labour policy and intervention is that children below a specified age can be protected by removing them from economic work. Yet opportunities are lost to disadvantaged children if intervention and policy attend only to removing risks of harm, and neglect to balance these against material and developmental benefits that work can convey.

Current evidence suggests that international standards and complying national legislation based on a general[3] minimum age of employment fail to protect children and are often inimical to their best interests and well-being.[4] There are three principal reasons for this. First, prohibiting work attends to none of the reasons why children work; it addresses symptoms rather than causes of problems, and so has limited chance of resolving them. Second, minimum-age laws do not target work that is harmful to children, which is where the problem lies (in employment and elsewhere). Third, they prohibit even work that is beneficial to children and contributes to their development, where there is no problem to be prevented. This illogical, labour-oriented approach is blind to children's situations, and to expect protection from such an approach is to court illusion.

A more reliable approach to protection, focussed on children's well-being and considering their rights, treats children's development holistically and targets specifically work and work situations having adverse

---

[3] We criticise only general minimum-age laws and recognise merit in putting age limits on specific types of hazardous work as a valuable tool in some situations.

[4] There is a growing literature on this topic, which is discussed in Bourdillon et al. (2009) and Bourdillon et al. (2011). Examples of more recent studies are Edmonds and Shrestha (2012) on failure of legislation significantly to affect children's time use, Bharadwaj et al. (2013) on perverse effects of legislation increasing time spent on work, Maconachie and Hilson (2016) on international standards exacerbating poverty, and Dammert et al. (2017) questioning the effectiveness of market-oriented policies.

effects on their lives. International human rights conventions following the Second World War together comprise what is commonly known as the "International Bill of Rights" and are today the primary foundation of global social policy, including policy for the protection of children. Specifically, in regards to children, the most authoritative human rights convention is the 1989 United Nations Convention on the Rights of the Child (UNCRC), which instructs on how the spectrum of basic human rights should be applied to young persons up to 18 years of age. In Article 3, it stipulates, "In all actions concerning children, whether undertaken by public or private social welfare institutions, courts of law, administrative authorities or legislative bodies, *the best interests of the child shall be a primary consideration*" [emphasis added]. In effect, children are to be protected by prioritising their well-being over other concerns that might be preferred by adults. Article 27 suggests that children's well-being requires "a standard of living adequate for the child's physical, mental, spiritual, moral and social development". Such holistic development is the goal. Article 32, which addresses children's work specifically, lists what work-related threats children should be protected against: "economic exploitation and from performing any work that is likely to be hazardous or to interfere with the child's education, or to be harmful to the child's health or physical, mental, spiritual, moral or social development". This carefully phrased language does not reject non-exploitative work that is safe and developmental. Its reference back to Article 27 obliquely suggests the acceptability and even desirability of work that benefits children.[5]

This approach suggests that good policy should be based on the analyses of the differential effects of work on children's lives considered holistically. Health scientists have achieved spectacular success in saving and improving the lives of many millions of children every year through a process of regularly monitoring the well-being and development of children, diagnosing problems, and applying preventative and curative remedies fitting the diagnosis. UNCRC Article 32 enables an extension of

---

[5] We are aware of Sect. 2a of article 32, which requires that states parties shall "Provide for a minimum age or minimum ages for admission to employment". We notice, first, that this wording allows for different ages for different kinds of employment, and second, assumptions arising from the history of minimum-age legislation, which we discuss above, influenced thinking at the time the Convention was constituted. Our argument stands that a general minimum age for employment fails to meet the goals set out in Sect. 1 of the article.

this proven good practise into matters of work by providing a checklist of threats to children's well-being and development against which protection may be necessary. Although incorporating the list of work-related threats into this effective approach raises some technical difficulties about specific indicators and methods in cross-cultural contexts, skills developed in the expanding field of childhood indicators could be adopted and applied to work-related threats to children, enabling a reliable process of monitoring, diagnosis and remedy for the benefit of children. This should be the natural institutional response to threats.

Since the UNCRC has been in force for over 30 years, one might by now expect to find programmes all over the world routinely monitoring the well-being and developmental impacts of work on children, spotting where there are problems, and stepping in to correct unacceptable situations in context-sensitive ways. But while some local community-based projects mount activities of this type, we are not aware of any major national or international agency having made a serious attempt to systematically observe how children's work affects their multi-dimensional well-being and development, and then intervene accordingly.[6] In practise, the most fundamental and widely ratified international policy to protect children in relation to their work has been ignored even by those agencies within the child protection regime who are responsible for promoting it as part of the UNCRC. It is hard to imagine a more complete or puzzling breakdown of international responsibility to protect children.

Why this failure? We think the main explanation is simply overhang from history. Children's work was the subject of the very first attempt at protection of children through the use of international conventions, in 1919, long before the modern "Bill of Human Rights" and the UNCRC. Among other provisions, the Treaty of Versailles ending the First World War established the International Labour Organisation (ILO)

---

[6] One indicator often cited to justify prohibition of children's work is the widespread inverse correlation between school outcomes and work. This is misinterpretation of the data, often a direct product of faulty research designs. Such studies need to consider bi-directional causality (work can interfere with school and school system failures can drive children to work) and to control for such background variables as poverty, household structure and education level, economic environment, and children's aptitudes, all of which are known to strongly affect both work and school (see Bourdillon et al., 2011, pp. 108–132). Formal education on its own is not an adequate indicator of child well-being: multi-dimensional indicators sensitive to specific situations of children are needed.

and included the elimination of child labour as part of its mandate for labour and economic justice.

This first well-meaning experiment got off on the wrong foot and has never recovered. The international system at that time conceived of children's work as a labour issue to be mediated by standardised law (hence the term "child labour" and the mandate to the ILO), rather than as a child protection issue to be addressed by meeting the different needs of children in diverse situations. The approach articulates and enforces behavioural norms in the workplace that are assumed to benefit workers; it does not inquire into what children need nor monitor their well-being and development. Desire to protect children from industrial employment became fused with desire to protect adult industrial employment from children. The prevailing fear was that cheap labour provided by children would undercut adult employment and wages and lead to working-class poverty (still a fear much later), notwithstanding the fact that poor families needed at least some productive work from their children to survive. The answer was to sharply limit and control the presence of child workers in labour markets, giving them a piece but not too much, which hopefully would also help children by keeping them safer and in school.

To that purpose, the international community emerging from the First World War adopted an 80-year-old European model that addressed exploitation in child labour through national laws regulating the age at which children could start work, their hours and working conditions, the payment of their wages, and so forth—a model that fails to attend to the economic, social, and educational changes that so radically improved the lives of families and their children and enabled a move from work to school over time (see Cunningham & Stromquist, 2005). Although it was expected that children would benefit from these laws, this labour-oriented approach starts out by seeing workers who are children, and proceeds to ask how those young workers fit into the existing world of adult work. The child-centred perspective of the UNCRC, on the other hand, sees children who work and asks how that work affects their well-being and development. These two views start and end at very different places, and policies based on them head in different directions. Yet both are simultaneously in force today and compete with each other, even inside the most relevant UN agencies, UNICEF and the ILO. We look briefly at the evolution of this conflict.

The 1919 mandate to protect children was given to a labour and economic justice agency, not to a child protection organisation. The first

ILO convention on child labour (Convention 5) forbade the employment of children under 14 in an "industrial undertaking". It was intended to protect children by removing them from certain kinds of work or working conditions, and it was followed by similar conventions addressing children's work at sea and in agriculture.

These moves were partly influenced by romantic ideas of childhood as a time for learning and play, and there was some push-back from those relying on children's work for survival. In 1924, the League of Nations adopted the Geneva Declaration of the Rights of the Child, which granted that "the child must be put in a position to earn a livelihood, and must be protected against every form of exploitation". "Exploitation" refers to children being under-compensated for their work. Higher wages for children would reduce the incentive to hire them over adults, thereby buffering adult employment from the competition of children. Children retained a right to work, but not to undermine adult labour markets.

Subsequent ILO conventions on child labour chipped away at the presence of children in labour markets, starting with those areas thought to pose more dangers for children. In 1973, the "Minimum Age Convention" (No. 138) banned most work by children under certain stipulated minimum ages. Beyond some concern to keep children from unsafe work, this Convention indicated its intent to protect children's schooling. However, since there was scant evidence that banning children from work effectively kept them in school, it is unclear whether that rationale served as purpose or pretext. This Convention is understandably regarded by many as, like its predecessors, about protecting labour markets as much as protecting children.

It was not until 1999, ten years after the adoption of the UNCRC and partly in response to it, that the ILO produced a convention that clearly prioritises protection of the well-being of children: no. 182 on The Worst Forms of Child Labour (WFCL). Only since the UNCRC in 1989 and ILO Convention 182 in 1999 has international law governing child work got around to attempting to protect child well-being as assiduously as it has protected adult jobs. But the older laws banning children from jobs remain assertively in effect, as Samuel Okyere's chapter here describes (Chapter 2). The consequence of this of course is to limit the positive potential impact of the CRC and WFCL Convention.

Today we have competing international approaches to children's work: one new, incorporating post-WWII human rights, and reflecting a more modern understanding of children; and the other, focussing on removing children from the labour market, outdated and not well adapted to consider children and contemporary rights. The international system is so highly invested in the old approach, which it has nursed and for which it has built legal and institutional infrastructure since 1919, that it lacks incentive, will, and means to easily change to the far more reasonable modern alternatives authorised and promoted under the UNCRC and to an extent also the WFCL convention. We urgently need to find a practical way to move the international community beyond the constricted and often counterproductive labour perspective, and towards a far broader focus that contextualises children's work in ultimate concern for their well-being and development, and their human rights. There has been much informal discussion about how to make this move, but politically viable means have not been identified. Current discussions between experts and organisations exploring the possibilities of incremental change within current agency structures are in progress, but do not seem to us at this point particularly promising. One reason why the labour perspective dominates policy and intervention rests in where expertise is deemed to lie and the kind of expertise available there.

The Illusion of Expertise

For nearly a century, the international community has promoted the conventional policy of banning children below a legal minimum age from working without ever evaluating it to find out whether it does in fact protect the well-being and development of children. Without such evaluation there can be no certainty that the policy is beneficial for children, but agencies continue to promote this untested treatment. Why do UNICEF, the ILO, and major INGOs comprising the international child protection regime seem so unable or unwilling to change from an outdated, labour-oriented, law-enforcement approach that barely pays attention to the needs of children, to the more modern, child-centred, human rights approach focussed on children's well-being and development?

Perhaps what looks like poor expertise is in fact a problem of information and communication; the agencies do not know what critics know, and visa-versa. Against this suggestion, the main international, national, and NGO agencies involved in advocating, making, and implementing child labour policy have easy access to the same published literature cited by critics, and for over 20 years been actively and explicitly informed by researchers (including a good number in this book) that some of their most important and long-standing policies are more likely to harm children than to help them. Indeed, that information has sometimes come from within their own organisations (for example, Boyden et al., 1998, jointly supported and published by UNICEF and Radda Barnen).

Another possibility is that these agencies are not adequately staffed to recognise and review important information. In our experience with major agencies such as UNICEF, the ILO, and the major international child advocacy NGOs, their staff may not always have time to read and keep up with the literature or may lack expertise in particular fields important to understanding key factors relating to children's work. For example, even major governmental and non-governmental organisations involved in child labour often seem under-informed about child development, especially for middle childhood and adolescence, and may not realise how much lack of familiarity with that field can limit understanding of children's work in terms of their well-being and development. Nevertheless, all such agencies have the capacity to engage consultants to fill these specialised needs. There is no shortage of social scientists and other information resources in most places where such agencies have head or regional offices. Moreover, as we write, researchers and other experts on children's work are in planned, systematic conversation with agency personnel to identify and fill information gaps. To the extent that information differences may be an issue, it may not be for long. We suggest that the crux of the expertise problem lies elsewhere.

We suggest that the biggest obstacle to true expertise, and the ultimate source of all the illusions we discuss in this chapter, is the dysfunction commonly known in organisational psychology as "groupthink" (Myers, 2017). It is a powerful factor in determining what information people consider important and are willing to pay attention to. Groupthink is a product of our natural mental processes and arises especially when people work in groups with which they wish to get along. "Groupthink occurs when a group with a particular agenda makes irrational or problematic decisions because its members value harmony and coherence over accurate analysis and critical evaluation".[7] The hallmark of groupthink is the assumption that group agreement on an issue indicates that the group is also correct: "Can so many colleagues I know and trust be wrong?" Unfortunately, they can.

[7] Definition from Psychology Today website, https://www.psychologytoday.com/search/site/groupthink (accessed 12 June 2018).

Humans as social animals evolved to survive through complicated cooperation; they are psychologically programmed to blend their thinking to promote easy cooperation. That drive reduces individual curiosity and critical thinking in directions that might impede cohesion for group goals. Group norms prevail and dampen individual qualms, hindering individual willingness to pursue different lines of thought or ask probing questions. The result is that attention is powerfully filtered to unconsciously select what is comfortable and exclude what is not. This is especially likely in group dynamics in which evidence-based and research-based questioning of an official or otherwise common position is discouraged by the group or its leadership.[8] Unanimity becomes the criterion for truth, and what does not achieve unanimity is discarded. Overlooked errors might be obvious to outsiders not caught in the dysfunctional illusion, but they are hidden from those participating in groupthink. There are no villains and victims in this scenario; it is an inconvenient side-effect of the brain processes we evolved to survive and thrive first as hunter-gatherers, and later as town dwellers with complicated social structures. Organisations need to be aware of this dysfunction, recognise when it may be occurring, and take steps to keep it under control.

We see much of what looks like groupthink in child protection policy in general, and in the treatment of working children in particular, where there are many ideas that have become presumed truths with little in the way of evidence to support them. Sophisticated organisations are these days aware of groupthink and its dangers, and they often take steps to prevent it. The most common and effective of these is to ensure that all important issues are identified and thoroughly researched, with evidence well documented, and discussed from different perspectives, including contrary views and arguments, all of which can be discomforting. Some organisations go so far as to designate a "devil's advocate" responsible for arguing contrary and neglected points of view. Courts of justice are structured that way to make sure all evidence comes to the surface and is properly considered through a process of formal debate.

A feasible institutional structure for testing positions on children's work through evidence may already exist. The ILO, together with UNICEF and the World Bank, supports a joint research project entitled

---

[8] For an example of how this works in practise in relation to child protection, see Howard (2017, pp. 97–123).

"Understanding Children's Work" (UCW), which collects detailed statistical and other data describing the incidence and patterns of child labour for a number of countries. UCW tends to "understand" children's work primarily in terms of descriptive statistics about who is doing how much of what kind of work, where, and for how much remuneration, etc. Other researchers from academic institutions are often more interested in understanding how participation in work affects children's lives, investigating how work and interventions in work promote or impede their overall well-being and development. These two perspectives are complementary, and the UCW focus could readily be expanded to include broader questions. With proper programming, it could be established as a mechanism, among other things, to test organisational assumptions, doctrines, and ideas against evidence, thus raising the quality and effectiveness of policy debate. Perhaps it could provide a valuable service in bridging the abyss between restrictive labour-oriented perspectives inherited from the past and more child-centred perspectives mandated for the present. We need not drop one kind of research to expand to the other.

One way of overcoming groupthink in organisations concerned with child protection would be to establish as a matter of course more and better quality contact with the children to be protected and the communities in which they live. When organisations are dominated by people who, though formally highly qualified, have little contact with the people the organisation is intended to serve, the danger of an unrealistic group perspective is greater. Contact with the perspectives of communities is important also for research techniques adopted. While data collected from large-scale surveys are important for indicating trends, the information is largely governed by predetermined questions, and surveys have limited ability to explore the perspectives of those being surveyed. Moreover, large-scale data deal with the majority and often miss what happens to particularly vulnerable children. Good communication with local communities requires intensive qualitative research. In particular, in the field of children's work, an obvious—and often neglected—way of checking organisational groupthink is to pay attention to what the affected children think about policies and interventions. They often have views well informed by their experience of work and of how policies and interventions affect their lives, as we saw clearly in Jessica Taft's chapter (Chapter 3).

The Illusion of Incompetent Children

Deriving from a notion of childhood arising from the Romantic Movement in nineteenth-century literature is the assumption that children are too naïve, suggestible, and dependent to handle work situations. Even as they enter their early teens, young people are often assumed to lack the experience necessary to understand and deal with exploitation. Such assumptions of incompetence relate to particular cultural expectations of children; they do not reflect the actual increasing competence of children as they grow. Psychologist Barbara Rogoff (2003) has shown how children develop competencies differentially, depending on cultural training and expectations. In particular, children growing up in high-risk situations (the most common of which is poverty) can benefit by being guided through difficult situations rather than avoiding them.

Western societies often assume that the only significant competence available to children is that which is acquired through schooling (and formal, classroom-based schooling at that) and that the many skills acquired through activities in the home and elsewhere outside school are unimportant. But in other cultures, children are expected to grow in responsibility and to develop through practise a range of competencies from an early age—including being responsible for the care of even younger children and for the family wealth invested in domestic herds. Too heavy an emphasis on school, therefore, especially where schooling is competitive rather than co-operative, can result in children losing social and environmental values and skills that could be useful in the present, in their adult lives, and to the societies in which they live (see for example, Alcalá et al., 2014; Katz, 2004, pp. 113–117, 174; Serpell, 2011; White, 2011, p. 6).

Failing to acknowledge the competence of children results in disrespect of their rights and their persons. Working children are frequently treated as passive victims to be rescued (something also seen in relation to migrant children, as Chapter 8 suggests). It is assumed that they have no control over their own lives, whereas the majority choose to work, albeit often under the duress of poverty, and regard work combined with schooling as a normal feature in growing up. Their opinions and reasons are frequently ignored in campaigns against child labour, in defiance of their right to have a say in decisions that affect them (UNCRC, article 12). Trades unions and the ILO persistently refuse to recognise children as legitimate and competent workers, and so deny them the protection of workers' unions, or even the right to form their own unions.

The competence of children is particularly evident when those living and working on city streets, often having migrated unaccompanied from impoverished rural areas, successfully make decisions to survive – and even thrive in comparison to alternative lives available to them (e.g. Baker, 1998; Banerjee et al., 2017; Invernizzi, 2003). They often develop a variety of life skills, which they share in support of each other. When the attempts of any working children to improve their own lives are ignored or dismissed as unimportant, they are thereby insulted and their self-esteem and resilience can be damaged.

Certainly, children's knowledge and experience are limited. They cannot always know about the long-term consequences of what they do; long-term medical effects of, for example, lead from traffic fumes are not evident to them. They are unlikely to be fully aware of a multitude of career options that might be open to them and the appropriate preparation for such options. But neither are adults always knowledgeable about these things, whether because they too are unaware of possibilities or because they fail to understand limitations arising from particular situations. Children usually have clear ideas of what work is reasonable for them to do and what is harmful or exploitative and may sometimes accept hazards that are outweighed by perceived benefits in their work. Children's perceptions of the problems they face can be more accurate and nuanced than those even of adults in their own communities.

Failure to recognise the growing competence of children relates to a notion of childhood in which their competencies have little value.

The Illusion of Universal Childhood

At least since the seminal work of James and Prout (1990), students in childhood studies have been aware of different socially constructed childhoods in different social and cultural contexts. Nevertheless, a Romantic notion of childhood, as a time of happy innocence, play and learning, and free of responsibility, remains a popular ideal, especially among elite groups who can afford such a childhood and who populate international child protection institutions. Such a notion frequently influences discourse on "child labour".

Child labour to be abolished, is often defined as "work that deprives children of their childhood".[9] This is a misleadingly emotive phrase. Since childhood is the time of being a child, the only thing that can strictly deprive someone of childhood is early death. Studies of children in different cultures and different places have shown that children can grow and develop in many different ways; what is deemed appropriate for children in some cultural contexts may appear inappropriate to people in others. So this worry about stolen childhoods reveals an ethnocentric notion of what childhood *ought* to be like and deprives different childhoods of their value.

In most of the world, and in many rural and working-class families in the West, work continues to be accepted as a normal part of childhood, contributing significantly to child development and even to child happiness (Bourdillon et al., 2011, pp. 88–107; and more recently Babo, 2019, the essays in Correa-Chávez et al., 2015, especially Jiménez, 2015; Lancy, 2017, 2018). Children grow into their communities and societies from an early age by participating in the social activities around them, among which work is key. Parents have the responsibility to bring their children up to be responsible and industrious with an increasing range of competencies, rather than lazy. Through work, children learn to exercise responsibility to themselves and to others, acquire social and technical skills, and expand and strengthen social networks. In this way work is properly considered educational, complementary to schooling rather than opposed to it; indeed, the vast majority of working children combine work with school. At the psycho-social level, work can contribute to self-esteem, especially important for children with little aptitude for school or poor access to useful schooling, and to children who are stigmatised by poverty or other social hierarchies. In cases of poverty or crises, children's work may be important to fulfil the basic needs of the child and the family—even contributing to school expenses. Some children work because they enjoy it, often in the company of peers. When work is a net benefit to children in any of these ways, preventing them from working hinders their well-being and development.

---

[9] See, for example, www.ilo.org/ipec/facts/lang-en/; http://www.theworldcounts.com/stories/Child_Labour_Definition.

In the twentieth century, colonialism, international organisations, and later the globalisation of ideas, spread the Romantic notion of childhood to elites in other parts of the world. While poorer families need the traditional contributions of their children, elites can manage without. So a work-free childhood has become associated with progress, development, and status; working children become widely perceived as a sign of backwardness. The ideology that children should not work became a pervasive idea, notwithstanding empirical evidence against it—evidence that is widely known among students of childhood, but largely unknown or ignored by those within the international child protection regime who influence children through policies and programmes and who are often too busy interfering in the lives of children to learn about the effects of the changes they instigate.

The Illusion of Moral Superiority

Some regard a prohibition of all forms of child labour as a moral issue: child labour is so abhorrent (somewhat like "slavery", Okyere argues in Chapter 2) that it cannot be tolerated in any circumstances. Moreover, they aim to prohibit as wide a range of work as possible so as to leave little chance of children being damaged by working. Attention to children's development, however, suggests that much work so eliminated could otherwise contribute to children's overall growth and that even prohibiting undesirable work can leave children worse off.

We question the view of morality as comprising conformity to a set of rules or principles irrespective of the consequences of this conformity in people's lives; we find more convincing the argument that judgements of morality, like those of ethics, must take account of outcomes.[10] In the case of children's rights and interventions on behalf of children, therefore, an essential component of moral judgement is how these rights and interventions affect children and whether they are accountable to children. If

---

[10] We are aware of philosophical discussions of various strands of ethical consequentialism, and of different components that make up morality. For the purpose of this essay, we simply assert our conviction that consideration of expected consequences is necessary for deciding what kinds of action are moral, and that moral judgements that ignore expected consequences are thereby flawed.

stopping children from working deprives them of chances for development, or in any other way leaves them worse off than when they were working, this is unethical and the antithesis of moral intervention.

Since the UNCRC demands that the work of children be assessed according to its effects on their holistic development, it suggests that States Parties are accountable for outcomes in the lives of children. This is an ethical as well as a legal imperative because lack of accountability is unethical, especially when it disregards human rights law; accountability to children's welfare is what justifies any legal intervention. What practical right should governments and social organisations have to circumscribe children's freedom—as does ILO C. 138—except to protect the children involved? If the well-being and development of children cannot be shown to have benefited from an intrusive intervention, how can that intervention be justified as either legal or ethical? It is not sufficient just to follow international standards or national laws, which can be considered unethical if they burden children without achieving a life-improving purpose. Compliance with children's human rights and the basic standards of ethical behaviour must be measured not by passing and implementing laws, but by the consequences of those laws in the lives of identifiable children. The legal process might be pertinent to making things happen, but it is how the result of that process plays out in children's well-being and development that defines whether their human rights have been met. This is the one fundamental criterion by which ethical compliance with children's human rights must be measured.

We have pointed out that experts in the major agencies involved in child labour policy and intervention have been informed of documented research findings questioning the outcomes for children of the dominant established policy. There has been no published refutation of such literature from these organisations. To ignore evidence that policies are counterproductive, and to insist on these policies in the face of such evidence, is not morally superior.[11]

A further problem with taking a moral stance to the elimination of all forms of child labour is that the term is used in different ways to suit

---

[11] Something similar happened in development studies. William Easterly (2013) explains how a particular model of development became prominent and widely practised with disastrous results for many of the poor it was supposed to help, because influential people ignored contrary evidence and kept contrary views out of conferences and discussions.

different agendas (see Ennew et al., 2005). "Child labour" is commonly a pejorative term connoting unacceptable work that is in some way harmful to children or interferes with their development, and the term is often formally defined in this way; such definition justifies campaigns to eliminate child labour. However, agencies and national laws complying with the ILO's *Minimum Age Convention* prohibit work or employment below a certain age. While many such agencies (notably the ILO, UNICEF, and others following their lead) formally define "child labour" in terms of work that is harmful to children, they effectively extend the meaning of the term to include employment below the legal minimum age for employment, even in work that is safe and beneficial for children.[12] This extended use has infiltrated some public and popular thinking, with the result that work is allowed or banned on criteria that bear little relation to the well-being of children, and products to which children's work has contributed are sometimes boycotted as a principle of business ethics. Indeed, in the name of business ethics, we find great efforts to remove children from supply chains, with little regard for local cultural values or children's interests (see the example in Bourdillon et al., 2011, pp. 181–190; or more recently Babo, 2019). Since economic work is by no means always harmful, and indeed is often beneficial to the broad development even of young children, stopping "child labour" with this extended meaning impinges on children's rights to holistic development and can itself become a human rights violation.

---

[12] For example, UNICEF (following the ILO) suggests as a classification for 'child labour':

a) children 5 to 11 years of age that during the week preceding the survey did at least one hour of economic activity or at least 28 h of domestic work, and.

b) children 12 to 14 years of age that during the week preceding the survey did at least 14 h of economic activity or at least 42 h of economic activity and domestic work combined. (http://www.unicef.org/infobycountry/stats_popup9.html (accessed 11 June 2018).

There is no empirical justification for regarding 27 h of chores as benign or one hour a week of economic activity as harmful to school-going children of any age.

Non-Illusory Protection of Children from Harmful Work

There are many tried and successful ways of protecting children from harmful work that can be brought to bear under more flexible approaches to protecting working children. Poverty relief programmes, particularly cash transfers, reduce demands on children to work (De Hoop and Rosati, 2013). Since benefit and harm are related to specific contexts in which we find children, protection can be achieved through working with and empowering local communities (for example, Bourdillon et al., 2011, pp. 194–200). Working children can be empowered to protect their own interests, especially through organisations (as Jessica Taft's contribution, Chapter 3 in this volume, demonstrates; see also Liebel et al., 2001 and Taft, 2016). Some programmes have ensured that school and work are compatible and complementary; schools can take account of work experience and can undertake internship programmes (Myers, 2001). Children can be protected by finding safe income-generating work for them (Promoting and Protecting the Interests of Children who Work, n.d.). We mentioned earlier that good policy should be based on the effects of work on children's lives, revealed through careful monitoring in different contexts, in turn producing a checklist of work-related threats, and developing context-appropriate remedies. All such initiatives are more likely to protect children than the imposition of general rules enforced by punitive sanctions.

For the human rights goal of effectively promoting and protecting human flourishing, the broader and richer children-centred vision demanded by the UNCRC offers at least three important advantages over the thinner gruel generated from ILO conventions.

- First, the child-centred vision treats children, and their well-being and development, as ends in themselves, as citizens rather than primarily as means or obstacles to a more prosperous future society. The future merits careful consideration, to be sure, but not necessarily more than the exigencies of the present.
- Second, the broader child-centred vision addresses children more completely. We have pointed out that the UNCRC requires work of children to be assessed in terms of its effects not only on their immediate safety from exploitation but also on their broader "physical, mental, spiritual, moral and social development", for which they have a right to adequate sustenance. Adequate physical development

would at a bare minimum entail freedom from debilitating injury, disease, or malnutrition. Mental development is normally interpreted to include both cognitive development (primarily acquisition of literacy, critical thinking, and life skills) and emotional development (such as self-awareness, self-regulation, and empathy). Spiritual and moral development encompass, among other things, growth in love, respect, compassion, solidarity, and fairness shown towards others. Social development involves abilities to successfully negotiate culture and key social structures and institutions, abilities which are necessary to become a fully engaged and productive citizen. Work that is appropriate for children has demonstrable beneficial effects on any or all of these aspects of child development (Aufseeser et al., 2018), just as work that is inappropriate for children may threaten them. The UNCRC demands that children be viewed holistically, with the objective of realising their full human potential, and the ILO conventions fail to do this.
- Third, the UNCRC, as a fundamental human rights document endorsed by the full body of the United Nations, has by custom higher status and prestige than do narrower conventions that set standards for particular organisations. This means that where there is ambiguity or conflict between the UNCRC and less comprehensive conventions, the rights provisions are commonly taken to prevail even though, technically, they do not inhabit a legal hierarchy.[13] Perhaps more could be done to boost the claim of the UNCRC to higher authority and the recognition of governments to the more evolved approach encoded within it.

Once the primacy of the human rights goal of promoting human flourishing is accepted, assessment of interventions must be in terms of outcomes in children's lives rather than simply in terms of achieving a policy goal. Intervention to eliminate harmful work must be assessed by whether the children are better off rather than by numbers of children taken out of the workforce.

Further, principles and rights, many of which originally derive from Europe, should be assessed against the effects of their application in particular contexts. When the Committee for the Rights of the Child asked for a critique of minimum age for employment to be based on principles rather than practical outcomes, it was possible to respond in these

---

[13] For discussions of this topic, see Wet and Vidmar (2012), especially chapter 2, Jure Vidmar, "Norm conflicts and hierarchy in international law; towards a vertical international legal system?" pp. 13–41.

terms,[14] but the request bypasses the most fundamental principle, namely, to ensure positive outcomes for children. Balancing of costs and benefits of any intervention is essential for a moral and principled approach.

Assessment of costs and benefits of work in specific contexts, and of outcomes of interventions in these contexts, requires detailed knowledge of the lives of the children concerned. The best source of such knowledge is the communities and the children themselves, who should therefore be collaborators in research and in designing policy. That poses a special challenge to the research community. It needs to overcome its distance from the world of practical policy, and directly engage with practitioners and policymakers in designing, organising and conducting the kinds of field research that needs to become a routine element in ensuring that policy is accountable to the needs and well-being of children. Bringing together practitioners, policymakers, academics, and children and their communities in their mutual concern for children's protection, well-being, and development will demand new ways of doing things and new structures for doing them.

We have in this chapter challenged conventional ideas and illusions behind much current intervention relating to children's work, demanding that the application of principles and defence of rights must be accountable to the well-being of children. Legal conformity is not adequate: the efficacy of rights must take account of the realities in children's lives. This requires serious effort to break through the assumptions and principles of institutions and organisations, to examine through inclusive research what enhances and what hinders the flourishing of children in the particular situations in which they live. It most of all demands that we work together to discard the many entrenched illusions that now impede real protection of working children and to replace them with evidence-based interventions accountable to children in demonstrated support of their well-being and development.

REFERENCES

Alcalá, L., Rogoff, B., Coppens, A. D., Mejía-Arauz, R., & Dexter, A. L. (2014). Children's initiative in contributions to family work in indigenous-heritage and cosmopolitan communities in Mexico. *Human Development.*, *57*(2–3), 96–115.

---

[14] https://www.opendemocracy.net/beyondslavery/open-essay-better-approach-to-child-work (accessed 11 June 2018).

Aufseeser, D., Bourdillon, M., Carothers, R., & Lecoufle, O. (2018). Children's work and children's well-being: Implications for policy. *Development Policy Review, 36*(2), 241–261.
Babo, A. (2019). Eliminating child labour in rural areas: Limits of community-based approaches in South-Western Côte d'Ivoire. In J. Ballet & A. Bhukuth (Eds.), *Child exploitation in the global South* (pp. 65–90). Palgrave Macmillan.
Baker, R. (1998). Runaway street children in Nepal: Social competence away from home. In I. Hutchby & J. Moran-Ellis (Eds.), *Children and social competence: Arenas of action* (pp. 46–63). Falmer Press.
Banerjee, A. V., Bhattacharjee, S., Chattopadhyay, R. & Ganimian, A. J. (2017). *The untapped math skills of working children in India: Evidence, possible explanations, and implications*. Unpublished manuscript.
Bharadwaj, P., Lakdawala, L. K., & Li, N. (2013). *Perverse consequences of well-intentioned regulation: Evidence from India's child labor ban*. National Bureau of Economic Research.
Bourdillon, M. (1999). *Earn-and-learn: Work for education in the Eastern Highlands of Zimbabwe*. https://www.academia.edu/6328045/Earn-and-learn_Work_for_Education_in_the_Eastern_Highlands_of_Zimbabwe
Bourdillon, M., Levison, D., Myers, W., & White, B. (2011). *Rights and wrongs of children's work*. Rutgers University Press.
Bourdillon, M., Myers, W., & White, B. (2009). Reassessing working children and minimum-age standards. *International Journal of Sociology and Social Policy, 29*(3/4), 106–117.
Boyden, J., Ling, B. & Myers, W. (1998). *What works for working children*. Rädda Barnen & UNICEF.
Burr, R. (2006). *Vietnam's children in a changing world*. Rutgers University Press.
Correa-Chávez, M., Mejía-Arauz, R., & Rogoff, B. (Eds.). (2015). *Children learn by observing and contributing to family and community endeavors: A cultural paradigm (Advances In Child Development and Behavior)*. Elsevier.
Cunningham, H. and Stromquist, S. (2005). Child labor and the rights of children: historical patterns of decline and persistence. In B. Weston (Ed.), *Child labor and human rights: Making children matter* (pp. 55–83). Lynne Reiner.
Dammert, A. C., De Hoop, J., Mvukiyehe, E., & Rosati, F. C. (2017). *Effects of public policy on child labor: Current knowledge, gaps, and implications for programme design* (Policy Research Working Paper no 7999). World Bank.
De Hoop, J., & Rosati, F. C. (2013). *Cash transfers and child labour*. Understanding Children's Work Programme Rome.
Easterly, W. (2013). *The Tyranny of experts: Economists, dictators, and the forgotten rights of the poor*. Basic Books.
Edmonds, E. V., & Shrestha, M. (2012). The impact of minimum age of employment regulation on child labor and schooling: Evidence from UNICEF MICS countries. *IZA Journal of Labor Policy, 1*(14).

Ennew, J., Myers, W., & Plateau, D. P. (2005). Defining child labor as if human rights really matter. In B. Weston (Ed.), *Child labor and human rights: Making children matter* (pp. 27–54).
Howard, N. (2017). *Child trafficking, youth labour mobility and the politics of protection*. Palgrave Macmillan.
Invernizzi, A. (2003). Street-working children and adolescents in Lima: Work as an agent of socialization. *Childhood, 10*(3), 319–341.
James, A., & Prout, A. (1990). *Constructing and reconstructing childhood*. Routledge.
Jiménez, R.C. (2015). Learning and human dignity are built through observation and participation in work. In M. Correa-Chávez, R. Mejía-Arauz, & B. Rogoff (Eds.), *Children learn by observing and contributing to family and community Endeavors: A cultural paradigm* (pp. 289–301). Elsevier.
Katz, C. (2004). *Growing up global: Economic restructuring and children's everyday lives*. University of Minnesota Press.
Lancy, D. F. (2017). *Raising children: Surprising insights from other cultures*. Cambridge Univesity Press.
Lancy, D. F. (2018). *Anthropological perspectives on children as helpers, workers, artisans, and laborers*. Palgrave Macmillan.
Liebel, M., Overwien, B., & Rechnagel, A. (Eds.). (2001). *Working children's protagonism*. Verlag für Interkulturelle Kommunikation.
Maconachie, R., & Hilson, G. (2016). Re-thinking the child labor "problem" in rural sub-saharan Africa: The case of Sierra Leone's half shovels. *World Development, 78*, 136–147.
Myers, W. (2001). Can children's work and education be reconciled. *International Journal of Educational Policy, Research and Practice, 2*(3), 307–330.
Myers, W. (2017). Bizarre bureaucratic dysfunction in child labour. *Beyond trafficking and slavery*. https://www.opendemocracy.net/beyondslavery/william-myers/bizarre-bureaucratic-dysfunction-in-child-labour
Promoting and Protecting the Interests of Children who Work. (n.d.). *Children working with smelters and scrap collecting in Qalubaya: Project Report*. Centre for Development Services, Cairo.
Rogoff, B. (2003). *The cultural nature of human development*. Oxford University Press.
Serpell, R. (2011). Social responsibility as a dimension of intelligence, and as an educational goal: Insights from programmatic research in an African society. *Child Development Perspectives, 5*(2), 126–133.
Taft, J. K. (2016). Supporting working children as social, political, and economic agents. *Beyond slavery*. https://www.opendemocracy.net/beyondslavery/jessica-taft/supporting-working-children-as-social-political-and-economic-agents
Wet, E., & Vidmar, J. (Eds.). (2012). *Hierarchy in international law: The place of human rights*. Oxford University Press.
White, B. (2011). *Who will own the countryside? Dispossession, rural youth and the future of farming*. University of Rotterdam.

CHAPTER 5

Children Born of Wartime Captivity and Abuse: Politics and Practices of Integration in Northern Uganda

Allen Kiconco

INTRODUCTION

This paper analyses the integration and socialisation experiences of Children Born in Captivity (henceforth CBIC) in northern Uganda. Over time, researchers, policymakers and the international community have justifiably placed great attention on wartime sexual violence against girls and women. In contrast, children born to such females have been ignored or overlooked in many debates and interventions (Apio, 2016; Carpenter, 2007, 2010; Lee, 2017). The focus continues to be on their parents. On the one hand, their fathers are perceived as perpetrators and criminals who should be prosecuted, including those abducted as children and turned into 'forced fathers'. Viewed as potential aggressors of post-conflict peace,

A. Kiconco (✉)
Department of Political Studies, School of Social Sciences, University of the Witwatersrand, Johannesburg, South Africa

they are given priority in the design and implementation of rehabilitation and reintegration programmes. On the other hand, their mothers are perceived and treated as only hapless victims who need saving; "the presence of 'war babies' can worsen their situations…" (McKay, 2004, p. 19; see also Jareg, 2005). Important policy documents on child soldiering recognise 'child/girl mothers' as a particularly vulnerable group, needing explicit attention and consistent follow-up within post-conflict societies (see e.g. Paris Principles, 2007; UNICEF, 2009). Such perspectives are informed by the reproductive rights agenda whose advocates see children as a side effect of their mothers' experiences (see e.g. Coulter, 2009; McKay et al., 2006). Children born as a result of wartime sexual violence are yet to be recognised and appreciated in their own right. Very little is known about how their integration in post-conflict societies unfolds. Their unique and complex needs remain unacknowledged and undiagnosed. Available help and intervention are still directed at their mothers. Using the case of the Acholi sub-region of northern Uganda, this chapter contributes to filling this important knowledge gap. The findings detailed below suggest that CBIC experience stigmatisation and discrimination in post-conflict settings. Thus, their integration and socialisation need specialised attention and intervention, posing a major challenge to the international child protection regime.

One of the legacies of the Lord's Resistance Army (LRA) insurgency in northern Uganda is the birth of thousands of children by girls, abducted and subjected to forced marriage and early pregnancy by commanders (see Apio, 2016). Born in the LRA camps in northern Uganda, South Sudan, the Democratic Republic of Congo, and recently the Central Africa Republic, many children find their way to receptor communities in the north of Uganda. They join these communities to seek survival, comfort and protection.

Studies have explored these children's integration in northern Uganda (e.g. Apio, 2016; Atim et al., 2018; Shanahan & Veale, 2016; Stewart, 2017). The children are not explicitly included in DDR and post-conflict recovery programmes. The government provided women returnees with a basic reintegration package and no additional support for women returning with children. The debate for a national reparations programme addressing these children and their needs, including land ownership and access to specialised rehabilitation, continues.

The consensus in the literature is that stigmatisation is the dominant challenge facing these children and their integration in northern

Uganda. They receive stigmatisation from sections of society, making their lives unbearable and excluding them from mainstream society (e.g. Shanahan & Veale, 2016; Stewart, 2017). They are perceived as close associates of the LRA, symbols of misfortune and stereotyped as violent. They are segregated in the host families and have a lower status compared to their mates with never-abducted parents. Their stigmatisation is compounded by everyday broader patriarchal discriminatory socio-cultural ideas, norms and practices.

This chapter examines stigmatisation problem facing children born within the LRA from a socio-cultural perspectives. It focuses on processes of socialisation, establishing social relations and kinship ties to ensure survival and safety in post-conflict northern Uganda. It draws from ethnographic fieldwork and interview with 40 formerly abducted mothers in the Acholi region, focussing on their children's integration. Therefore, the findings presented and discussed in this chapter are based on mothers' perspectives of their children's situation. The findings show that the children's rebellion background has led to no easy integration arising from problems associated with their stigmatised identity, both as children and former members of the LRA. Four key sources of stigmatisation emerge in the data: born in the bush, association with the rebellion, polluted background and illegitimacy at birth. The chapter reveals the messiness of integration in northern Uganda by unpacking these sources. In Uganda's patriarchal and patrilineal social systems, children with no paternal lineage are viewed as of lower status. Stigmatising and criminalising their parents condemn CBIC to this status, consequently excluding them from mainstream society.

To appreciate the context within which this discussion is situated, it is perhaps important at this point in the discussion to chart the events and the situation leading to the abduction of these children's mothers (and sometimes fathers) from their communities in northern Uganda into the LRA rebellion.

Wartime Captivity and Abuse in Northern Uganda

The Acholi sub-region (also known as Acholiland) was the centre of the conflict in northern Uganda (see Behrend, 1999; Branch, 2011; Dolan, 2009). The region was deeply scarred by many abuses, including the now-notorious practice of the Lord's Resistance Army (henceforth LRA) abducting adolescents and teenagers (see Annan et al., 2008; Blattman &

Annan, 2010; Pham et al., 2007). These abductions frequently resulted in years of captivity, with victims being forced to become agents of terror and violence against their own families and communities (see Branch, 2011; Dolan, 2009; Human Rights Watch, 2005). Also, abductees (especially girls) were socialised and forced to serve as sexual slaves and forced labourers. This was orchestrated through a system of forced conjugal associations between male commanders and female combatants. Most of these female abductees bore children (see also Annan et al., 2008; Baines, 2014; Carlson & Mazurana, 2008; Watye Kin Gen, 2014).

In an attempt to restore peace, on 16 December 2003, the Ugandan government referred the situation in the North to the International Criminal Court (ICC) (see Branch, 2007). On 6 December 2016, Trial Chamber IX of the ICC commenced its trial against Dominic Ongwen, one of the five LRA indicted commanders (see ICC, 2016). Ongwen was accused of 70 counts of war crimes, crimes against humanity and both. On 6 May 2021, the court sentenced Ongwen to 25 years of imprisonment (Sentencing available at: CR2021_04230.PDF (ICC-cpi.int). The trial was the first in which the ICC convicted a rebel commander for forced pregnancy as a war crime and a crime against humanity. It was also the first time that the ICC convicted forced marriage (charged under the category of 'other inhumane acts), constituting a crime against humanity (ICC, 2016). Ongwen is the first ex-militia commander to be charged of forced marriage and forced pregnancy against his 'forced wives' (ICC, 2016). Being the first person to be tried for crimes "of which he is also a victim" (Baines, 2009, pp. 163–164), Ongwen also represents tens of thousands of LRA ex-combatants holding such conflicting statuses in northern Uganda.[1]

The ICC, human rights and child protection organisations have been applauded for strengthening criminalisation of child recruitment and involvement in armed conflicts. But in situations where all parties involved in forced conjugal associations happen to be minors turned into combatants, the conventional explanations and ensuing responses may be deficient. Moreover, the neglect of children born as a result of forced conjugal associations between child combatants and girls forced to marry them complicates the task. In patriarchal and patrilineal social systems like those of the Acholi, children who have no paternal lineage are viewed as

[1] See also the trial of Thomas Kwoyelo in the International Crime Division (ICD) of the Ugandan High Court (Macdonald & Porter, 2016).

of a lower status. Part of the problem with criminalising and stigmatising their fathers, then, is that it condemns these children to this lower status. Findings from Acholi suggest that local contexts must inform external reintegration and justice interventions if they are to be successful. Without appreciating the local context, realities and social mechanisms, external interventions will continue to fail.

Research Methodology

In 2012–2013, I carried out six months of field-based research in the Acholi sub-region.[2] I interviewed and held conversations with 170 participants in Gulu, Kitgum, Lamwo, and Pader districts. From the number of participants above, in-depth interviews were conducted with 57 abducted women. These women were identified and recruited through a rehabilitation centre, Kitgum Concerned Women's Association (KICWA), and through referral via already interviewed women. Among the 57 women, 40 had had a total of 68 CBIC, including some who died in the LRA camps or once subsequently back home. At the time of the study, 58 children were still alive (28 girls and 30 boys). Their age at the time of joining their mothers' receiving communities ranged between 0 and 8 years, averaging 1.8 years. At the time of the study, age ranged between 6 months and 17 years, averaging 9.5 years. Most of these children lived with their mothers and maternal kin. The focus in this chapter is on the perspectives of 40 mothers on their children's integration. Because I was not ethically equipped to interview the children, the study limited itself to observing them while working with their mothers. Therefore, the data on the children presented and discussed below was generated via interviews with their mothers.

The research relied on a qualitative thematic content analysis approach to analyse the data. It applied Nvivo10 to organise, manage and analyse the data. First, the analysis process included familiarising with the data by repeatedly reading interview scripts, comparing with field notes, and

---

[2] This paper is based on research undertaken for my doctoral thesis at the University of Birmingham. The thesis focused on issues of the LRA captivity and abuse, rehabilitation and reintegration. It particularly looked at lived experiences of abducted women in the Acholi region. The arguments of this paper emerged from this research as a key insight. The research received ethical approval from the University of Birmingham and Uganda National Council for Science and Technology (UNCST).

making notes on potential themes, patterns, and categories. Secondly, all the transcribed interviews were transported from Microsoft word to the Nvivo10 for organising, managing, and bringing order to the data. The move facilitated the inductive thematic/focussed coding and analysis. The theme of stigmatisation emerged as a significant integration problem. The final analysis focussed on finding the meaning behind this response to help understand the situation of the LRA captivity children. I draw on mothers' perspectives to provide evidence for the argument, using quotations to illustrate the broader set of life stories.

STIGMATISATION INSTEAD OF INTEGRATION

My findings suggest that stigmatisation dominates CBIC's integration experiences in post-conflict Acholi communities. Many studies highlight this problem but do not elaborate on its source or persistence (see e.g. Apio, 2007, 2016; Atim et al., 2018; Shanahan & Veale, 2016; Stewart, 2017). Emerging anecdotal information suggests that some CBIC living with their fathers/paternal kin also experience stigmatisation and discrimination (see e.g. Stewart, 2017). But interviews show that this is more common in the maternal family and their villages. In this section, I explore a number of the main sources of stigmatising, including these children's association with 'the bush' and the LRA, their perceived 'haunted'/ 'polluted' background, and their illegitimacy.

Anton Dijker and Willem Koomen (2007, p. 6) define stigmatisation as "the process by which an individual's or group's character or identity is negatively responded to on the basis of the individual's or group's association with a past, imagined, or currently present deviant condition, often with harmful physical or psychological consequences for the individual or group". Thus, when 'stigmatisation' is used in the present paper, it means stigma promotion, including any off-putting thoughts, feelings, inappropriate language or actions intended to constitute defamation or slander of this category of children in the Acholi region.

Having *olum-olum* ('people of the bush'—LRA combatants) as their natal parents is one of the main sources of stigma for CBIC. Although *olum* means 'grass' in Acholi, it also means 'bush': an unsafe, fearful and mysterious place that should not be visited without good reason. People who live in the bush—as in the case of the LRA militia—are considered to be dangerous, mentally unsound or criminal. The bush is a place where wild animals, criminals and evil spirits live. So there is tension between bush and village/home spaces (see also, Oloya, 2010). And as a consequence, like their parents who were abducted and taken to the bush, being born in the bush 'qualifies' CBIC as *olum-olum*.

In Acholi cosmology, two parallel worlds exist for these children—the bush world and the 'normal' world. Although they may have complete access to the normal world and live in close physical proximity to other 'normal' people, they are nevertheless conceptualised as inhabiting the bush world. And because of their 'bush' experience, they are singled out and labelled as different, strange or even dangerous. In my research, mothers often reported that their CBIC are viewed through the prism of their birth in the bush, and their character is understood therefore as 'bush-like'. They are teased, scorned and stigmatised about this background. Two mothers shared their experiences as follows:

…my child faces a lot of stigmatisation from the community. When referring to him, people use negative descriptions ranging from 'born in the bush' to 'rebel'. These things greatly affect us [formerly abducted persons] and our children. We did not choose to be abducted, it was not our wish and these [words] give us and our children a lot of pain.[3]

…The biggest challenge is the stigma that people direct towards all of us [mother and two CBIC]. They [the children] keep telling me about how sad and stressed they feel. To cheer them up, I tell them how hurt I also feel and that if there was a way of returning to the bush, we would, just to be free…The same things [bad-mouthing] are being said to them at schools as well. I have visited their schools to try and discuss with their teachers to protect them against stigmatisation from their mates, but the stigmatisation persists. They are still being branded as rebels…[4]

Beyond being born in the bush, their association with the LRA is clearly also a source of stigmatisation for CBIC. Villagers call them 'Kony', 'Kony's children', or 'rebels', claiming that they are 'wild', 'mentally unsound' or 'evil spirit possessed'. Villagers blame them for the hated practices of their fathers (see also Apio, 2007, pp. 98–103), assuming that they are 'useless' like Kony and his militiamen, who are perceived as useless fathers that inflicted uncountable pain on their own society

---

[3] Interview, abductee mother no.9, Amida, Kitgum district, October 2012.

[4] Interview, abductee mother no.50, Lokung, Lamwo district, December 2012.

and with no remorse. Male children are viewed as having inherited their fathers' evil and wild behaviour and are thus more commonly stereotyped as 'criminals'. As one mother put it, "I do not have any bad feelings towards my child because I am the mother. But other people stigmatise him a lot saying his father is a rebel and that he will have no future use to the community...."[5] Another mother shared the following sad story:

> I abandoned my marriage after only eight months because I could not stand stigmatisation directed at me and my children. People used to say that if my boys grow up, with the bush mentality inherited from their father, they will break the man's [stepfather's] home...[6]

Similarly, compared to their peers not born in captivity, CBIC are viewed as more stubborn and uncontrollable (see also Apio, 2007, p. 102), with girls understood to have inherited their mothers' perceived 'weak points'. Stepfathers in particular were reported to use insulting words like 'stupid', 'senseless', 'bush mentality/behaviour' or 'unsound mind' in relation to them and their mothers.

This language all serves to highlight and reinforce the difference and distance between CBIC and the local population. It underlines local awareness of CBIC's social origins and shows how CBIC are seen as inferior or of lower status, posing a putative danger to the local social order and its accompanying harmony. It scarcely needs to be said that this treatment reduces CBIC's well-being and life opportunities, particularly given that their stigmatisers are not strangers who come into contact with them for the first time, but rather acquaintances, neighbours and intimates.

To make matters worse, CBIC are also viewed as coming from a background that is contaminated, haunted or polluted. According to Acholi custom, being haunted arises from having been in close contact with unresolved murder, accidental death or the body of someone who has been killed violently. Because LRA combatants are thought to have killed, seen people being killed, or passed through areas where murders were committed, they are believed to be haunted by evil spirits including potentially deadly *cen*, which are 'vengeful spirits of the dead'. If a person is not exorcised or cleansed in Acholiland, it is believed that these *cen* will

---

[5] Interview, abductee mother no.9, Amida, Kitgum district, October 2012.

[6] Interview abductee mother, no.30, Kitgum town Kitgum district, November 2012.

haunt them over a long period and even become contagious or transferable to the second generation of the 'possessed'. As such, a baby may be born with *cen* if either parent was possessed (see Finnström, 2008, p. 160; Liu Institute & Gulu NGO Forum, 2005, p. 12). Thus, like their parents, CBIC are seen as vehicles through which *cen* might enter the community and destroy its social order and harmony. Although ritual cleansing (including of their mothers) is meant to purify CBIC of these sprits and the related guilt and shame, their association with *cen* nevertheless remains and impacts upon their successful integration.

Moreover, CBIC face stigmatisation in Acholi villages due to the 'illegitimacy' of their birth circumstances. Being born out of wedlock sees Acholi children negatively perceived and devalued, while having an unknown father makes this even worse. Acholi society is organised along patriarchal, patrilineal and interdependent clan lines, with marriage playing a crucial role in unifying clans and ensuring social integration. Customary marriages are completed with the payment of 'bridewealth', which serves to cement the contract between the girl's and boy's families/clans. When the groom's clan pays its 'bridewealth', it "establishe[s] a right to a productive womb in the woman's family" (Girling, 1960, p. 72). The married woman then joins and becomes part of her husband's family/clan, while the children born of the union become part of their father's clan and lineage (Baines & Gauvin, 2014, p. 287; Finnström, 2008, p. 192). Where the levied 'bridewealth' has not been paid in full, the relationship is not recognised, any resultant children are viewed as illicit, and ultimately they belong to their mother's clan and lineage (see also Baines & Gauvin, 2014, p. 287). This is such a socially undesirable outcome that a process exists (called '*luk pa latin*') whereby the paternal family pays a customary fine for care taken to raise the child in order to affiliate it to its father's lineage.

Although deeply affected by war, displacement and the accompanying crises of social reproduction (see Dolan, 2009), these customs remain crucial to Acholi social order and therefore to individual psychological well-being. For Acholi children, knowing and belonging to one's paternal family/clan is a critical element in their social belonging, protection and provision. By contrast, children who have no paternal lineage are viewed as of lower status and treated accordingly. Unfortunately, this necessarily applies to the majority of CBIC, whose fathers never paid 'bridewealth' and are largely absent from their children's lives. As such, CBIC typically exist as social others who are illegitimate within the Acholi order of things. So much so that some reintegrating mothers have reported being criticised for leaving the LRA with their children: "I am constantly told that I should not bother raising a child of no father", one woman said.[7] Another expressed the dilemma facing her child in this way:

> People stigmatise and talk about it [fatherhood] to him. That makes me angry and anxious. I am always thinking and worrying that, when he grows older, this issue will be a big concern. If he was a girl, at least it would have been better. I had wanted to tell him that his father died but he is still too young to understand. For now, he calls my elder brother his father...[8]

While it may theoretically be possible for an LRA father or his family to claim custodianship of a CBIC through *luk* negotiations, this has rarely been pursued by families, clans and child protection institutions, in large part because doing so may be challenging and require comprehensive coordination among families, clans and the wider community. As such, in the present sample, only eleven children knew their paternal families at the time of interviews.[9] This suggests that most of CBIC in the region are attempting to integrate into their maternal clan systems, unable to rely on their paternal kinship networks for support, survival and integration in post-conflict Acholiland.

When the LRA conflict began many years ago, practices of abduction and wartime forced conjugal association were new to the people of northern Uganda. Many suffered enormously during the conflict. Now, as children and their mothers attempt to reintegrate, many people do not appreciate being asked to accept those fathered by rebels. The consequence of this is rejection and stigmatisation. CBIC are held accountable for the crimes of their fathers and are thus often victims of societal

---

[7] Interview, abductee mother no.9, Amida, Kitgum district, October 2012.

[8] Interview, abductee mother no.25, Omiya Anyima, Kitgum district, November 2012.

[9] Six lived with their mothers and fathers after the two mothers had exited the LRA and been joined by the LRA fathers, who paid the customary bridewealth for the mothers and the *luk* for each of the children. Two other children had joined their fathers. One belonged to a mother who returned with two children by the same LRA father but only one was taken by the father, after paying *luk*. The mother was in a new relationship. The second child lived with the maternal grandparents because the father was yet to pay the second *luk*. Two final children stayed with their mothers, but their fathers often visited. One mother exited the LRA with three children by two combatants: one had been taken by his paternal family (grandparents) and the other two lived with maternal grandparents, with no knowledge of their paternal family.

violence. This, in turn, hampers the building of self-confidence, self-esteem and trust. It also limits relationships with their communities and hinders integration. This is further compounded by the cultural practice that eschews 'illegitimate' children born out of wedlock. In the following sections, I explain how development and child protection agencies are overlooking these issues and even making them worse through their approach to reintegration.

External Interventions Exacerbating Integration Problems

How to ensure rehabilitation and reintegration for women and girls abducted and forced into wartime conjugal relationships? How to integrate the children born of their unions, with or without their fathers? These are the questions faced by the large number of organisations working in this space in northern Uganda, particularly the International Non-Governmental Organisations (INGOs) and UN agencies who flooded the area to support with reintegration via the provision of interim care centres (Dolan, 2009, p. 239).[10] Unfortunately, my data show that there are a number of problems plaguing what they do. In this section, I show not only that agencies are failing to mitigate the socio-cultural issues documented above, but that at times the biases within their approaches are even making things worse. This raises major questions for the ongoing work of the international child protection regime.

The first issue with the mainstream approach to protection and integration concerns the conception of childhood predominant within intervening agencies. In Acholiland, neither childhood nor adulthood is reducible to biological age. Adolescence is considered to be the phase between the ages of 10 and 18. *Orobo* ('youth'/'young-persons') are people between the ages of 15 and 30. But particularly in rural areas, a girl becomes a woman upon experiencing menstrual cycles, developing breasts, or being sexually active. Girls within the age range of 12 and 16 are therefore typically seen as ready for marriage and bearing children. A girl becomes a woman *as soon as* she marries or gets pregnant,

---

[10] Notable centres included, Kitgum Concerned Women's Association (KICWA), Gulu Support the Children Organization (GUSCO), World Vision Rehabilitation Centres, Concerned Parents Association (CPA), Christian Counselling Fellowship (CCF), Caritas Canter, Rachele Centre and Kitgum Women Peace Initiative (KIWEPI).

even if this occurs at age 12 or 13. A pregnant girl, therefore, though still young in biological age, will begin self-identifying as *Dako matidi* ('young mother/woman/wife'). Thus marriage and motherhood—not age—are the pathways to womanhood and adulthood in this context (Dolan, 2005, p. 282; Finnström, 2008, p. 235; p'Bitek, 1986).

By contrast, for rehabilitation agencies, children and childhood are biological phenomena and each implies an inability to consent to sexual activity or resulting pregnancy. As such, agencies constructed all females returning from LRA captivity as 'child mothers'. Reports in fact showed that "...the majority of those classified as 'child mothers' at reception centres [were] over the age of 18" (Allen & Schomerus, 2006, p. 24), so they were adults in both the Western and Acholi sense of that term. Yet agencies aimed at reproducing 'children' in line with the Romantic Western standards discussed in Chapter 4 by Bourdillon and Myers—innocent, helpless, vulnerable, dependent, in need of rescue, etc.—no doubt in part because this is what played with donor sympathies. However, by viewing and treating such young women as children, "...they [staff at the centres] cared for us but treated us as children even when some of us already had children".[11] This limited the cultural appropriateness of their interventions and ultimately alienated many. Furthermore, the focus on 'mothers-as-children' meant that their CBIC were entirely invisible in the design and implementation of programmes, limiting the quality of the support available to them. As Susan Alal, then Manager of the World Vision Rehabilitation Centre in Gulu town, put it:

> There is no direct intervention for this category of children [CBIC] in northern Uganda. During the conflict, there were some agencies that helped them with basic scholastic materials but these have also moved out of the region. They have integration challenges and make their mothers' reintegration process hard.

Beyond such primary difficulties, the exceptionalism inherent to the targeted focus on returning 'child mothers' also contributed to their stigmatisation and alienation, in turn worsening the situation of their CBIC. This happened for a number of reasons. First, the preference for the initial phase of reintegration taking place in centres run by foreign agencies as opposed to within community settings gave the impression

---

[11] Interview, abductee mother 18, Omiya anyima, October 2012.

to many communities that they were seen as unable to offer appropriate support. This bred resentment among many Acholi, made worse by the way that reintegration agencies advocated on behalf of mothers, voicing their concerns as if criticising the public for not protecting them. Additionally, the Western approach to childhood and womanhood highlighted above alienated people through its implicit disregard for local understandings. While the sole focus on child mothers vexed people by ignoring the parallels between their difficulties and those of the wider region. In Allen and Schomerus' (2006) words, "...so many adolescent girls in northern Uganda [were] living vulnerable and impoverished lives, and [were] likely to end up becoming pregnant at a very early age" (p. 24). Provision of support and opportunities in a manner that did not address the needs of these other vulnerable populations therefore made returnee mothers (and, by extension, their children) stand out in a way that entrenched resentment against them, and thus isolation and stigmatisation.

Agencies pursued the 'child mother' policy for legal reasons and for moral reasons of responsibility and accountability. But in their attempt to restore 'lost childhoods', they prioritised returning women, who were now mothers, to the communities they left before they became mothers. This flew in the face of the local customs outlined above and overlooked the fact that some CBIC would not be accepted by their mothers' families. Because in a patriarchal and patrilineal society like the Acholi, "as a mother you cannot stay with a child who does not know their father or paternal home. It is very important for the child to know their father's home...".[12] In the words of one mother, "my relatives bluntly told me that I should have left the child with the LRA since the father was not around to take care of the child, so it was useless coming home with the child. And this would only bring more problems for my reintegration. This hurt me a lot".[13] As a consequence, both CBIC and their returning mothers faced stigma, preventing meaningful reintegration.

Relatedly, although for certain mothers, the identity of their children's father was not an issue ("it does not affect our relationship because her father is also an Acholi who was abducted and he grew up from there"),[14] protection agencies discouraged the continuing of relationships with LRA

---

[12] Interview, abductee mother 56, Gulu town, February 2013.

[13] Interview, abductee mother 12, Kitgum town, October 2012.

[14] Interview, abductee mother 9, Amida, Kitgum, October 2012.

combatants or the tracing of paternal families in the early days of return. This influenced many mothers against tracing fathers. One of the mothers reported:

> ...I did not attempt to do anything like that because we were advised from World Vision rehabilitation centre that there was no need to do that since we suffered in the bush carrying and delivering them. They [the children] were our consolations and blessings that God had given us and that we should never let their fathers' relatives know. Even about the mere fact that the children were related to them and had come back home with us.[15]

Some agencies even went so far as to interfere with details that could have helped fathers or their lineages identify and trace their children. Following the Acholi naming custom, male LRA combatants named their children after themselves or their families/clans. Some male children were named after their fathers' brothers or uncles and some girls after their paternal grandmothers. It is possible that this was viewed as a way of eventually identifying the child in the future. And certainly, had the father's family members wanted to trace the child, these names would have been crucial. As such, agencies advised mothers to rename their children. In some cases, they came up with new names:

> While in captivity, he was named Binaisa Samuel Arwai [a pseudonym] after his Dad Arwai. But when we were at KICWA Rehabilitation centre, the name Arwai was deleted from his names. The management advised me that the name Arwai would make people stigmatise him in the village. So I decided to stop calling him Arwai.[16]

Since they acted as the critical broker reintroducing returnees to civil society and preparing them for community-based reintegration, agencies held a fundamental position in society. Besides offering rehabilitation interventions, they could have advocated for CBIC social visibility and customary rights pertaining to paternal descent and in line with Acholi custom. Instead, they sponsored interventions that contributed to the

---

[15] Interview, abductee mother 25, Omiya Anyima, Kitgum, November 2012.
[16] Interview, abductee mother 25, Omiya Anyima, Kitgum, November 2012.

predicaments around identity and social belonging currently facing these children.

I do not wish to suggest here that it is a *sine qua non* for CBIC to know their paternal families in order to be integrated into Acholi villages. But from what was explained above about the Acholi social order, we can assume that this is likely. Furthermore, from a basic material standpoint, mothers facing severe impoverishment (see e.g. Kiconco, 2021) need the support that they could receive from biological fathers or/and paternal relatives in order to meaningfully integrate their children: "... If Dominic [Ongwen] would come back, he and I could join hands and raise our two children", stated one of Ongwen's former forced wives who appeals for his forgiveness. Indeed, confronting though it may be to many, she pleads for reconciliation and not the prosecution of such LRA fathers.[17]

CONCLUDING SUGGESTIONS

Despite their evident good intentions, many child protection agencies operating in Northern Uganda have demonstrably failed to offer the best support possible to reintegrating mothers and their CBIC. In my view, there are various ways that what they do could be improved. Above all, instead of stigmatising and criminalising LRA fathers, these fathers should be encouraged to come forward and take part in the raising of their children. At the very least, this would address CBIC's inability to access the most important resource in the Acholi region, which is land. In Acholi practice, land is customarily owned, with male children expected to inherit it from their fathers so as to establish their own families and farming livelihoods. Having no relationship with their biological fathers, CBIC lack inheritance rights and claims to land. This leaves them vulnerable and at the mercy of their maternal kin, which is necessarily uncertain given the stigma they face due to their socially unorthodox positions.

> My future plan is to have a place of my own, for my children to call home. Even if we are living at my aunt's home, in the future, as human beings, people will get tired of my children and expect them to find their own places. I have to plan for them before they become adults by finding a piece of land, constructing a house on it. For agricultural land, if I find

---

[17] An interview with Mail & Guardian. Retrieved from: https://mg.co.za/article/2015-02-16-uganda-the-thin-line-between-victim-and-perpetrator.

a Good Samaritan to allow me to rent their land, we can grow some food...[18]

Reuniting with their paternal families does not mean CBIC will be guaranteed the safety of belonging and land accessibility. They will still surely have to manoeuvre amidst the land wrangles engulfing most of the Acholi region (see e.g. Adoko & Levine, 2004; McKibben & Bean, 2010). But paternal lineage networks will at least offer them the basis of the safety net that most vulnerable children in Uganda rely on to survive.

CBIC do not need to know their fathers and paternal clans to be integrated into societies of northern Uganda. But to deny them this option and right is to condemn them to a lower social status and to deepen their socioeconomic vulnerability. CBIC are approaching teenagerhood and adulthood. Their sense of social identity, a need for acceptance and belonging, are fast evolving. They are sensitive to stigmatisation and emotional abuse from immediate surroundings. To achieve meaningful integration, it is crucial for them to come to a better understanding of their social identity and the belonging realities that surround their existence.

Despite the fact that paternal family/clan reunions may help with reconciliation and redress, this has not been the focus in northern Uganda. The focus and target of reintegration agencies and programmes remains to return and keep LRA combatants in their villages of origin. Also, the emphasis on mothers continues to drive the reintegration intervention. This is done with the perception that 'empowering' mothers will improve the well-being of their children. But this approach leaves many gaps. Many mothers stipulate the desire to re-marry with non-LRA men, leaving their children with maternal grandparents or/and relatives. Some mothers do not have immediate relations alive or willing to take on their children. With CBIC unable to join their mothers in new marriages/relationships, they are left at the mercy of extended relatives or stranded with well-wishers. This gap can be filled by tracing and connecting CBIC to their fathers and paternal lineages. In patriarchal and patrilineal contexts like the Acholi, it seems that a CBIC and/or their mother has limited control over integration success or failure due to the processes of communal validation and response. The avenue of tracing and connecting with paternal lineages can be pursued through

---

[18] Interview, abductee mother 32, Kitgum town, November 2012.

empowering Acholi traditional leaders to head this mission. Particularly mothers and LRA combatants should be encouraged to embrace it. Also, with some mothers facing post-captivity marital problems (see e.g. Kiconco & Nthakomwa, 2018), traditional leadership should encourage those who are willing, to continue their relationship with the returned LRA combatants. These interventions will support CBIC to lead 'normal' lives. CBIC are significant as symbols of assimilation needs and complexities. Paradoxically, they are also a potential for community reconciliation. Reintegration stakeholders should thus start viewing and addressing their predicament as a redress issue for them, their parents and the community at large.

References

Adoko, J., & Levine, I. (2004). Land matters in displacement: The importance of land rights in Acholiland and what threatens them. *Africa, 60*(1), 39–68.

Allen, T., & Schomerus, M. (2006, June). *A hard homecoming: Lessons learned from the reception center process on effective interventions for former "abductees" in Northern Uganda*. USAID & UNICEF.

Annan, J., Blattman C., Carlson, K., & Mazurana, D. (2008). *The state of female youth in Northern Uganda: Findings from the survey of war-affected youth (SWAY), phase II*. Survey of War-Affected Youth (SWAY).

Apio, E. (2007). Ugandan forgotten children. In C. Carpenter (Ed.), *Born of war: Protecting children of sexual violence survivors in conflict zones* (pp. 94–109). Kumarian Press.

Apio, E. O. (2016). *Children born of war in northern Uganda: Kinship, marriage, and the politics of post-conflict reintegration in Lango society*. PhD Dissertation. The University of Birmingham. http://etheses.bham.ac.uk/6926/.

Atim, T., Mazurana, D., & Marshak, A. (2018). Women survivors and their children born of wartime sexual violence in northern Uganda. *Disasters, 42*(S1), S61–S78. https://doi.org/10.1111/disa.12275

Baines, E. (2009). Complex political perpetrators: Reflections on Dominic Ongwen. *Journal of Modern African Studies, 47*(2), 163–191. https://doi.org/10.1017/S0022278X09003796

Baines, E. (2014). Forced marriage as a political project: Sexual rules and relations in the Lord's Resistance Army. *Journal of Peace Research, 51*(3), 405–417. https://doi.org/10.1177/0022343313519666

Baines, E., Gauvin, L., & R. (2014). Motherhood and social repair after war and displacement in Northern Uganda. *Journal of Refugee Studies, 27*(2), 282–300. https://doi.org/10.1093/jrs/feu001

Behrend, H. (1999). *Alice Lakwena & the holy spirits: War in Northern Uganda 1986–97*. James Currey Ltd.

Blattman, C., & Annan, J. (2010). On the nature and causes of LRA abduction: What the abductees say. In T. Allen & K. Vlassenroot (Eds.), *The Lord's Resistance Army, myth and reality* (pp. 132–155). Zed Books.

Branch, A. (2007). Uganda's civil war and the politics of ICC intervention. *Ethics & International Affairs, 21*(2), 179–198. https://doi.org/10.1111/j.1747-7093.2007.00069.x

Branch, A. (2011). *Displacing human rights: War and intervention in Northern Uganda*. Oxford University Press.

Carlson, K., & Mazurana, D. (2008). *Forced marriage within the Lord's Resistance Army*. Tufts University.

Carpenter, R. C. (Ed.). (2007). *Born of war: Protecting children of sexual violence survivors in conflict zones*. Kumarian Press.

Carpenter, R. C. (2010). *Forgetting children born of war: Setting the human rights agenda in Bosnia and beyond*. Columbia University Press.

Coulter, C. (2009). *Bush wives and girl soldiers: Women's lives through war and peace in Sierra Leone*. Cornell University Press.

Dijker, A. J. M., & Koomen, W. (2007). *Stigmatisation, tolerance and repair: An integrative psychological analysis of responses to deviance*. Cambridge University Press.

Dolan, C. G. (2005). *Understanding war and its continuation: The case of Northern Uganda, 1986–2004*. PhD Thesis. London School of Economics. http://etheses.lse.ac.uk/832/

Dolan, D. G. (2009). *Social torture: The case of Northern Uganda, 1986–2006*. Berghahn Books.

Finnström, S. (2008). *Living with bad surroundings. War, history, and everyday moments in Northern Uganda*. Duke University Press.

Girling, F. K. (1960). *The Acholi of Uganda*. Her Majesty's Stationery Office.

Human Rights Watch. (2005). *Uprooted and forgotten: Impunity and human rights abuse in northern Uganda*. Author.

International Criminal Court. (2016). *The situation in Ugandan in the case of the Prosecutor V. Dominic Ongwen*. Author. https://www.icc-cpi.int/CourtRecords/CR2016_02331.PDF

Jareg, E. (2005). *Crossing bridges and negotiating rivers-The rehabilitation and reintegration of children associated with armed forces*. Save the Children.

Kiconco, A. (2021). *Gender, conflict and reintegration in Uganda: Abducted girls, returning women*. Routledge.

Kiconco, A., & Nthakomwa, M. (2018). Marriage for the 'New Woman' from the Lord's Resistance Army: Experiences of female ex-abductees in Acholi region of Uganda. *Women's Studies International Forum, 68*(May–June), 65–74. https://doi.org/10.1016/j.wsif.2018.02.008

Lee, S. (2017). *Children born of war in the twentieth century.* Manchester University Press.

Liu Institute for Global Issues and Gulu District NGO Forum. (2005). *Roco Wat I Acoli. Restoring relations in Acholi-land: Traditional approaches to reintegration and justice.* Gulu, Authors.

Macdonald, A., & Porter, H. (2016). The trial of Thomas Kwoyelo: Opportunity or spectre? Reflections from the ground on the first LRA prosecution. *Africa, 86*(4), 698–722. https://doi.org/10.1017/S000197201600053X

McKay, S. (2004). Reconstructing fragile lives: Young mothers' social reintegration in Northern Uganda and Sierra Leone. *Gender and Development, Peacebuilding and Reconstruction, 12*(3), 19–30.

McKay, S., Robinson, M., Gonsalves, M., & Worthen, M. (2006). *Girls formerly associated with fighting forces and their children: Returned and neglected.* Coalition to Stop the Use of Child Soldiers.

McKibben, G., & Bean, J. (2010, December). *Land or else: Land-based conflict, vulnerability, and disintegration in Northern Uganda.* International Organisation for Migration, UNDP, and Norwegian Refugee Council.

Oloya, O. (2010). *Becoming a child soldier: A cultural perspective from the autobiographical voices.* PhD Dissertation. Department of Education, York University.

p'Bitek, O. (1986). *Artist the ruler: Essays on art, culture and values.* East African Educational Publishers.

Paris Principles. (2007). *The principles and guidelines on children associated with armed forces or armed groups.* United Nations.

Pham, N. P., Vinck, P., & Stover, E. (2007). *Abduction: The Lord's Resistance Army and forced conscription in northern Uganda.* The University of California.

Shanahan, F., & Veale, A. (2016). How mothers mediate the social integration of their children conceived of forced marriage within the Lord's Resistance Army. *Child Abuse & Neglect, 51*(January), 72–86. https://doi.org/10.1016/j.chiabu.2015.11.003

Stewart, B. W. (2017). *'I feel out of place': Children born into the Lord's Resistance Army and the politics of belonging.* PhD Dissertation. The University of British Columbia. https://open.library.ubc.ca/cIRcle/collections/ubctheses/24/items/1.0363006

UNICEF. (2009). *Machel study 10-year strategic review: Children and conflict in a changing world.* Office of the Special Representative of the Secretary-General for Children and Armed Conflict in collaboration.

Watye Kin Gen. (2014). *The Lord's Resistance Army's Forced wife system.* Watye Kin Gen Children and Youth as Peacebuilders (CAP). Gulu, Uganda.

CHAPTER 6

Protection Versus Reintegration of Child Soldiers: Assistance Trade-Offs Within the Child Protection Regime

Jaremey R. McMullin

This chapter critically assesses and analyses the assumptions and practices of the international child protection regime, focussing on the relationship between the criminalisation of recruitment and re-recruitment of children into armed forces and groups on one hand and programmes to provide children with post-war reintegration assistance on the other. Notwithstanding the rhetoric of child protection actors in the wake of recent investigations and convictions at the International Criminal Court (ICC), international legal triumphalism about the protection of child soldiers is premature, not least because there is little evidence that criminalisation

J. R. McMullin (✉)
School of International Relations, University of St Andrews, St Andrews, Scotland, UK
e-mail: jrm21@st-andrews.ac.uk

© The Author(s), under exclusive license to Springer Nature Switzerland AG 2022
N. Howard and S. Okyere (eds.), *International Child Protection*, Palgrave Studies on Children and Development,
https://doi.org/10.1007/978-3-030-78763-9_6

of recruitment and use has reduced actual recruitment and use.[1] The gap between the rhetoric and reality of deterrence calls into question whether prioritising criminalisation is the best way to protect children during conflict, and whether developments at The Hague can have any real impact on the lived everyday experiences of young people caught up in structures of war-making. Indeed, these are still boom times for the business of recruiting and using children in war. The Child Soldiers World Index, launched in 2018, reports that children were used in war in at least 18 countries since 2016 (Child Soldiers International, 2018). The participation of large numbers of child soldiers in conflict continues in almost every region of the world (Human Rights Watch, 2008, 2012b). It is also clear that the three goals of child protection and assistance—release of children from armed forces and armed groups, reintegration of former child soldiers into civilian life, and prevention of recruitment or re-recruitment into armed forces and groups—are not conceptualised or pursued with equal commitment of resources.

This chapter presents three arguments which demonstrate that prevailing protection strategies do not merely distract from assistance but also impede it. First, the deterrence impact of criminalisation strategies has not been demonstrated and is likely negligible. Second, protection efforts produce direct trade-offs with the quality, duration, scope, and reach of child reintegration. The trade-offs emanate from a paradox of international criminalisation strategies, that by penalising those who admit to using child soldiers during war, the international child protection regime creates incentives for armed forces and armed groups to disguise their recruitment and use of children, which in turn hurts efforts to identify, target, and assist children during and after war.[2] Third, the basic concepts, assumptions, and practices of child protection strategies simultaneously infantilise and pathologise young people, and especially young people in sub-Saharan African contexts. Discourses dependent on the vulnerability and securitisation of children, combined with the criminalisation of their recruitment and use in conflict, actively inhibit more effective and just reintegration strategies from emerging.

---

[1] For examples of such triumphalism, see Child Soldiers International (2012) and Human Rights Watch (2012a).

[2] I examine this particular effect of the international child protection regime in relation to failures to include children in DDR programming in Angola, in McMullin (2011).

Trade-offs between protection and reintegration can be traced back to the child rights architecture itself, which sets up competing goals and embeds contradictions about child rights during post-war transitional processes. That architecture gives child ex-combatants, unlike their adult counterparts, an international legal right to reintegration assistance but provides little guidance about what the nature, duration, and goals of such assistance should be. Additionally, it does not give children standing or recognition to challenge key decisions made for them, even though it does call for their voices to be heard and taken into account. And, it gives little if any guidance about how to resolve competing priorities or interpret and implement key rights (what constitutes the 'best interests of the child', who decides, and how). As a result, the child rights architecture enshrines unenforceable or difficult-to-enforce goals as rights.

At the same time, a way out of the impasse might be located within the child rights architecture, starting with greater and more meaningful consultation and participation of child soldiers themselves in decisions that affect them. Also crucial are programmes that reflect the understanding of how children are already engaged in efforts to reintegrate themselves that exist outside of formal disarmament, demobilisation, and reintegration (DDR) processes. At present, however, commitment to honour children's participation in decisions that affect them is rhetorical rather than actual. Ensor and Reinke (2014) identify a lack of commitment to meaningful child participation as the principal reason why many child rights and child protection approaches emphasise paternalistic protection over child empowerment. In other words, and as I argue throughout this chapter, the elevation of securitised protection strategies does not just distract from meaningful post-war reintegration assistance policies; it thwarts them.

To provide context for these arguments, the chapter first traces the emergence and development of dominant intervention and enforcement modalities. It then moves on to identify and analyse the ways in which strategies adopted to prevent recruitment and use of children in hostilities have frequently come at the expense of reintegrating children recruited into and used in hostilities. In locating trade-offs between protection and reintegration, the chapter collates key findings from the ethnographic literature on child soldiers and draws empirically from diverse contexts across Africa, including Mozambique, Sierra Leone, Liberia, Angola, and the Democratic Republic of the Congo (DRC).

The argument that protection assumptions and practices produce trade-offs with reintegration assistance is not abstract or academic but has real impacts for youth beneficiaries. In this chapter, I hope to tip the scales from 'protection via criminalisation' towards 'reintegration' in part because the bulk of scholarly analysis and advocacy has focussed on protection, to the detriment of an understanding of the assumptions and practices underpinning child reintegration. I am not arguing that protection or criminalisation should be discarded. Nor am I advocating for the allocation of resources away from one activity towards the other. Instead, I assert that new ways of 'seeing reintegration' become possible when the complex impacts of protection practices on reintegration are foregrounded. Crucially, critical opportunities for re-thinking key child rights standards (such as 'maximum development', 'best interests of the child', and 'participation') become possible only through a critical examination of prevailing protection and reintegration approaches. In contrast, pretending that observed and persistent trade-offs between protection and assistance do not exist will do little to protect children from future recruitment and use, and will miss opportunities to improve assistance. Ultimately, the discursive monopoly that criminalisation strategies exercise over protection and assistance policy will need to be broken up if reintegration assistance is to be more effective and correspond with the lived experiences of children caught up in conflict. But such a breakup will likely be impossible without radically enhancing the frequency and quality of child participation in key decisions that affect them.

The Codification of Simultaneous Rights to Protection and Reintegration

The human rights instruments and legal institutions that are the focal point of child protection and assistance policy include the CRC, the 2000 Optional Protocol to the CRC on the Involvement of Children in Armed Conflict (Optional Protocol), the Paris Principles, the Rome Statute, and trial judgments of the ICC. Article 38 of the CRC commits states not to recruit children under 15 into their armed forces, to ensure that children under 15 'do not take a direct part in hostilities', and to ensure the 'protection and care' of all children affected by armed conflict (United Nations, 1989, p. 3). The Optional Protocol commits signatory states to four enhanced obligations. Article 1 commits states not to recruit children under 18 for use in hostilities. Article 2 commits states not to conscript soldiers under 18 (a distinction is made between voluntary recruitment and coercive conscription, such as a military draft). Articles 3 and 6 require states to draft legislation and take all other necessary measures to prohibit and criminalise recruitment and use of children in hostilities. And, Articles 6 and 7 require that states demobilise those under 18 and provide them with physical, psychological, and social reintegration support. The Optional Protocol (United Nations, 2000) further prohibits non-state armed groups from recruiting or using children under 18 in hostilities (Article 4).

The CRC text itself, however, waters down the commitments of states and other actors. Article 3(2) establishes the 'best interests of the child' as the primary consideration in 'all actions concerning children' but then dilutes the standard in two ways, first by limiting interpretation of 'all actions' to those actions undertaken by state entities ('public or private social welfare institutions, courts of law, administrative authorities or legislative bodies') and second by stipulating that various parental 'rights and duties', not enumerated, ought to prevail over other actors' determinations about best interests, including children's own. Elsewhere, the CRC text frequently defers to states' own interpretations of feasibility and desirability in enforcing child rights. For example, Article 6(2) commits states to ensure child rights to survival and development but only 'to the maximum extent possible'. The same feasibility default dilutes the Optional Protocol, where the responsibility of states to provide reintegration support for children is an 'obligation of means' (Vandewiele, 2005, p. 48). According to Article 6(3) of the Protocol, state responsibility is limited to taking 'all *feasible* measures' to ensure children's release and demobilisation and to providing 'all *appropriate* assistance' for reintegration and recovery (United Nations, 2000, emphasis added). The result? It is not possible to locate within the Convention or Protocol concrete guidance about the contours, duration, or scope of reintegration assistance. Instead, states, international child protection agencies (UNICEF), and the Committee on the Rights of the Child are given wide latitude in interpreting the feasibility, extent, and appropriateness of their own efforts to safeguard and promote children's survival and development, reintegration, and recovery.

These same actors retain considerable discretion when it comes to enforcement, too. International enforcement of rights codified within the CRC and Optional Protocol has taken four principal forms: state reporting, UN monitoring, negotiation of bilateral action plans between states and the UN, and criminal investigation and prosecution at the ICC of *individuals* (not *states*) alleged to recruit or use children in hostilities. First, in terms of state reporting, the CRC mandates that States Parties submit reports to the Committee on the Rights of the Child every five years on the actions they have taken/are taking to safeguard CRC and Optional Protocol rights. The Committee's enforcement powers are limited to raising concerns or making recommendations in response to a state's report, or to making recommendations to the General Assembly.

Second, the UN Security Council monitors compliance with the CRC and Optional Protocol and authorises various enforcement measures through Security Council Resolutions (UNSCRs), including through stabilisation missions and peace enforcement operations authorised under Chapter VII of the UN Charter. Numerous UNSCRs address the issue of children and armed conflict.[3] Resolutions have urged member states and the UN system to end recruitment and use of children in hostilities and promote alternative livelihoods for children (UNSCR 1261, 1999, para. 13). Resolutions have also recalled obligations under international law not to use schools for military purposes (UNSCR 2143, 2014, para. 18), required certain states to complete 'action plans' with the UN to end recruitment and use of child soldiers (UNSCR 1612, 2005, para. 3), and mandated protection of children as part of UN peacekeeping operations (UNSCR 1612, 2005, para. 12; UNSCR 2143, 2014, para. 24). Reflecting the latter enforcement option, peace operations increasingly authorise child protection and assistance under Chapter VII. And, provision for child protection and assistance, including release and demobilisation of child soldiers, child reintegration assistance, or other support for children's rights, is present in all ongoing mission mandates in sub-Saharan Africa: CAR (MINUSCA), Mali (MINUSMA), DRC (MONUSCO), Sudan-Darfur (UNAMID), Liberia (UNMIL), South Sudan (UNMISS), and Côte d'Ivoire (UNOCI).[4]

---

[3] See UNSCR 1261 (1999), UNSCR 1314 (2000), UNSCR 1379 (2001), UNSCR 1460 (2003), UNSCR 1539 (2004), UNSCR 1612 (2005), UNSCR 1820 (2008), UNSCR 1882 (2009), UNSCR 1998 (2011), UNSCR 2068 (2012), UNSCR 2143 (2014), and UNSCR 2225 (2015).

[4] See the child protection mandate of the UN Multidimensional Integrated Stabilization Mission in Mali (MINUSMA), reiterated in UNSCR 2227 (2015, para. 24). The original child protection mandate of MINUSMA is found in UNSCR 2100 (2013, para.16(a)(v)).

Third, UNICEF and the Special Representative to the Secretary-General on Children and Armed Conflict monitor and assist states and non-state armed groups that have signed action plans with the UN to prevent recruitment and use. As of 2016, 26 listed parties (11 state governments and 15 non-state armed groups) signed 27 action plans with UNICEF and the SRSG (United Nations Office of the SRSG for Children and Armed Conflict, 2017a). Since 2014, UNICEF and the SRSG have de-listed nine signatories, deeming them to have completed their agreed action plan.[5] Most action plans stipulate that the signatory issue military command orders prohibiting the recruitment and use of children, release all children identified in its ranks, ensure reintegration assistance, criminalise future recruitment and use, and adopt age-verification mechanisms in recruitment procedures. Action plans might also call for the investigation and prosecution of those who recruit and use children in hostilities, the appointment of child protection specialists, and state-wide information campaigns. The SRSG credits action plans with the criminalisation of child recruitment in Afghanistan, the appointment of a presidential adviser in the DRC to address child sexual violence and child recruitment, and Somalia's ratification of the CRC in 2015 (United Nations Office of the SRSG for Children and Armed Conflict, 2017b).

These various enforcement actions are relatively toothless. States that fail to implement action plans face few, if any, sanctions. States largely determine the feasibility and appropriateness of their own strategies to demobilise and reintegrate child soldiers, regardless of recommendations from the Committee on the Rights of the Child to the General Assembly. And UN monitoring efforts, even when accompanied by Security Council condemnation or action, lack enforcement heft or sustainability, particularly when broader efforts to manage or end conflict stall. Consequently, the fourth enforcement strategy—criminalisation—has emerged as the dominant one.

---

[5] Delisted parties are the ANT in Chad, the FAFN, FLGO, MILOCI, APWe, and UPGRO in Côte d'Ivoire, the UCPN-M in Nepal, the TMVP in Sri Lanka, and the UPDF in Uganda. Ongoing action plans involve state armed forces or non-state armed groups in Afghanistan, Central African Republic, Democratic Republic of the Congo, Myanmar, Philippines, Somalia, Sudan, South Sudan, and Yemen (UNICEF, 2015, p. 31; UN Office of the SRSG for Children and Armed Conflict, 2017a).

The Prioritisation of Criminalisation as a Child Protection Strategy

Enforcement of criminalisation rests with the ICC. Per the 1998 Rome Statute creating the ICC, the Office of the Prosecutor of the ICC can open and conduct investigations against individuals and can initiate prosecution by filing charges against such individuals. From there, the Trial Chamber of the ICC can convict and sentence individuals and issue reparations judgments to aid and assist victims.[6] The Rome Statute (1998: Article 8(2)(b)(xxvi) for state armed forces and Article 8(2)(e)(vii) for non-state armed groups) also made recruitment and use of children in conflict a war crime.

As it happens, the ICC's first case was for the crime of recruitment and use of child soldiers in the conflict in eastern DRC from 2002 to 2003.[7] The case resulted in a conviction, on 14 March 2012, against Thomas Lubanga Dyilo. The Trial Chamber sentenced Lubanga to 14 years of prison, and the Appeals Chamber confirmed the conviction and sentence (International Criminal Court, 2012). Human rights groups and victims' advocates have criticised the judgement as being too narrowly focussed on the single crime of recruiting and using child soldiers, ignoring the other human rights abuses and war crimes they allege Lubanga to have overseen or committed and therefore limiting the scope of victims' participation in the ICC's first case (Coleman, 2007, p. 780; Gambone, 2009; Graf, 2012).

---

[6] The issue of reparations stemming from ICC judgments is a potentially positive development that could redress the persistent trade-offs between protection and reintegration. On 15 December 2017, the Trial Chamber II of the ICC ordered payment of $10 million USD in reparations to child soldiers in the DRC who had been recruited by the convicted warlord, Thomas Lubanga Dyilo. Dyilo, the Trial Chamber acknowledged, is incapable of paying the amount and so it said payment would come from a court Trust Fund for Victims, which should be funded from the government of the DRC. The ability of the ICC to enforce payment of reparations and ensure that they are put to effective and therapeutic use for young victims, remains to be seen. Also missing from the judgement is provision for child participation and consultation in administration of the funds. See International Criminal Court (2017).

[7] Prior to the Lubanga case, the Special Court for Sierra Leone also issued judgements that set important precedents for international criminalisation of child soldiering, including the conviction and sentencing of Charles Taylor (Novogrodsky, 2005).

Legal scholars, meanwhile, have focussed on two problems with the Lubanga judgement.[8] First, the Trial Chamber in Lubanga distinguished the Rome Statute acts of conscription and enlistment, associating conscription with coercion to join an armed force or group and enlistment as voluntary recruitment into a force or group.[9] In any case, however, it also ruled that the distinction is irrelevant to adjudicating the war crime of recruitment because, it argued, the admission of a child into an armed group or force 'with or without compulsion' was a war crime under the Statute (Amann, 2013, pp. 421–422). Some legal scholars see benefits in emphasising that structural constraints make any claim of voluntary enlistment by children suspect, whilst others have decried the denial of child agency, along with the broad longstanding legal tradition of according 'each term in a statute… a separate meaning' and the more specific legal treatment of juvenile autonomy (Amann, 2013, p. 422).[10] The ruling coincides with the view put forward in the SRSG for Children and Armed Conflict's amicus brief to the Court (the SRSG also testified as an expert witness), which argued that any distinction between voluntary and forced recruitment is 'without meaning in the context of armed conflict because even the most voluntary acts can be a desperate attempt to survive by children with a limited number of options in the context of war' (International Criminal Court, 2008). Many child rights advocates prefer a narrative of clear-cut coercion to complicated agency, which indeed can also be detected in the evidence presented in Allen Kiconco's chapter in this volume (Chapter 5).

---

[8] At the time of principal writing, four other major cases before the ICC have involved the charge of recruitment and use of child soldiers, and two of these cases have since resulted in convictions. In 2019, Bosco Ntaganda, Commander of Operations for the FPLC in DRC, was found guilty on 18 counts of war crimes and crimes against humanity, including conscription and use of children under 15. The Ntaganda case also, and unlike the Dyilo judgement, extended protection to children raped or sexually enslaved by their own armed group. In 2021, the LRA Brigade Commander Dominic Ongwen, himself a former child soldier, was convicted of 61 war crimes and crimes against humanity, including conscription and use of children.

[9] Throughout this chapter, I have used the shorthand term 'recruitment' for both 'conscription' and 'enlistment' for ease of reference but also to underscore the blurred lines between the two distinctive acts, a topic dealt with in greater detail in section three of this chapter.

[10] Amann herself sees merit in the approach of the Lubanga judgement. For the view in favour of agency and juvenile autonomy, see Drumbl (2012, pp. 13–17). See also Drumbl and Barrett (2019).

The second problem concerns the use of child soldiers. Numerous international agreements (including the Cape Town and Paris Principles) disallow a narrow conceptualisation of use that is limited to arms-wielding fighters engaged in battlefront combat. They call instead for a broad interpretation recognising that children play a variety of roles on the front lines and in base camps. One of the Lubanga judges affirmed this broad view, echoing three arguments in the amicus brief and testimony of the SRSG in the case. First, the amicus brief described children as fulfilling a variety of roles during war, including as spies, messengers, porters, scouts, and cooks. Second, it argued that all of these roles make children targets of violence and place them in or near violence during hostilities. Children face injury or death for dereliction of duty or attempts to escape, and face reprisal violence by rival groups and forces, regardless of their conflict roles. Third, it argued forcefully that sexual violence, abuse, and exploitation of children all constitute 'active use' of children in hostilities, again acknowledging the lived reality of girl and boy combatants under 18 who experience sexual abuse as use (International Criminal Court, 2008). But the majority of the Lubanga Court affirmed only the SRSG's first two points, explicitly excluding the third point about the inclusion of sexual violence from any consideration of active use. The majority ruled only that use meant exposure of children 'to real danger as a potential target' even outside of 'the immediate scene of the hostilities'. In reaching this majority view, the Court drew on some evidence of maltreatment of child soldiers 'outside the immediate scene of hostilities' (e.g., corporal punishment) but excluded other evidence of maltreatment (sexual violence, abuse, and exploitation) (Amann, 2013, pp. 422–425).

Criminalisation has impacted child protection and assistance, but not always for the better. The impacts of protection strategies on child soldiers and their post-war reintegration are analysed next, starting with an assessment of whether criminalisation has a deterrent effect on recruitment and use.

Do Protection Enforcement Strategies Deter Recruitment and Use?

The deterrent impact of the ICC is in doubt, in part because of its slow pace and limited reach. It took the Court almost a decade to investigate and prosecute one defendant for the crime of recruiting and using child soldiers. The reach of the ICC, and its resources, are extremely limited and there are pressures on the Court to demonstrate that it can and will investigate and convict cases across the spectrum of Statute jurisdiction crimes and across geographical contexts. These limitations call into question the extent of any deterrent effect on recruitment and use of children in hostilities. Any potential deterrent effect is also clouded by the ongoing confusion and contestation around concepts such as enlistment, recruitment, and use. Deterrent effects rely on widespread and diffuse information campaigns that clearly demarcate proscribed activity. If per the controversial Lubanga judgement, the above concepts continue to divide jurists and advocates, then the criminal culpability for these three crimes remains in doubt. Furthermore, there is a perception problem. Populations in states with ongoing or recently concluded hostilities arguably place recruitment and use of child soldiers low on the priority list of needs and concerns that result from long-term, devastating violence.

The selectivity of justice at the ICC also precludes deterrence. The cases successfully prosecuted at the Special Court and the ICC were against defendants of non-state armed groups. Such a focus sidesteps widespread *state* use of children under 18. For example, whilst there is little doubt that Joseph Kony's LRA recruited and used children in hostilities, the SRSG for Children and Armed Conflict has also drawn attention to the Ugandan government's own child recruitment into pro-state militias and the army, including through abduction and coercion (IRIN, 2006). But the ICC has not been willing to investigate or prosecute state recruitment and use.

Meanwhile, recruitment and use of children continue, with no perceptible decrease since the creation of the ICC in 2002 or the issuance of the Lubanga judgement in 2012. Reports of child recruitment and use continue in all states with active action plans (Kohm, 2014, pp. 232–233). The UN Security Council has frequently condemned the recruitment and use of child soldiers, but that condemnation has not deterred states and armed groups from recruiting and using them. In 1999, the Security Council, expressed 'its grave concern' at the impact of conflict on children and 'strongly condemn[ed]' recruitment and use of children in conflict (UNSCR 1261, 1999, paras. 1, 2). Fifteen years later, the Security Council remained 'deeply concerned over the lack of progress on the ground', and again expressed 'deep concern' about and 'strongly condemn[ed]' recruitment and re-recruitment of children (UNSCR 2143, 2014), just as it had in resolutions almost annually since 1999. The 'urges', 'reiterates', 'calls upon', and 'encourages' outnumber the 'decides'. Nor have UN peacebuilding missions proved to be an effective deterrent, with ongoing instances of abduction and recruitment of young people into armed forces and groups consistently reported in Secretary-General's reports on *current* UN missions in Mali, CAR, and South Sudan (United Nations Human Rights Council, 2016, paras. 67–70; United Nations Security Council [UNSC], 2016a, para. 207; 2016b, paras. 41–42; 2016c, paras. 26, 28, 34–36; 2016d, paras. 13, 40).

Protection Trade-Offs with Reintegration

More importantly for the welfare of actual young people caught up in structures of war-making, the enforcement strategies that the UN and ICC pursue end up denying many children access to reintegration assistance. In case after case, child soldiers released and 'reintegrated' from armed forces and groups during conflict have been excluded from formal reintegration assistance after the conflict ends.

Because of the strong norms against recruitment and use of child soldiers, actors who have recruited and used child soldiers have incentives to disguise such use in ways that end up excluding children from protection and assistance (Vandewiele, 2005, p. 50).[11] In Sudan, military and militia officials denied the existence of children in armed forces and groups, and such denial prevented UNICEF from designing and implementing a pilot project for children there. Furthermore, UNICEF found that armed forces and groups in Sudan released children ahead of planned disarmament and demobilisation efforts to avoid acknowledging their presence within the ranks (UNICEF Sudan, 2004, pp. 2, 20). In Somalia, international pressure against the detention and prosecution of children, combined with the 'catch and release' policy for pirates captured at sea, denies children their rights to reintegration under the CRC (Kohm, 2014, p. 334).

In Angola, the wholesale exclusion of children from the reintegration process can be traced to the very protection regime designed to include them. Absorption into the new military was a precondition for access to demobilisation and reintegration assistance under the peace agreement there. The Angolan government did not want to be seen as validating

---

[11] An estimated one-third of child combatants do not enter formal DDR processes (UNSC, 2000, para. 23).

entry of underage boys and girls into its new force, even if such individuals were immediately demobilised, and so instead decided to treat all child combatants not as combatants but as dependents of combatants. The decision resulted in children's exclusion from formal reintegration benefits. Subsequent efforts to re-locate and assist excluded children failed (McMullin, 2011, pp. 744, 746–749).

In Mozambique, the post-war government awarded pensions to its own soldiers (no pensions were awarded to RENAMO fighters, unless they were disabled) but only to those who had completed ten years of military service. Again, reacting to strong international norms against recruitment and use of children in hostilities, the government would not recognise start-dates for soldiers recruited whilst underage because it refused to admit its recruitment and use of children during the long civil war. The UN deferred to the government, but donor states applied pressure, and the government eventually relented to approve pension applications for soldiers whose military service start date occurred before they were 18, but without recognising recruitment and use of children. But the government waits for claimants to petition it for pensions, and veterans' assistance organisations in Mozambique estimate that most child soldiers have not presented themselves for the assistance to which they are now entitled (McMullin, 2013, p. 134).

The mandates and authorising language of Chapter VII peacebuilding missions underscore how the prioritisation of child protection comes at the expense of post-war reintegration assistance for child soldiers. Children's right to receive reintegration assistance is qualified in mission mandates: children are promised support sufficient only to guarantee that they are not at risk of re-recruitment and that they do not threaten their communities with violence. Consequently, children's rights to access DDR assistance are not about realisation of social, political, and economic integration as ends in and of themselves, but rather such rights are securitised, extending assistance to children only insofar as child beneficiaries threaten or are threatened. Their right to reintegration assistance is similarly securitised: it is circumscribed temporally as short term, to end once threats subside, and substantively, where threat estimates determine the nature and contours of the assistance offered.

The gendered practices of the child protection regime further entrench trade-offs between protection and reintegration. The policy and academic literature on DDR has criticised the exclusion of children, and especially girls, from DDR benefits in Sierra Leone because of the way programmes were designed and administered (Coulter, 2009; MacKenzie, 2009). Because cash payments hinged on combatants turning in either a weapon or ammunition at demobilisation sites, many commanders simply cut loose the children in their ranks and distributed guns and ammunition to family members or associates instead so they could benefit.[12] Only a fraction of the girls estimated to have been abducted or recruited into armed groups in Sierra Leone registered for DDR assistance (506 girls of an estimated 8,600 to 11,400) (Williamson, 2005, pp. viii–ix). The public nature of DDR enrolment deterred girls and women, due to the stigma attached to publicly identifying as having participated in the conflict (Coulter, 2009, p. 155). In Liberia, DDR actors worked to avoid the exclusion of girls from programmes as occurred in Sierra Leone by adopting open and flexible eligibility requirements, but evidence suggests that commanders there still excluded bona fide child soldiers from formal DDR assistance, and publicly visible registration policies recurred (McMullin, 2013, pp. 203–204).

The gendered nature of DDR that chronically eludes practitioners in their reintegration programming is not just about whether elite actors pay attention to gender dynamics or not; rather, it is about whether they sufficiently understand the complex and multiple roles that girls play during conflict. The UNICEF guide to the Optional Protocol illustrates the widespread misunderstanding of such roles. The guide's breakaway text box on DDR in Sierra Leone gives the reader the impression that all girls used in the conflict there were 'camp followers', recruited to 'provide sexual services to armed groups'. A guide intended to give a specific account of the 'special needs of children' consequently fails to note or analyse the multiple roles that girls played during the Sierra Leonean conflict, including as active combat fighters (UNICEF, 2003, p. 19). The overall tendency and effect are to sexualise and infantilise girl soldiers during war and conflate a variety of individualised wartime experiences with a kind of 'ultimate' victimhood. If the protection regime assumes that all girl soldiers are universally and equally victimised during hostilities, then a difficult question is skirted; i.e. whether a gendered approach to DDR involves treating all girls recruited and used in hostilities the same or whether reintegration assistance should account for the *different* roles that individual girls may have played during conflict.

---

[12] Author's interview (2005) UNICEF Official, Freetown, 7 July. See also Vandewiele (2005, p. 51).

Integration or Stigmatisation?

Gendered infantilisation of child soldiers illustrates a further trade-off between protection and criminalisation approaches on one hand and sustainable reintegration assistance on the other. Both protection and assistance are frequently rationalised on the basis of presumed child vulnerability. International legal and policy frameworks that govern assistance for child soldiers often rest on romantic notions of childhood that do not correspond with children's own lived experiences and aspirations. Such frameworks treat war as an interruption to an otherwise secure, peaceful home life. Similarly, they treat children's return home after war as a return to a nurturing idyll that can facilitate a child's development provided the disruptive consequences of war can be managed (Pauletto & Patel, 2010). Both portrayals erase forms of violence that children encounter before and after war, including inside the home. Also typical of the mainstream treatment of children is to contrast the kind, happy children encountered by international intermediaries with the disruptive violence perceived as at odds with children's natural innocence. Take the following presentation of a child soldier in Liberia found within a UNICEF report: 'With his big round eyes, toothy smile and spindly…frame Tommy looks more like a mischievous schoolboy than a cold-blooded killer. Yet—at age 16—that's exactly what Liberia's warring adults have turned him into' (Kelly, 1998, p. 8). Because of the way in which legal frameworks position children (inherently victims and not culpable for the violence they commit in war) and the way in which child protection policy frameworks construct them (in need of adult guidance in order to return to a pre-war status quo), their agency and motivations for participating in conflict are obscured, as is the structural violence they experience within their home and communities.

Child rights advocates frequently anchor tropes about why and how young fighters are recruited into conflict to narratives about child victimisation and immaturity. Such narratives discount children's own perceptions of war-making as a tool to promote their own security and survival in contexts where they felt dangerously insecure and unprotected pre-war. For example, a UNICEF report discusses youth involvement in the first Liberian civil war with the following:

> Although children were forcibly recruited by all of the warring factions, the participation of boys and youths in Liberia's war was characterised

by a particularly high number of volunteers. Few, however, joined for ideological reasons or even understood the roots of the conflict. Instead many...initially joined for revenge. Others succumbed to peer pressure...A few others were looking for adventure and a chance to be in control...But most joined for one simple reason...security. (Kelly, 1998, p. 13)

Although underage volunteers are said to outnumber those coercively recruited, the report nevertheless presumes that 'few' of these volunteers 'understood the roots of conflict'. And yet the same report acknowledges that 'most' youth joined for security reasons, suggesting that young people did indeed 'understand the roots of conflict' as being intrinsically tied to their own pursuit of security. The report neglects to anchor the 'simple reason' of 'security' to a political context. Instead, it associates the security concerns of youth with non-political, individualised motivations such as 'revenge', 'peer pressure', power, and adventurism. Tropes about the immaturity of children, incapable of knowing what they are doing or why, also exist paradoxically alongside tropes that assert their 'innate' skills as fighters, where children are thought to be immune to the complicating factors of morality and mortality that might inhibit 'normal', but non-'innate', adult fighters (Kelly, 1998). Assumptions about child vulnerability and victimhood like the ones on display in this particular report also seem to resist sustained critique. In other words, they persist despite a large volume of ethnographically informed research that challenges such universal conceptions and that instead emphasises young people's coping skills and resistance strategies (Seymour, 2012, p. 374).

Much of the ethnographic critique of the child protection regime has focussed on the either/or bind that tends to locate children during war *either* as victims *or* as perpetrators. Ann Sagan's deconstruction of the Lubanga trial proceedings and judgement notes how the prosecution relied 'on patronising and criminalising stereotypes of African child soldiers in order to make their case', portraying children in the DRC as incapable of moral agency unless properly guided by good adults, who are assumed to be too few in number. In such scenarios, children are always 'ripe' and the global south always a 'breeding ground' for recruitment (Sagan, 2010, pp. 17–18). The ethnographic critique also calls into question portrayals of children's innocence. Verma (2012) juxtaposes what she calls 'daytime' and 'nighttime stories' of Ugandan children who were abducted into the Lord's Resistance Army and were then taken into rehabilitation camps for war returnees. She found that children's daytime stories hued closely to the expectations of NGO workers, UNICEF, donors, and international media outlets, all of whom expected a standardised narrative of children's involuntary recruitment into war and subsequent victimisation by war. Meanwhile, in children's nighttime stories, after aid workers had gone home or to sleep, '[e]vents changed like that, plots were inversed, moralities altered, and loyalties cast in doubt'. In children's nighttime stories, they complicated their own agency in war, presenting themselves 'neither as a child nor as victim' (Verma, 2012, p. 443). She also identifies diverse strategies that the children used in the reception centres, sometimes employing standardised daytime stories to gain trust or resources, and instructing their peers in how to do the same, but occasionally resisting dominant narratives, too, including in the presence of aid workers (Verma, 2012, pp. 451–452).

Narratives of child soldiering rooted in victimisation end up gatekeeping children's access to assistance after war. Utas (2005) argues that aid discourse repeatedly and consistently encourages war-affected women in Liberia to present themselves as victims. His research on young people during conflict has sought to complicate notions of youth agency and victimhood during and after war, such as portrayals of children who were not child soldiers but who claimed identity as child soldiers to escape poverty, or child soldiers who tweaked their recruitment stories so they would more closely align with aid workers' expectations (Utas, 2005, 2011). Utas advocates movement away from the victim/perpetrator dichotomy that characterises so much of international jurisprudence and assistance practice for youth. Instead, he conceptualises young people's complicated 'victimcy' as a relational construct in between the lived experiences of youth, on the one hand, and the expectations, constructs, and material and social structures that define and control post-war assistance and the individuals (usually, adult internationals) who perpetuate them, on the other. He then highlights and accentuates the 'tactical agency' of youth, or the way in which young people move between worlds of war-making and post-war survival.

The ethnographic and critical literature on child soldiering has brought necessary attention to the victimisation discourse prevalent in child rights and child protection practices. Through that literature, it becomes possible to understand how DDR discourse and practice are not consistent about where children get located along the victim-perpetrator spectrum. On one hand, the suffering of child soldiers is meticulously catalogued and detailed, and children are exempted from culpability normally associated with war-making, including the policies that prohibit prosecution of children for crimes they may have committed whilst (illegally) soldiering during hostilities. But on the other hand, practitioners often treat child soldiers in any given context as collectively capable and guilty of war crimes and take exception to targeted assistance for them, arguing that any assistance should be available instead to all war-affected children without prejudice to whether or not they soldiered. Such advocacy tends also to assert that non-combatant children and civilian communities generally suffered just as much or more. Thus, whilst child protection discourse insists on child combatants' 'special needs' and repeatedly calls for their 'special treatment' in relation to adult combatants, it also simultaneously decries 'special treatment' of child soldiers in relation to other war-affected children. Such ambivalence signals latent hostility towards child soldiers as assistance beneficiaries and scepticism about whether child soldiers 'have earned' or 'deserve' the very specialised assistance to which they are legally entitled.

Stigmatisation and infantilisation of child soldiers work against children's post-war integration, as we also saw in Allen Kiconco's chapter (Chapter 5). The CRC holds that a child's assumption of a 'constructive role in society' is paramount in assessing that child's post-war integration. But consistent victimisation of children suggests that children's assumption of a constructive role is either *premature* (they are not ready for it or they are too traumatised to be able to play a visible and productive role in post-war society) or *dangerous* (they are too volatile and violent to be allowed to play it). Alison Watson argues that, in this regard, the victim label can be 'deeply othering', with portrayals dependent on the representation of marginalised groups as victims directly impacting on the ability of those groups 'to become political agents and thus claim rights' (Watson, 2015). Of course, that impact will not always be the same for all children; in fact, Watson suggests that young men and women are increasingly likely to reject the narrative of victimhood thrust onto them by outside others. Instead, they are always already engaged in modes of self-representation and action that challenge and complicate their identity as victims.[13]

---

[13] Regarding this latter point, Watson cites Spalek (2006).

Pathologisation of Southern Youth and States

Prevalent protection strategies, especially clustered around criminalisation of recruitment and use of children, also work to pathologise young people and their communities in poor states of the Global South, raising questions about whose justice interests are promoted via the current child protection regime (Wells, 2016). Drumbl (2012, p. 9) argues that the concepts and practices of the child protection regime reflect the 'international legal imagination', which tends to fixate in particular on young victims of war and tends to substitute its own 'standards and desires...for the aspirations of victims themselves'. Others see self-congratulation and ethnocentrism behind the pathologisation of child-rearing and child protection in the South (Dillon, 2008, p. 145, cited in Kohm, 2014, p. 342). Such dynamics are not new or unique to the particular challenge of child soldiering, as much of this book has argued. The silencing of African voices and absence of African perspectives extends to the development of international law more broadly.[14]

As of early 2018, there have been 23 cases before the ICC, all of them with defendants from African states, which ensures the continued 'reproduction of the criminal-victim dichotomy in the representation of African subjects in the discourse of international criminal law' (King, 2015, pp. 130–131; Sagan, 2010, p. 4).[15] The ICC's prosecution thus far of perpetrators targeted exclusively from African contexts risks African states' withdrawal from its jurisdiction entirely, or from associated conventions, statutes, and treaties. In February 2017, the African Union approved a non-binding resolution calling on member states to withdraw from the ICC, and South Africa and Burundi subsequently announced decisions to withdraw.[16] The Court's focus on Africa also has real impacts on child

---

[14] For a critical historical treatment, see Haslam (2014).

[15] As of 2018, the ICC Prosecutor was investigating crimes in Georgia and undergoing preliminary examination of crimes in Afghanistan, Burundi, Colombia, Gabon, Guinea, the UK (crimes alleged in Iraq), Nigeria, Palestine, Ukraine, and registered vessels of Comoros/Greece/Cambodia.

[16] South Africa subsequently revoked its withdrawal, whilst Burundi because the first state to leave the ICC in 2017. Nigeria, Senegal, and Cape Verde entered formal reservations to the resolution that the AU's heads of state adopted. Many African states subsequently reaffirmed their commitment to the ICC, and the resolution includes various caveats, including a call to research further the idea of collective withdrawal from ICC and to negotiate with the Security Council for reform of the ICC (Keppler, 2017).

soldiers there. One impact, already discussed in this chapter, is the exclusion of children from assistance due to the refusal of states and groups to acknowledge their use. Another is that the Africa focus normalises the state-sponsored co-involvement of underage men and women in the militarisation of culture and the structures of war-making in Northern states.

Arguably, the child protection regime does not apply a universal understanding of childhood to all states in the world, but instead uses a particular standard of childhood and expends great resources in applying that standard selectively to only some states. In protecting children from recruitment and use, child rights discourse 're-conceptualises the plight of children as the fault of the adult population' (Pupavac, 2001, p. 102). But then, during the shift from releasing children from armed groups to their post-war reintegration, the presumed innocence of children and presumed guilt of their Southern adult guardians and communities are reversed. As if overnight, in certain contexts, the community transitions from having failed to protect children from recruitment to being regarded as the font of wisdom about children's best interests, the arbiter of children's reconciliation with their communities, and the decider of the norms that will govern children's integration. Children also shift from being innocents in need of saving in wartime to being deviants who are considered threats to the transition from war.

More participation by children themselves in shaping and designing the forms that social, political, and economic reintegration take could be palliative. Collins (2017) believes that children's participation could also redress the ethnocentrism that pervades child rights discourse, allowing movement away from rigid understandings of children's experiences of war and post-war integration.[17] As Watson (2015) suggests, children's work to shape their own identity and navigate their own post-war transition is always already under way. Currently, however, dogmatic narratives and practices of child reintegration fail to engage more meaningfully with children. Instead of designing avenues for more genuine consultation and participation of child beneficiaries, programmes end up miming participation. They marginalise the productive, peaceful efforts of children to navigate their own reintegration, and securitise the efforts deemed unproductive or threatening. Each action consigns children's participation to a

---

[17] See also Ensor and Reinke (2014).

world of informal DDR, whilst the formal structures of DDR reflect paternalism and total control, not just over the prospects and futures available to children, but also the benefits available to them, and even the way in which they are encouraged to process and remember experiences of soldiering.

REFERENCES

Amann, D. M. (2013). Children and the first verdict of the International Criminal Court. *Washington University Global Studies Law Review., 12*, 411–432.

Child Soldiers International. (2012). *ICC Lubanga conviction: A positive step to end impunity for recruitment of children.* https://www.child-soldiers.org/News/press-release. Accessed 11 June 2018.

Child Soldiers International. (2018, February 21). *Child Soldiers World Index reveals shocking scale of child recruitment around the world.* Reliefweb. https://reliefweb.int/report/world/child-soldiers-world-index-reveals-shocking-scale-child-recruitment-around-world. Accessed 11 June 2018.

Coleman, J. (2007). Showing its teeth: The International Criminal Court takes on child conscription in the Congo, but is its bark worse than its bite? *Penn State International Law Review., 26*(3), 765–785.

Collins, T. M. (2017). A child's right to participate: Implications for international child protection. *The International Journal of Human Rights., 21*(1), 14–46.

Coulter, C. (2009). *Bush wives and girl soldiers: Women's lives through war and peace in Sierra Leone.* Cornell University Press.

Dillon, S. A. (2008). What human rights law obscures: Global sex trafficking and the demand for children. *UCLA Women's Law Journal., 17*, 121–186.

Drumbl, M. A. (2012). *Reimagining child soldiers in international law and policy.* Oxford University Press.

Drumbl, M. A., & Barrett, J. C. (Eds.). (2019). *Research handbook on child soldiers.* Edward Elgar Publishing.

Ensor, M. O., & Reinke, A. J. (2014). African children's right to participate in their own protection: Perspectives from South Sudan. *The International Journal of Children's Rights., 22*(1), 68–92.

Gambone, L. (2009, July 22). *Failure to charge: The ICC, Lubanga & sexual violence crimes in the DRC.* Foreign Policy Blogs Network, Foreign Policy Association. http://foreignpolicyblogs.com/2009/07/22/failure-to-charge-the-icc-lubanga-sexual-violence-crimes-in-the-drc/. Accessed 1 March 2017.

Graf, R. (2012). The International Criminal Court and child soldiers: An appraisal of the Lubanga judgment. *Journal of International Criminal Justice, 10*(4), 945–969.

Haslam, E. (2014). Silences in international criminal legal histories and the construction of the victim subject of international criminal law: The nineteenth century slave trading trial of Joseph Peters. In C. Schwöbel (Ed.), *Critical approaches to International Criminal Law: An introduction* (pp. 180–195). Routledge.

Human Rights Watch. (2008, December 3). *Facts about child soldiers, Background Briefing.* https://www.hrw.org/news/2008/12/03/facts-about-child-soldiers. Accessed 1 March 2017.

Human Rights Watch. (2012a, June 14). *ICC: Landmark verdict a warning to rights abusers.* https://www.hrw.org/news/2012/03/14/icc-landmark-verdict-warning-rights-abusers. Accessed 11 June 2018.

Human Rights Watch. (2012b, March 12). *Child soldiers worldwide, Background Briefing.* https://www.hrw.org/news/2012/03/12/child-soldiers-worldwide. Accessed 1 March 2017.

International Criminal Court. (2008, March 18). The Prosecutor v. Thomas Lubanga Dyilo. Case No. ICC- 01/04-01/06-1229-AnxA, written submissions of the United Nations Special Representative of the Secretary-General on Children and Armed Conflict submitted in application of Rule 103 of the Rules of Procedure and Evidence. https://www.icc-cpi.int/RelatedRecords/CR2008_01287.PDF. Accessed 1 March 2017.

International Criminal Court. (2012). The Prosecutor v. Thomas Lubanga Dyilo. Case No. ICC-01/04-01/06-2842, judgment pursuant to Article 74 of the Rome Statute. https://www.icc-cpi.int/drc/lubanga. Accessed 1 February 2017.

International Criminal Court. (2017, December 15). *Lubanga case: Trial Chamber II issues additional decision on reparations* (Press release). https://www.icc-cpi.int/Pages/item.aspx?name=pr1351. Accessed 12 June 2018.

IRIN. (2006, June 13). *Interview with Radhika Coomaraswamy, Special Representative for Children and Armed Conflict.* http://www.irinnews.org/report/59296/uganda-interview-radhika-coomaraswamy-special-representative-children-and-armed-conflict. Accessed 1 March 2017.

Kelly, D. (1998). *The DDR of child soldiers in Liberia, 1994-1997: The process and lessons learned.* UNICEF. http://repository.forcedmigration.org/show_metadata.jsp?pid=fmo:3259. Accessed 26 January 2017.

Keppler, E. (2017, February 1). *AU's 'ICC withdrawal strategy' less than meets the eye: Opposition to withdrawal by states.* Human Rights Watch Dispatches. https://www.hrw.org/news/2017/02/01/aus-icc-withdrawal-strategy-less-meets-eye. Accessed 3 March 2017.

King, V. (2015). Constructing victims in the International Criminal Court: A critical discourse analysis. *Pursuit – The Journal of Undergraduate Research at the University of Tennessee, 6*(1), 129–139.

Kohm, L. M. (2014). Brief assessment of the 25-year effect of the Convention on the Rights of the Child. *Cardozo Journal of International and Comparative Law., 23*, 323–351.

MacKenzie, M. (2009). Securitization and desecuritization: Female soldiers and the reconstruction of women in post-conflict Sierra Leone. *Security Studies., 18*(2), 241–261.

McMullin, J. R. (2011). Reintegrating young combatants: Do child-centred approaches leave children – and adults – behind? *Third World Quarterly., 32*(6), 743–764.

McMullin, J. R. (2013). *Ex-combatants and the post-conflict State: Challenges of reintegration*. Palgrave Macmillan.

Novogrodsky, N. B. (2005). Litigating child recruitment before the Special Court for Sierra Leone. *San Diego International Law Journal, 7*, 421–426.

Pauletto, E., & Patel, P. (2010). Challenging child soldier DDR processes and policies in the eastern Democratic Republic of Congo. *Journal of Peace, Conflict and Development, 16*, 35–57.

Pupavac, V. (2001). Misanthropy without borders: The international children's rights regime. *Disasters, 25*(2), 95–112.

Rome Statute of the International Criminal Court. (1998, July 17). A/CONF.183/9 [entry into force 16 January 2002].

Sagan, A. (2010) African criminals/African victims: The institutionalised production of cultural narratives in international criminal law. *Millennium: Journal of International Studies, 39*(1), 3–21.

Seymour, C. (2012). Ambiguous agencies: Coping and survival in eastern Democratic Republic of Congo. *Children's Geographies., 10*(4), 373–384.

Spalek, B. (2006). *Crime victims: Theory, policy and practice*. Palgrave Macmillan.

UNICEF. (2003). *Guide to the Optional Protocol on the involvement of children in armed conflict*. UNICEF.

UNICEF. (2015). *Annual report 2015*. UNICEF.

Sudan, U. N. I. C. E. F. (2004). *Children associated with fighting forces (CAFF) in Sudan: Rapid situation analysis for demobilization and reintegration of CAFF in government controlled areas*. UNICEF.

United Nations. (1989, November 20). Convention on the Rights of the, Child Treaty Series 1577 [entry into force 2 September 1990].

United Nations. (2000, May 25). Optional Protocol to the convention on the Rights of the Child on the Involvement of Children in Armed Conflict. GAR A/RES/54/263 [entry into force 12 February 2002].

United Nations Human Rights Council. (2016, January 21). Report of the Independent Expert on the situation of human rights in Mali. A/HRC/31/76.

United Nations Office of the SRSG for Children and Armed Conflict. (2017a). *Action plans with armed forces and armed groups*. https://childrenandarmedconflict.un.org/our-work/action-plans/. Accessed 26 January.

United Nations Office of the SRSG on Children and Armed Conflict. (2017b). *Children not soldiers campaign.* https://childrenandarmedconflict.un.org/children-not-soldiers/. Accessed 26 January.

United Nations Security Council (UNSC). (2016a). Letter dated 5 December 2016 from the Panel of Experts on the Central African Republic extended pursuant to Security Council Resolution 2262 (2016) addressed to the President of the Security Council. S/2016/1032, 5 December, Annex 6.7.

UNSC. (2016b, September 29). Report of the Secretary-General on the situation in Mali. S/2016/819.

UNSC. (2016c, September 29). Report of the Secretary-General on the situation in the Central African Republic. S/2016/824.

UNSC. (2016d, June 20). Report of the Secretary-General on South Sudan (covering the period from 1 April to 3 June 2016). S/2016/552.

UNSC. (2000, February 11). The role of United Nations peacekeeping in disarmament, demobilisation and reintegration. S/2000/101.

UNSCR 1261. (1999, August 25). S/RES/1261.

UNSCR 1314. (2000, August 11). S/RES/1314.

UNSCR 1379. (2001, November 20). S/RES/1379.

UNSCR 1460. (2003, January 30). S/RES/1460.

UNSCR 1539. (2004, April 22). S/RES/1539.

UNSCR 1612. (2005, July 26). S/RES/1612.

UNSCR 1820. (2008, June 19). S/RES/1820.

UNSCR 1882. (2009, August 4). S/RES/1882.

UNSCR 1998. (2011, July 12). S/RES/1998.

UNSCR 2068. (2012, September 19). S/RES/2068.

UNSCR 2100 (2013, April 25). S/RES/2100.

UNSCR 2143. (2014, March 7). S/RES/2143.

UNSCR 2225. (2015, June 18). S/RES/2225.

United Nations Security Council Resolution (UNSCR) 2227. (2015, June 29). S/RES/2227.

Utas, M. (2005). Victimcy, girlfriending, soldiering: Tactic agency in a young woman's social navigation of the Liberian war zone. *Anthropological Quarterly., 78*(2), 403–430.

Utas, M. (2011). Victimcy and social navigation: From the toolbox of Liberian child soldiers. In S. Podder & A. Özerdem (Eds.), *Child soldiers: From recruitment to reintegration* (pp. 213–230). Palgrave Macmillan.

Vandewiele, T. (2005). *Optional Protocol: The involvement of children in armed conflict.* Brill.

Verma, C. L. (2012). Truths out of place: Homecoming, intervention, and storymaking in war-torn northern Uganda. *Children's Geographies, 10*(4), 441–455.

Watson, A. M. S. (2015). Resilience is its own resistance: The place of children in post-conflict settlement. *Critical Studies on Security, 3*(1), 47–61.
Wells, K. (2016). Governing the global child: Biopolitics and liberal subjectivities. In N. Ansell, N. Klocker, & T. Skelton (Eds.), *Geographies of global issues: Change and threat* (pp. 237–255). Springer Singapore.
Williamson, J. (2005). *Reintegration of child soldiers in Sierra Leone*. USAID.

CHAPTER 7

Children's Rights and Child Prostitution: Critical Reflections on Thailand in the 1990s and Beyond

Heather Montgomery

INTRODUCTION

This chapter is written as a reflection on work I carried out over twenty years ago with a small group of children in Thailand who sold sex to foreigners. I went there at a time of intense media interest in such children and determined campaigns by NGOs to end the problem of child prostitution. The stories they produced of the abuse of children by foreigners were heart rending and the need for these children to be 'saved' appeared unquestionable. Yet when I started doing fieldwork it quickly became apparent that the children in whose name these campaigns were being fought understood their lives and actions very differently, describing their

H. Montgomery (✉)
School of Education, Childhood, Youth and Sport, WELS, The Open University, Milton Keynes, UK
e-mail: heather.montgomery@open.ac.uk

© The Author(s), under exclusive license to Springer Nature Switzerland AG 2022
N. Howard and S. Okyere (eds.), *International Child Protection*, Palgrave Studies on Children and Development, https://doi.org/10.1007/978-3-030-78763-9_7

experiences not necessarily in terms of abuse but through wider cultural ideas about kinship and social relations and the ways in which ideas of prostitution and filial obligation were intertwined (Montgomery, 2001). There appeared to be a large gap between the victims of the campaigning literature and the lives and experiences of child prostitutes on the ground. Equally significantly there was a space between the rhetoric of universal children's rights and the lived realities of children themselves. In this chapter I will discuss these lacunae, contrasting the image of the 'perfect victim' inherent in the media and NGOs campaigns with the somewhat more complicated experiences, understandings and explanations of the children that I knew. This gap echoes those documented by Kiconco and McMullin in Chapters 5 and 6 and points to a wider issue within the international child protection regime. After discussing it, I will then go on to analyse how a selective emphasis on certain aspects of children's rights overshadowed more holistic interpretations in ways that were not always helpful to children, before concluding with some tentative suggestions for understanding and implementing the rights of very vulnerable children more productively.

STORIES OF CHILD PROSTITUTION IN THE 1990S: THE SEARCH FOR THE PERFECT VICTIMS[1]

I went to Thailand in 1993 as a PhD student in social anthropology.[2] My aim was to investigate children who worked in the sex industry, an issue which was coming to international prominence, particularly through

---

[1] There has been much debate about what to call children who sell sex. Some commentators prefer terms such as 'the commercial sexual exploitation of children', 'sexually exploited children' or 'prostituted children' which emphasise victimhood and exploitation (see Ireland, 1993). Others prefer words which frame the situation in terms of exploitative labour rather than sexual abuse, such as 'child sex worker' or 'child prostitute', to allow some discussion of agency (Ennew, 2008). The phrase 'child sex worker' is certainly an unsettling one which implies that the selling of sex by children is a legitimate way of earning money and it is disliked because it ignores the obvious, and very large, power imbalances between children and adults and the vast disparities in social, structural, political and economic resources between prostitute and client. I remain conflicted about which term to use although I tend to use 'child prostitute' for convenience and clarity.

[2] When I started to think about my PhD, I had little interest in children. I wanted to work in Southeast Asia but I was not entirely sure of what I wanted to focus on. Two things changed my mind. Firstly, the international media coverage of the problem which is

reports in the international English-language media and through NGO campaigns about young Thai girls (and less often boys) selling sex (or being forced to sell sex) to foreign men. These campaigns were led in Thailand, in the early 1990s, by ECPAT (End Child Prostitution in Asian Tourism, later End Child Prostitution, Child Pornography and Trafficking of Children for Sexual Purposes) which developed quickly from a small offshoot of the Ecumenical Council on Third World Tourism (ECTWT) into the foremost international campaigning group against the commercial sexual exploitation of children.

Typically, both journalistic and NGO reports would tell of a girl who was tricked into leaving home, or sold by impoverished, ignorant or greedy parents into a brothel, where she was repeatedly raped and terrorised into servicing many foreign clients a night, before being rescued by a charitable organisation or a journalist, only to discover she was HIV positive and had a limited time left to live. After a while, the reports became repetitive, even stereotyped, the narratives based on repeated patterns of betrayal, abuse, rescue, and death with the foreigner the ultimate cause of the misery. The child prostitute was presented as the perfect victim of foreign perversion, tricked into a world she should have been protected from, traumatised by heartless foreigners, rescued by good NGO workers, before dying quietly off stage with no promise of redemption or rehabilitation (see Bishop & Robinson, 1998; Montgomery, 2001 for a fuller discussion of the portrayal of child prostitution in the international media).

This narrative was highly effective in terms of awareness-raising but the stereotype it relied on had two major consequences for the way that child prostitution came to be understood and the policies that were put in place to combat it; firstly, the problem become almost exclusively associated with the sexual abuse of Thai children by foreigners and stories were stretched to fit a pre-determined model which included the foreign folk devil, regardless of the realities. One example of this was the way a fire in

---

the focus of the first half of this chapter and secondly, but probably more importantly, the presence in Cambridge of the late Judith Ennew, a charismatic anthropologist and author of *The Sexual Exploitation of Children* (1986). Since the opening for signature of the CRC in 1979, Judith had been interested in the anthropological study of children, focusing on promoting children's rights and developing ethical methods of studying children. She was also a passionate advocate of children's rights and believed that their implementation could transform children's lives. It was an appealing notion which resonated deeply with me and influenced my choice of research project.

1984 at a brothel in Phuket was reported. Newspaper accounts told how, on entering the burnt-out building, fire fighters discovered the charred remains of five young prostitutes who had been unable to escape the blaze because they had been chained to their beds (Rattachumpoth, 1994). This case generated a public outcry, and the pimps and procurers of these girls were prosecuted and made to pay compensation to the victims' parents. It was a gruesome story and one that was endlessly repeated to show the 'typical' horrors of brothel life. Yet at no point was there any evidence that these girls had Western clients or that the brothel catered to tourists. The pimps and procurers were local men and so, in all probability, were the clients. This, however, did not stop it from becoming part of the anti-child-sex-tourism mythology. The story found its way into an ECPAT book, *The Child and the Tourist*, and was also fictionalised by Thai women's-rights group, The Foundation for Women (1990), in their book *Kamla*, which was distributed among girls considered to be at risk of becoming prostitutes and which warned them against taking jobs away from their homes because such jobs were likely to involve selling sex to foreigners and the outcome of this was almost certainly death.

Secondly, practical ways to help such children were totally sidestepped through this narrative because their death was seen as inevitable. Even if the children had somehow escaped infection or fire, they were seen as lost causes. In the words of one of the founders of ECPAT, 'When boys and girls have been forced to receive several customers a night seven days a week, they will be so traumatised that very little can be done to help them resume anything like a normal life' (O'Grady, 1992, p. 1).[3] There were also limited means of 'rescuing' children and young women and when pressure was put on the Thai government and the police to protect children, the result was often high-profile rescues of children and young women from brothels. Such raids were widely reported in the Thai and international press and normally involved the police raiding brothels and dragging out girls and young women in the full glare of the media. Newspaper reports were usually accompanied by pictures of the rescued victims trying to hide their faces and protect their identities, thereby creating the

---

[3] It is also worth pointing out that Thailand at that time had very few rehabilitation centres for such children and the few that existed were set up by outside evangelical Christian organisations or were hampered by names such as Homes for Socially Handicapped Women that resembled prisons and stigmatised those taken there (Hantrakul, 1983).

unfortunate impression that their rescue was as coercive as their recruitment. What happened to these children and young women afterwards was less frequently discussed. However, given the perfect victim narrative it was often widely assumed and reported that these children were HIV positive and therefore likely to die very soon (Baker, 2007; Montgomery, 2001).

These two facts—that children were abused primarily by foreigners and that nothing could be done for them once they were abused—led inexorably to one solution. NGOs claimed that the only way to solve the problem was prevention and this could only be achieved by targeting foreign abusers. From the outset, ECPAT publicised the cases of Western men in Thailand who were arrested for molesting children but were then released, jumped bail or let off on technicalities. In 1992, a Swedish man, Bengt Bolin, was caught with a naked boy in his bed, but claimed that he had been led to believe that the boy was over fifteen and therefore of legal age. Before he could be prosecuted, he applied for a new Swedish passport and left the country. Three years later, in 1995, *The Bangkok Post* reported the case of a Frenchman who had been found guilty in a Thai court and sentenced to four years' imprisonment yet had been bailed in order to launch an appeal. Instead of doing so he simply left the country having had his passport returned to him by the French Embassy. The idea that men who sexually abused Thai children could simply leave Thailand without consequences was widely condemned. ECPAT and other NGOs throughout Asia began to argue that the best, and indeed the only way, of protecting children was to petition the national governments of tourist sending countries to change their laws to allow for extra-territorial legislation so that if men had escaped justice in Thailand they could still be prosecuted in their home countries. In 1994, Australia became the first country to introduce extra-territorial legislation, which brought in penalties of up to seventeen years' imprisonment for those convicted of sexual crimes against children overseas. Over the next five years, Norway, Germany, France, Belgium, New Zealand, Sweden and even the UK (which initially resisted the move) all passed similar laws and successful prosecutions were quickly obtained in 1996 in Australia and in 1997 in France (Montgomery, 2010). Interestingly, the first case to be successfully brought before the Swedish courts was that of Bengt Bolin, mentioned above, who was sentenced to three months' imprisonment in 1995 for his crime of having sex with a teenage boy in Thailand.

Child Prostitution and Children's Rights

The dominant discourse of the 1990s presented the problem of child prostitution entirely in terms of its morality and through un-nuanced binaries: wicked foreigners versus innocent Thai children. It was a straightforward narrative but lacked crucially important details in that it took no account of either the socio-economic or historical context or of children's rights, which I will now look at briefly in turn. The history of prostitution in Thailand is highly politicised with some commentators claiming that organised prostitution began only with the influx of Chinese migrants in the 1930s and was expanded by the American military in the 1960s during the Vietnam War, when the Thai government gave permission for the United States to station troops in Thailand and allowed American servicemen to use Thailand as a base for 'R & R' (Rest and Recreation—which quickly became known as 'I & I'—Intercourse and Intoxication). Others however have argued that these influences simply mapped onto pre-existing social institutions and that prostitution was long regulated, taxed and condoned by the Thai authorities even after they criminalised it in 1960 as part of a wider plan to rid the country of 'undesirables' such as beggars and prostitutes (see Boonchalaksi & Guest, 1994; Montgomery, 2001 for a fuller discussion of these arguments). Whatever its antecedents, it is undeniable that prostitution expanded and changed dramatically in the 1960s and the large numbers of young Western men with money to spend led rapidly to the creation of bars and brothels set up to cater explicitly to foreigners.

This occurred however against a complex backdrop of industrialisation, globalisation and urbanisation and their impacts on poor, socially marginalised, communities who could no longer make a living from family farms and were pushed into wage migration, both within Thailand and overseas. Between the 1970s and 1990s, Thailand had undergone a period of rapid industrialisation characterised by the proliferation of urban factories producing goods for export markets. Land no longer supported larger rural families and factories in urban settings offered the young the chance to migrate and live in rapidly growing cities and participate in a monetised economy (Hirsch, 1993; Mills, 1999). Tourism too was pursued as a strategy for development and by 1990 was the country's highest source of foreign currency revenue despite its basis in sex tourism. This was part of a deliberate plan and in 1980 the Thai Deputy Prime Minister made the extraordinary comment:

I ask all governors to consider the natural scenery in your provinces, together with some forms of entertainment that some of you might consider disgusting and shameful because they are forms of sexual entertainment that attract tourists ... we must do this because we have to consider the jobs that will be created for the people. (quoted in Ennew, 1986, p. 99)

Despite protests about the increasing visibility of sex tourism, as well as widely expressed fears that Thailand was losing its identity, this strategy for modernisation was followed by successive governments (Montgomery, 2001).

Children and young people were drawn into these new capitalist relations and while the focus has been on children with foreign clients, the institutionalisation of the sex industry in Thailand meant that there was (and still is) an indigenous market with Thai men using Thai prostitutes. The inconvenient fact remained throughout the 1980s and 1990s that the majority of prostitutes were not to be found in the tourist bars of Bangkok, Pattaya or Phuket but in the brothels of rural Thailand or the back streets of Bangkok. Life in such brothels could be harsh and even abusive (as the brothel fire in Phuket showed). These brothels did not, however, cater for tourists, and children with Western clients did not usually work in these places. Children were likely to work in the slums around the port area of Bangkok and or the Burmese border where there was a large population of transient, undocumented labourers from neighbouring countries (Asia Watch, 1993; Bureau of Democracy, Human Rights, and Labor, 2008). The vast majority of clients of these child prostitutes were local men, not because they were more 'depraved' than Westerners, but because it was often much cheaper to have sex with a child than with an adult woman (Ennew, 1986).

This context was significant and important but largely ignored as it would have led to the direct challenging of government policy. More surprising however was how children's rights were largely side-lined and unexamined when talking about child prostitution, although lip service was sometimes paid to particular articles in the United Nations Convention on the Rights of the Child (CRC). In 1996 The First World Congress against the Commercial Sexual Exploitation was held in Sweden and was attended by government representatives and royalty from across the world. Children's rights were supposedly central to the resulting Stockholm Declaration and Agenda for Action which stated explicitly and repeatedly that child prostitution was a violation of children's rights under the CRC, in particular Article 34 which states: 'State Parties undertake to protect the child from all forms of sexual exploitation and sexual abuse'. Yet this rhetoric seemed to have little impact on the ground and while the rights of children were presented as central to the campaign to end prostitution, understandings of them were patchy and at times misunderstood. It was undoubtedly the case that children were being exploited by Western men, that their rights were being violated by this abuse, and that the campaigns against these men were designed with the best of intentions to protect children from future harm. What these campaigns were not, however, were truly rights-based and the idea of a holistic set of indivisible and inalienable rights for all children, based on their humanity and dignity was never invoked. Instead children's rights in relation to prostitution were seen extremely narrowly in terms of protection: ideas of provision and participation were rarely mentioned, and focus was placed on a very limited, normative understating of rights by those seeking to operationalise one article of the Convention. In this case, it seemed that protection was conceived only in terms of preventing Westerners from exploiting children and nothing much beyond.

At the height of the media stories about Western men abusing Thai children, another story came briefly to prominence which highlighted some of the ethical and practical problems of understanding child prostitution without a full assessment of children's rights. In 1993, a human rights group, Asia Watch, reported on the widespread collusion of Thai officials in the indigenous sex trade and, in particular, of their treatment of Burmese girls who worked in brothels on the Thai side of the border. Asia Watch discussed at length a raid on a brothel near the Burmese border in Ranong in which the police found 148 underage Burmese girls who claimed to have been forced or tricked into prostitution. Rather than being rescued or released, they were immediately arrested as illegal immigrants (Asia Watch, 1993). Although this case attracted some attention in the Western press, the fact that it involved poor Burmese children having cheap sex with poor Burmese men rather than depraved Westerners indulging their tastes at high prices meant that the story quickly faded from view. Yet it exposed another side of the child sex industry in Thailand which was acutely embarrassing for the Thai government. The abuse and exploitation that occurred in Ranong, compounded by the women and children being jailed as illegal immigrants, was a gross abuse of human rights and was going on in the full knowledge of Thai officials. On 16 July 1993 in the Thai newspaper, *The Nation*, Pol. Lt. Gen. Sudjai Yanrat was quoted as saying: 'In my opinion it is disgraceful to let Burmese men frequent Thai prostitutes. Therefore, I have been flexible in allowing Burmese prostitutes to work here. Most of their clients are Burmese men'. In this case the rights of Burmese children to protection from sexual exploitation were ignored because their circumstances did not fit with the agreed narrative and they were very far from being perfect victims. Taking their rights as children seriously would have forced the government to look at issues of migration and citizenship, as well as rehabilitation. Similarly, it has often been reported that those children most at risk from prostitution are those from the hill tribes in the north of Thailand, due to their social and national marginalisation (Jeffrey, 2002). Many of these children lack citizenship but while this is recognised as risk factor drawing them into prostitution, there are few campaigns to implement their rights to citizenship, nationality or state protection.

Child Prostitution in Baan Nua

Against this background, I went to Thailand in 1993 wanting to find out more about children who sold sex: Who were they? To whom were they selling sex? What did the pathways into and out of prostitution look like? Did children want to be rescued and was it always in their best interests? I was determined to find a community of people where children were currently working as prostitutes rather than those who had already been 'rescued'. I also wanted to work with children who had non-Western as well as Western clients, although in the end this was not possible. After a few months of searching I came across a small NGO which worked with a community, which I have called Baan Nua, on the edge of a large tourist resort. There were 65 children there of whom 35 worked regularly or occasionally as prostitutes; this number included both boys and girls aged between six and 14.[4] The people of Baan Nua had migrated to this resort in the early 1980s to look for work in the informal economy, including prostitution, and had put up makeshift houses of corrugated iron and scrap wood. It was a poor community without running water and only

---

[4] Both boys and girls sold sex in Baan Nua, although as I tended to get on better with girls and could share their interests (I knew nothing about the football clubs the boys liked to talk about or computer games), I found I had much stronger rapport with the girls and a deeper understanding of their lives.

intermittent electricity, which the inhabitants patched into illegally from the supply of a local supermarket. The number of households fluctuated throughout the year as partners changed, children moved out or houses collapsed. One of the most striking facts about the children in Baan Nua, however, was that they remained with their parents who were well aware of, and even encouraged, what their children did. In contrast to the image presented in the media, they had not been trafficked, debt bonded or tricked and were therefore technically 'free' and able to exercise a certain amount of control over their clients.

There was no formal organisation for prostitution in Baan Nua; children entered it through the encouragement of friends or older siblings, who introduced them to clients, showed them what acts they had to perform and looked after them afterwards. The clients of these children were exclusively Western, from a variety of European countries with three in particular having the most contact with the children. On the whole, the children stayed in the village and lived with their families but sometimes stayed out overnight with clients. In a few cases, the older children (those over 14), stayed for a period of a month or two with visiting men but frequently returned to the village during the day.

I found that perhaps the most obvious answer to the question of why children sold sex and why their parents allowed them to do so, was that they lived in deep poverty and selling sex paid the most amount of money that a poor, uneducated, marginalised child could hope to earn. It paid them considerably more than scavenging on local rubbish dumps, working in sweat shops, or begging, and was perceived as less physically demanding. While they never claimed to like prostitution, children sometimes described it as better and easier than other jobs they had tried. Although they seemed wilfully ignorant of the threat of pregnancy and sexually transmitted diseases, they argued that prostitution gave them access to benefits such as staying in good hotels or apartments, eating well and being given large, occasional payments. One of the 12-year-old girls in the community, Lek, said: 'I hated begging and getting beaten up the older street children or the police. John [my boyfriend] will marry me one day and give my family a big house. He has already given us a new roof. When we are rich, I won't regret anything. Now, things are not so good but one day, they will be good for us'.

The children's clients were mainly European men who came back to the slum several times a year and whom they claimed as 'friends'. These men were in contact with the children between visits and often sent money when requested to do so. Children strove to put these relationships on a more reciprocal basis and were continually struggling to include their clients in aspects of their lives outside the sexual/financial transaction. This enabled them to claim that they had some sort of reciprocal relationship with their clients of which sex was only a small part. Children always preferred to use terms such as 'having guests', 'being supported by a foreigner' or 'going out for fun with foreigners' rather than the term prostitution. They never set a price for sexual acts and money that was given to them after sex was always referred to as a present. Sometimes a client would not leave cash but would pay in kind, for example, through the rebuilding or refurbishing of a girl's house. Appeals would be made for loans, money to rebuild houses or for medical bills and when clients responded favourably, children saw the relationship as one of friendship rather than one of exchange. One man had been visiting Baan Nua for several years and gave several of the girls money. When I challenged one about it and said he was a bad man who was abusing her, she quickly put me right by saying: 'he is so good to me, he gives me and my family money whenever we need it, how can he be bad?'.

Children themselves however rarely talked of selling sex in terms of the money it brought in. Rather they used prostitution as a way of fulfilling what they understood to be their filial duties. The children felt that by earning money for their parents and keeping the family together they were acting in socially sanctioned roles as dutiful daughters and sons and that prostituting themselves with the 'right' intentions meant that there was less moral opprobrium around what they did. Within Baan Nua, as in much of rural Thailand, children were seen as a parental investment with an anticipated return and were expected to work for the family as soon as they were able. This emphasis on filial duty has been a constant theme in ethnographic studies of prostitution in Thailand and, in an influential article, Muecke (1992) has argued that while girls in the past would have earned money through market trading, contemporary young women were likely to earn money through prostitution, given its ubiquity. Phongpaichit (1982) made a similar point in an earlier study, showing that daughters who left their rural homes to work as prostitutes were not running away or discarding the principles of support and repayment, but were fulfilling them as best they could in a changed environment, by sending home remittances (see also Fordham, 2005; Rende Taylor, 2005).

Concepts of gratitude and obedience towards parents remained important cultural reference points and whenever I asked the children in Baan Nua about prostitution, they almost always referred to these concepts. I was constantly told that prostitution was a means to an end, a way of fulfilling the filial obligations that they felt were demanded of them by their families. In the children's own analysis of what they did, and why they did it, selling sex was about social relationships and fulfilling their filial obligations to their families. Although the children sometimes became annoyed with my questions about prostitution, they were happy to talk about the impact their money had on their families and their successful self-identification as moral people and dutiful daughters. 12-year-old Kob, for example, once told me with delight that a client had given her enough money to rebuild her parents' house. She said: 'I did this all by myself and someday I will be rewarded for looking after my parents'. A powerful mitigating circumstance for many of these children was thus that they were earning money to help their parents. They expressed love and affection for their parents and claimed to see nothing wrong with bringing in money by whatever means they could. Even when parents spent it on alcohol or gambling, no child ever criticised his or her mother for this behaviour. Instead they were keen to point out to me how their money had paid for their mothers' new houses, motorbikes or television.

Is It Possible to Make Children's Rights Relevant in Places Like Baan Nua?

Children in a community such as Baan Nua suffer from grave violations of their rights—not least and not only their right to be free from sexual exploitation. Yet, as we have seen, the rights of child prostitutes, as well as practical means of help, have been largely absent from discussions about them. The image of the perfect victim and indeed the perfect perpetrator have been delineated but the everyday experiences and lives of individual children, with all their messy complexities, have remained undocumented, insufficiently understood, and devalued, making rights-based interventions all but impossible.

Since its ratification, the CRC has been heavily criticised by many for reasons of its ethnocentrism and imposition of alien notions of childhood onto societies where parent/child relationships are understood very differently and where ideals of a safe, protected space of childhood separated from the adult world are unrealisable and undesired (Boyden, 1997; Burman, 1996; Montgomery, 2016). It has also been condemned as a form of neo-colonialism which ignores the realities of children's experiences and which gives Westerners the 'right' to interfere and intervene in other countries which do not support or properly enforce children's rights (Pupavac, 2001). Many scholars who have worked with vulnerable children both in and outside the West have been critical of the top-down imposition of the CRC by NGOs and governments and have exposed the gaps between the rhetoric of children's rights and the reality on the ground. They have raised uncomfortable questions about whether insisting on children's rights, at least in the hegemonic way translated and promoted by the agencies comprising the child protection regime, is the best way to support them or whether it could be counterproductive. Reynolds et al. (2006, p. 292) argue that 'there is a real risk that issues confronting children may be cloaked in a discourse on rights that, in effect, both diagnoses and prescribes and, thus, eclipses alternatives that may be more sensible, more realistic and more attractive to the children concerned…There may be a real danger that in the name of their rights positive aspects of children's lives are discarded and the alternatives, for the vast majority of them, may remain out of reach'.

Yet there are very few people who work with children, especially children in situations that make them vulnerable such as those in Baan Nua, in brothels on the Burmese borders of the backstreets of Bangkok (or indeed among children undertaking any form of hazardous of exploitative labour), who would not support the CRC's basic demands to protect children and prevent harm to them. Or indeed its insistence on children's dignity, humanity and the underlying principle that children's rights are inalienable human rights. The CRC was never designed as a practical policy blueprint and, whatever its flaws, its intentions and ideals are honourable. This does not make it easy to implement in practice but one possible way forward is to insist on looking at the CRC holistically, while acknowledging the sometimes irresolvable difficulties between local realities and global ideals. While it is important to understand the CRC as indivisible, it may also be necessary to recognise that 'even the most basic rights are not compatible in every situation and cannot always be simultaneously maximised' (Ennew et al., 1996, p. 33). For the children of Baan Nua for example, their rights (and desire) to live with the families and their right to be free from sexual exploitation appear at first to be mutually incompatible. Yet rather than jettisoning the universal model of rights entirely I would argue that Article 34 is not the only, or even the most important, right that needs to be enforced and that focusing exclusively on this one article may in fact be counterproductive. Articles which discuss the definition of childhood (Article 1) or children's identity and dignity (Articles 2 and 8) are vital to an understanding of children's rights with regard to sexual exploitation as they deal with the very aspects that are violated when sexual exploitation takes place. Likewise, Article 12, which gives a child the right to give or withhold consent or Articles 5, 8, 19, 26, and 27, which deal with family support, must be seen as inherently relevant.

In 1996 new laws came into force in Thailand designed to protect children and enforce their rights. Among other things, these allowed for the prosecution of parents, procurers and the customers of child prostitutes. While these may have been useful and much welcomed by some children, for those in Baan Nua they would have been disastrous. Given the emphasis the children placed on family relationships and filial obligations, such laws would have made it extremely difficult for the children to ask for help, even if they recognised they needed it. Keeping the family together was their primary justification for what they did, the prosecution and imprisonment of their parents their worst fear. In addition, neither children nor their parents had any interest in seeing their clients prosecuted, or even stopped from entering Baan Nua. In the absence of any social support or any form of welfare, these men were the only form of protection they had, no matter how damaging that might seem to outsiders. Without proper financial, physical and emotional support from the state (as envisaged under Articles 4 and 5, among others, of the CRC), these children turned to the only source of protection available.

From my own perspective, there is no doubt that child prostitution is physically and psychologically harmful to children and I believe the international community should take what steps it can to eradicate it. I have no sympathies with men caught abusing children and, although the numbers caught and prosecuted are still small (Montgomery, 2010), sending out the message that there are consequences for using child prostitutes is no bad thing. Yet all interventions carry consequences, often unintended, and there is anecdotal evidence that prosecuting men for abusing children in Thailand has not protected children but has simply shifted the problem elsewhere. Countries such as Cambodia or Vietnam, where law enforcement is laxer and the chances of being caught and prosecuted are lower, may now have become the preferred destination for those wanting to buy sex from children (see Montgomery, 2010). There are also as yet unanswered questions about the children who have to give evidence against their abusers. Will they be offered anonymity and support before, during and after giving evidence? What happens to them on their return home? Will their parents be prosecuted? Will they be placed in care, given counselling and alternatives to prostitution? Will they be stigmatised in the eyes of the government and their communities? Or will they simply be forgotten?

Conclusions

As is the case with the chapters in this volume by Allen Kiconco and Jaremey McMullin (Chapters 5 and 6), there are no easy answers to the many dilemmas raised here and I can offer no tried and tested suggestions to end child prostitution. It is not a problem confined to Thailand, or even to poorer countries outside the West. Europe has a problem with the commercial sexual exploitation of children as well as with child abuse within its institutions. Child prostitution flourishes in areas of social inequality and social marginalisation and cannot be understood without looking at global and national structures and hierarchies of power as well as at issues of inequality inherent in gender and age relations. Ending child prostitution would involve not only understanding the situation of individual communities very differently, it would also mean very different interventions, dependent on circumstances. In communities such as Baan Nua both parents and children would require support which would help them look after each other, emphasising the values of reciprocity while ensuring freedom from all forms of economic, social and sexual exploitation. None of this would be easy or cheap. Finding good jobs would be very difficult: in Baan Nua, both children and parents were barely literate, had problems with time keeping and their behaviour was erratic. Other studies on older women have suggested that while many in activist groups assume that given the option most women would rather leave prostitution and go back to menial but 'respectable' jobs such as food selling or hairdressing, sex workers themselves tend to vote with their feet and refuse to accept the huge drop in wages that they would incur by entering such professions. The failure rates of 'rehabilitation' programmes which train women in these skills are notoriously high (Truong, 1990). It is likely to be the same for children and training and rehabilitation programmes must reflect this, offering useful, relevant and well-paid jobs at the end.

This is not to argue that children have a right to prostitute themselves or that Thai culture somehow demands that they do. Rather it involves acknowledging local realities and looking beyond merely 'saving' children from prostitution by removing them from that imminent danger without any forethought beyond that. Although many children are at risk from HIV and other sexually transmitted diseases, not all have been or will become infected. Dying from AIDS may be convenient in terms of the neatness of the narrative, and the fact it absolves others from thinking of longer-term solutions, but it is not the fate of all children. Furthermore, even those children who are infected will need interventions and support and should not be expected to die quietly off stage. Medical and social help for affected children and their families is critical, no matter how dire their prognosis. Taking children's rights seriously involves looking at individual children's circumstances and imaginatively thinking about which interventions would help them, no matter how costly or counter-intuitive or politically unpopular, including keeping the family together and removing parents from the criminal justice system and dealing both with them and their children through the welfare rather than the legal system.

There have been some recent initiatives which have aimed to support children's ability to fulfil their filial obligations without turning to prostitution. For example, a system of scholarships to provide money to families who help their daughters in school until they are sixteen has been set up with input from the Thai royal family. Such a scheme recognises that family obligations, and the necessity of making an early economic contribution, are two important factors which have contributed to the ongoing problem. While they are welcome, however, Baker (2007) also notes that there have been criticisms from community groups who have claimed that the payments are too low, meaning that it is still more profitable for girls to enter prostitution. Conversely, such schemes can be seen to penalise parents who, despite poverty, keep their children out of prostitution and to reward parents who do not. They also take little account of children's own views and agency. Furthermore, there has been limited follow-up of this scheme and it is not known how successful it has been long term and whether it keeps girls out of the sex trade permanently or just until they leave school.

In terms of Baan Nua, my dilemmas over children's rights and the best ways to realise them have not gone away. I remain uneasy about claiming that these children did not view themselves as prostitutes and saw no abuse and that this perspective must take priority over all other interpretations. I am similarly wary of stating that rights were meaningless to these children because they were an outside imposition based on Western ideals. What I have tried to do is to find some way of acknowledging the validity of the children's statements, without dismissing them as misguided or wrong, while at the same time recognising the wider social and political issues of which the children may not be aware. The commercial sexual exploitation of children does not exist in a vacuum, nor is it attributable to any single cause such as poverty or lack of education. In keeping all these viewpoints in mind, it becomes easier to view the children's references to filial duty as statements which acknowledged different cultural conceptions of children and childhood but, at the same time, come into being as rationalisations of an economic strategy which enabled the families to stay together. Taking these elements together would suggest that these children do not need saving in the ways that some of their champions suggest and that they are not the popular victims of the public imagination. This does not mean that they do not need help and support, rather it means they must be seen as rational, economic and social agents who must be involved in decisions about their future and never be penalised if their own vision of the future does not match those who claim to know their best interests. This will continue to be a major challenge for international child protection, for the world is far more complex than the simplistic victim–perpetrator binaries that this and other chapters in this book have shown to structure regime thinking.

References

Asia Watch. (1993). *A modern form of slavery: Trafficking of Burmese women and girls into brothels in Thailand*. Human Rights Watch.

Baker, S. (2007). *'Child labour' and child prostitution in Thailand: Changing realities*. White Lotus Press.

Bishop, R., & Robinson, L. (1998). *Night marker: Sexual cultures and the Thai economic miracle*. Routledge.

Boonchalaksi, W., & Guest, P. (1994). *Prostitution in Thailand*. Institute for Population and Social Research.

Boyden, J. (1997). Childhood and the policy makers: A comparative perspective on the globalization of childhood. In A. James & A. Prout (Eds.), *Constructing and reconstructing childhood: Contemporary issues in the sociological study of childhood*. Falmer Press.

Bureau of Democracy, Human Rights, and Labor. (2008). *Human rights report: Thailand*. Washington: 2008 country reports on human rights practices. http://www.state.gov/g/drl/rls/hrrpt/2008/eap/119058.htm. Accessed 25 June 2016.

Burman, E. (1996). Local, global and globalized: Child development and international child rights legislation. *Childhood, 3*, 45–66.

Ennew, J. (1986). *The sexual exploitation of children*. Polity Press.

Ennew, J. (2008, November). Exploitation of children in prostitution. Thematic paper. Paper presented at the world congress III against the sexual exploitation of children and adolescents. Rio de Janeiro, Brazil. http://www.childcentre.info/public/Thematic_Paper_Prostitution_ENG.pdf. Accessed 25 June 2016.

Ennew, J., Gopal, K., Heeran, J., & Montgomery, H. (1996). *Children and prostitution: How can we measure and monitor the commercial sexual exploitation of children? Literature review and annotated bibliography for the world congress on the commercial sexual exploitation of children*. Childwatch International.

Fordham, G. (2005). *A new look at Thai AIDS: Perspectives from the margin*. Berghahn.

Foundation for Women. (1990). *Kamla*. Foundation for Women.

Hantrakul, S. (1983). *Prostitution in Thailand*. Paper presented to the women in Asia workshop, Monash University.

Hirsch, P. (1993). What is the Thai village? In C. Reynolds (Ed.), *National identity and its defenders: Thailand 1938–89*. Silkworm Books.

Ireland, K. (1993). *Wish you weren't here*. Save the Children Fund.

Jeffrey, L. (2002). *Sex and borders: Gender, national identity and prostitution policy in Thailand*. University of Hawaii Press.

Mills, M. B. (1999). *Thai women in the global labor force: Consuming desires, contested selves*. Rutgers University Press.

Montgomery, H. (2001). *Modern babylon? Prostituting children in Thailand*. Berghahn.

Montgomery, H. (2010). Child sex tourism: Is extra-territorial legislation the answer? In D. Botterill & T. Jones (Eds.), *Tourism and crime*. Goodfellow Publishing.

Montgomery, H. (2016). Anthropological perspectives on children's rights. In M. Ruck, M. Peterson Badali, & M. Freeman (Eds.), *Children's rights: Global and multidisciplinary perspectives*. Taylor and Francis.

Muecke, M. (1992). Mother sold food, daughter sells her body—The cultural continuity of prostitution. *Social Science and Medicine, 35*, 891–901.

O'Grady, R. (1992). *The Child and the Tourist*. ECPAT.
Phongpaichit, P. (1982). *From peasant girls to Bangkok masseuses*. ILO.
Pupavac, V. (2001). Misanthropy without borders: The international children's rights regime. *Disasters, 25*, 95–112.
Rattachumpoth, R. (1994, March 2). The economics of sex. *The Nation* (p. 3).
Rende Taylor, L. (2005). Dangerous trade-offs: The behavioral ecology of child labor and prostitution in rural Northern Thailand. *Current Anthropology, 46*, 411–432.
Reynolds, P., Nieuwenhuys, O., & Hanson, K. (2006). Refractions of children's rights in development practice: A view from anthropology. *Childhood, 13*, 291–303.
Truong, T. D. (1990). *Sex, money and morality*. Zed Books.

CHAPTER 8

Why Child Mobility Is Not Always Child Trafficking: The Moral Economy of Children's Movement in Benin and Ethiopia

Jo Boyden and Neil Howard

INTRODUCTION

Few topics are afforded greater attention in contemporary policy debates than that of human mobility. In the past decade alone, the UN has established a Global Commission on International Migration to examine the phenomenon of human movement, convened the High-level Dialogue on International Migration and Development to discuss the links between

J. Boyden
Department of International Development, University of Oxford, Oxford, UK
e-mail: jo.boyden@qeh.ox.ac.uk

N. Howard (✉)
Department of Social and Policy Sciences, University of Bath, Bath, UK
e-mail: n.p.howard@bath.ac.uk

© The Author(s), under exclusive license to Springer Nature Switzerland AG 2022
N. Howard and S. Okyere (eds.), *International Child Protection*, Palgrave Studies on Children and Development,
https://doi.org/10.1007/978-3-030-78763-9_8

movement and socio-economic change, established the UN Global Compact for Migration, and convened the Geneva Migration Group with the International Organisation for Migration, to explore how to manage and share information about migration.[1] These initiatives echo concerns among nation-state officials about un-sanctioned international migration which has, in turn, been associated with a spate of migration-restricting measures and an explosion of anti-migration rhetoric that has at times led to tragic consequences for would-be migrants in places such as the Mediterranean (discussed by, for example, Anderson, 2013; Huijsmans, 2006; O'Connell Davidson, 2015).

While migration in general attracts significant attention, the independent movement of children[2] has tended to cause particular disquiet (Hashim, 2003; Howard, 2016; Huijsmans, 2006; O'Connell Davidson & Farrow, 2007; Whitehead et al., 2007). Institutions across a variety of contexts have understood children's departure from the family home (whether for work, learning, or care) as a child protection violation—an involuntary act stemming, inescapably, from crisis or adult failure (be that neglect or exploitation), with negative consequences for children, their families and communities. A key part of this understanding has been the idea that child mobility either leads to or is essentially inherently the same as child trafficking. In some countries, this equation has seen laws passed specifically to prevent children from moving, and prominent figures and village committees have been put to work to 'sensitise' the population to the dangers of child mobility-cum-trafficking and to convince the young to stay at home (Dottridge & GAATW, 2007; Howard, 2016).

Based on primary data from Benin and Ethiopia, two countries that have formed a focus for intervention by agencies concerned both with child trafficking and with children's independent movement more generally, this chapter engages with and critiques this paradigm. Although we recognise that there have been some discursive advances over the past five years, with some recognition that not all child movement is bad and not every child on the move is a victim of trafficking, there

---

[1] See http://www.un-ngls.org/orf/international_migration.htm for details. Accessed 15 January 2011.

[2] Though we recognise the concept of 'childhood' to be a situational reality depending on socio-cultural context, we approach the 'child' here as any individual under the age of 18, since we are engaging with international norms and policies.

remains a common conflation of movement with trafficking, alongside a widespread assumption that movement is by necessity deleterious to child well-being. In keeping with arguments presented by several other authors from disciplines including geography, anthropology, sociology, and childhood studies (for example, Aitken, 2010; Crivello, 2008; Dobson, 2009; Hashim & Thorsen, 2011; Punch, 2007; Whitehead et al., 2007), our contribution here thus calls for greater recognition of the historical and contemporary importance of children's independent migration to domestic economies, to children's social integration and development, and to broader cultural transformation. Focusing on teenage boys from two communes in the Zou Department, the Benin data derive from doctoral research, using qualitative methods, on the relationship between discursive representations of 'child trafficking' and lived experiences of independent child labour migration. The Ethiopia data are from Young Lives, a mixed-methods study of childhood poverty that, over 15 years, tracked nearly 3,000 boys and girls in the country, as well as their families and communities.[3] The chapter does not draw on these two countries for comparative purposes, but rather to highlight the diversity of migratory practices among the young and to question policies pioneered by the global child protection regime that lump all forms of child mobility together under the banner of un-willed and injurious movement.

POLICY ASSUMPTIONS

The dominant policy paradigm around the independent migration of the young rests on two sets of assumptions, the first of which concerns children and child development and the second, children's movement. Starting with the first, emphasis is given to certain seemingly universal features of childhood. Among these is the idea that children are especially impressionable and hence at risk in the face of uncertainty or change; their healthy development depending on continuity of care and protection by adults (Boyden & Mann, 2005), with prominence given to the unique psychological and emotional bond that characterises the mother–infant dyad and to secure nucleated family structures. Consequently,

---

[3] Young Lives was core-funded by the UK Department for International Development (DFID) and the Netherlands Ministry of Foreign Affairs (DGIS) for the benefit of developing countries, with sub-studies funded by The Bernard van Leer Foundation, the International Development Research Centre (IDRC), the Oak Foundation and UNICEF.

children's departure from the home is perceived as severing familial ties and disrupting their development (for critical reviews see: Howard, 2016; Thorsen, 2007; Whitehead et al., 2007).

These pessimistic assessments are compounded by the second set of assumptions, according to which independent child movement is intrinsically exploitative. Seemingly, by leaving the protective domestic sphere, children are exposed to avaricious intermediaries and employers; in this way, child migration is increasingly conflated with child trafficking (Bales, 2005; Craig, 2010; Howard, 2008, 2016). Described by the International Labour Organisation (ILO) as 'a global problem' that 'strips children of their childhood' (Boonpala & Kane, 2001, p. 1), trafficking has now become one of the major policy concerns within international child protection, perceived in effect as encompassing all independent movement by the young (see De Lange, 2007; Dottridge & GAATW, 2007).

Hence, in the 'Palermo Protocol' of the UN Convention on Transnational Organised Crime, the crime of trafficking constitutes any involvement in the movement of persons that is based on deception or coercion for the purpose of exploitation. Importantly, coercion is irrelevant in the case of children since they are deemed unable to offer consent. All that matters therefore is the existence of an intention to exploit. Yet crucially, the Protocol does not specify what constitutes exploitation (beyond sexual exploitation, forced labour and slavery). Instead, when it comes to children, policy-makers rely on the anti-child labour framework of the ILO and discussed at length in Chapters 2, 3 and 4 of this volume, which prohibits any economic activity under the minimum age of employment and other work deemed to be 'harmful' and usually identified by economic sector. Consequently, in practice, whenever a particular activity or sector is judged exploitative or unsuitable for children, *all* migrant children involved in it are by default defined as victims of trafficking.

Challenges to this approach are, however, plentiful, especially within academia. Scholars from several disciplines have questioned the narrative of migration-as-trafficking and argued that not all migrant experiences are detrimental (De Lange, 2007; Hashim & Thorsen, 2011; Howard, 2016). They argue that the attachments and bonds that are imputed to be so central to children's development and thus integral to the anti-movement discourse are themselves in fact contextual, as Barbara Rogoff's work in psychology has demonstrated (see Alber, 2003; Mann, 2001 for important anthropological applications of this work). Indeed, many researchers contend that spatial separation does not lead inevitably to the breaking of bonds or the hindrance of developmental progression, pointing to the non-nuclear nature of family structures and to close familial ties that stretch across households and communities in many places (e.g. Verhoef, 2005). Studies of child-rearing practices have long highlighted the frequency of extra-parental guardianship practices, such as through child fosterage (Goody, 1982), or sibling care-giving (Weisner & Gallimore, 1977), which produce children characterised both by 'the diffusion of affect' and 'attachment to community' (Mann, 2001), and for whom extra-parental movement can be understood less as a collapse of the normal developmental process and more as its *direct articulation* (Howard, 2008; Whitehead et al., 2007). This evidence suggests that in non-nuclear familial environments, children's mobility is not only customary but constructive. This chapter takes these ideas as its point of departure.

Children's Mobility in Benin and Ethiopia

The Importance of the Moral Economy

We begin by using our empirical data to draw a vignette of mobility among young people in Benin and Ethiopia. We focus first on the localised realities that govern decisions around young people's independent movement. We find that even though some young people have choices and exercise their agency, their movement tends to be heavily structured by the political-economic forces impinging on them and their families, by intra-household dynamics, and by children's socio-culturally mediated pathways to adulthood.

The Economic Imperative

One of the key justifications for policies proscribing child migration is that the young are vulnerable, dependent and incapable of making judgements in their best interests; indeed, anti-trafficking policy discounts their decisions altogether. We begin by interrogating these assumptions, focusing on the rationale for young people's movement in our empirical samples, who decides they should migrate, and with what effect on their lives.

The motives behind children's movement are often associated with the form that movement takes. Most of the young migrants and former migrants interviewed in Benin had moved away from their homes in search of employment. Most of the child respondents in Ethiopia, on the other hand, had either relocated within the extended kin group, or, in the case of some pubescent girls, moved from home at betrothal or marriage. Regardless of the form it takes, our data show that there is a strong economic imperative driving the movement of children. In subsistence economies, migration by individuals or groups can be crucial to survival, opening up access to new livelihood sources and remitted income, bolstering households with labour shortages and providing for individuals who cannot be supported at home. Being less encumbered with dependents, less free to articulate their independent wishes and less restricted by gendered roles, the young are often more mobile than adults.

Benin is one of the world's poorest countries, with much of the population living on less than a dollar a day and survival dependent on subsistence or poorly remunerated farming activities. Adolescent male migrants and their communities in Benin thus frequently cited lack of resources and opportunities in their home environment as the major reason for moving away. For example, Freddy,[4] from the south of the country, reasoned that child mobility is 'a question of means – poor people…are the ones who send their children away'. Charley, who was the chief of Zelele and Chair of its local Anti-trafficking Committee, pointed out that in his village, 'there is poverty, and where there is poverty, people leave'. Winston deplored the dwindling of fish stock in the lake on which his community had depended for generations and explained that this forced many young people to move. Villagers in Tenga agreed that people leave 'to find something to eat, because they are poor and because there's money to be made in the city, Nigeria, or where the white man is from'.

In Ethiopia, also one of the poorest countries globally, children's movement is frequently precipitated by a crisis, such as drought, harvest failure or familial death (Dercon, 2002). By the time of the 2009 round of Young Lives data gathering, 34.5% of the younger children and 52% of the older ones were separated from at least one of their parents, with more fathers than mothers absent (Crivello & Chuta, 2013). And a full 20% of the children were orphaned of at least one parent (Young Lives, 2009). Yet, even with the high levels of mobility associated with economic hardship and orphaning, the extended family remained central to the care of the young. Only 1.4% of the older children in the sample

---

[4] Names of people and local places have been changed to protect the identity of research respondents in Benin and Ethiopia.

and 0.3% of the younger ones were living with non-kin (Crivello & Chuta, 2013). Paternal orphans were most likely to live with their biological mothers, whereas arrangements for maternal orphans are extremely diverse, grandparents being the most common caregivers.

Crisis is also a feature of child mobility in Benin, where the majority of the young people interviewed who were not living with their parents had come from poor households that had faced some kind of unexpected hardship. When Yomana's father died, for example, both of his older sisters migrated to Cotonou to live with relatives. Similarly, Jeg, a young man who had recently returned from a decade of working in Côte d'Ivoire, left Zelele because his father's long illness and ultimate death had resulted in his family's destitution and inability to care for him or his sister. Clearly, in resource- and capital-poor environments such as in Benin and Ethiopia, the economic imperative for child relocation within or outside the extended family is not insignificant. Families move their children in response to localised economic shocks, as well as to maximise household and family production. They are both reactive and pro-active, as is necessary in such a context.

We now consider whether or not children are able to exercise choice in their mobility. On this, there is great diversity in our findings, and certain general trends. While some children undoubtedly use their own judgement, the younger ones and girls are by and large less able to assert their preferences than are teenagers and boys (see also Abebe & Kjørholt, 2009). So, for instance, in Ethiopia, girls' experiences of departure from the home for early marriage commonly hinge on a sense of duty or on more direct compulsion, more than personal inclination (Boyden et al., 2013). Keleb Weyra's mother, for example, was in her early teens when her father decided that she should leave home and school to get married. Keleb's mother was very unhappy in the marriage and after giving birth to a baby girl, sought a divorce, returned home and went back to school. But her father insisted she re-marry and again removed her from school. This time, only a month into the marriage and unaware that she was already pregnant with Keleb, she ran away from her husband to return to her parents' home and to school. Forcibly removed from school and remarried a third time, she became pregnant once more, although this baby was stillborn. This marriage also failed and eventually, in despair, Keleb's mother migrated to Addis Ababa for good, leaving her daughters in the care of their grandparents.

Most of the male respondents in Benin made their own decisions to move, with or without parental consent, and some simply chanced their luck. This is consistent with norms in Southern Benin whereby younger children and girls tend to have their migration settled on by adults (often involving placement in domestic work within or outside the kinship-group), while adolescent boys are expected to earn a wage and so frequently migrate independently in order to do so. Didier, for example, decided to move with a friend to Cotonou to become a blacksmith's apprentice when his parents told him they could no longer afford his school fees. Similarly, having failed his latest year at school at age 14, Christophe determined that it was time to get a job. His father acceded to his wishes and helped him secure an apprenticeship with the Cotonou blacksmith who employs Didier. Ethan and a group of friends from his village, on the other hand, travelled to Cotonou to become ambulant scratch-card sellers after a young returnee migrant passed the word around that good money could be earned this way.

Since poverty and adversity are common impulses in the movement of the young in Benin and Ethiopia, and since many boys and girls have little or no say about migrating, the policy emphasis on the involuntary nature of the practice would appear to have some validity, but that is limited and depends on many contextual factors. Nevertheless, despite the picture elaborated above, we have not found the movement of the young to involve traffickers, nor have we uncovered a correlation between extra-kin work and 'exploitation'. Also, the young seldom move *simply* out of economic necessity, or following a crisis. Indeed, most children's movement is shaped not by material need alone but by a complex interplay of material and moral considerations, as discussed below.

Mutuality in Survival

We have argued that those opposed to children's migration emphasise how, when children move, their primary care relationship is disrupted, with adverse developmental consequences. However, our data do not support this position. Indeed, in exploring the moral economy of children's movement, we show that in fact relocation very often reinforces rather than disrupts mutuality between the generations of a family, ensuring a virtuous moral circle which secures both group and individual survival.

Central to this argument is the evidence that very often children's movement is more than simply about supplying labour or remitting income where most needed and is embedded within a nexus of practices that focus also on their care and socialisation. Thus, it is structured both by the material needs of the household (or related households), and by the opportunities available for children's informal learning and care in line with their gender and social age. In Ethiopia and Benin, as in the case everywhere, considerable importance is attached to young people building the social and life skills necessary to flourish in their particular milieus. Emphasis is given to self-sufficiency and supporting others in accordance with the child's maturity and gendered and generational expectations (Abebe & Kjørholt, 2009; Boyden, 2009; Okyere, Chapter 2, this volume; Rogoff, 2003). To this end, young people are encouraged whenever possible to tend animals, crops, or a small business, to cook, to collect fuel and water, or to look after the very young and infirm. In Ethiopia, girls are more likely to assume domestic responsibilities; boys to take on farm and paid work. Specific tasks are often assigned in line with the birth order and gender composition of siblings in a household (Boyden, 2009).

Intra-familial relocation is often crucial in providing for this kind of learning. Indeed, in Benin, children are normally sent to caregivers who are perceived most likely to ensure that the children develop valued social and life skills. Where an uncle is more authoritative than a father, a child viewed as errant or lazy might be sent to him for guidance, while if an aunt has more schooling, a studious child with a bright academic future might be sent to live under her watch. Women in one village explained that, in the advent of having nothing to do, it would be advisable for a young person to leave his home and find work in a related household or elsewhere, because 'he needs to learn how to contribute'. The social (and indeed practical) importance of learning such a lesson was underlined by the claim that, if he did not, 'he would end up becoming a thief'—a figure universally reviled in the community for taking without giving. As such, it was concluded, 'it is better for both the child and the community for him to depart'. The importance of children learning the attributes needed to contribute their labour power is thus clearly apparent within this understanding of what it means to be an active member of the community.

Relocation can therefore serve to enhance children's social integration. Often this is evidenced in the intense intergenerational mutuality that prevails in host households, as in Ethiopia where orphaned children move in with older relatives precisely to ensure both their protection and learning *and* to meet the labour and care needs of the elderly. For example, Mariam, a paternal orphan from Oromiya, went to live with her maternal grandmother, who is old and sick, on the grounds that she was the only family member available to care for the old woman. Mariam's mother was not herself able to assume this responsibility because she was fully occupied raising her youngest children. The grandmother outlined how the arrangement works: 'Before, she [Mariam] used to come and go, but now she has come to stay with me. So, her mother decided that she shall stay here and take care of me until I die. She takes care of me and I take care of her schooling'.

Acknowledgement of the reciprocal nature of intergenerational claims and duties is central to kinship mutuality and key to the success of young people's intra-familial relocation. This can be seen from the experience of Dawit, in Ethiopia, who, at age six was given over to the care of a widowed aunt when her son moved away to join the military. Dawit assumed the aunt's dead husband's name and in return for food and lodging, herded her cattle, fetched water and firewood and cleaned the floor. But he was made to work long hours, sometimes without food, and was forced to drop out of school twice because of his workload. He was denied medical attention when ill and on returning home from the army, the aunt's son started mistreating him. Unhappy, Dawit returned home and resumed use of his father's name. When asked why he had left his aunt, he said she had stopped communicating with him (using local idioms, 'because she left me' and 'she was not ordering me'), this in his view being evidence that she 'hated' him.

This brief example brings into sharp relief the unambiguous emotional expectations deriving from intra-familial relocation; for Dawit it was the lack of affective commitment rather than physical neglect that led him to abandon his aunt's house. Such evidence suggests that children's mobility invokes far more than mere material exigencies: it is also rooted in particular ideas about the appropriate nurture of the young. In other words, the practice does not denote a rupture in emotional bonds as implied by the dominant discourse so much as an expression of the powerful interconnectedness of moral and material relations.

Consequently, under these circumstances, intra-familial relocation is experienced as an entirely natural and indeed positive phenomenon. Of the ten children and young people in one Beninese household, for example, only two were the biological offspring of the household head, with the others having relocated for school or work. In one village, Adam had four young people living with him, all of whom were the children of his brother, while his own daughter had just returned from Lomé, where she had spent two years staying with her aunt. On another occasion, when a man was asked about how he would know that his daughter would be treated well in her uncle's home in Gabon, he replied: 'She's not going away...she's going to be with my brother and sister, my own flesh and blood, so she will be treated *just as if she were here*'.

A Vehicle for Transition and Transformation

So far, we have outlined the part played by children's movement in sustaining household livelihoods, kinship mutuality and personal development in precarious subsistence, or near-subsistence, circumstances. However, by accentuating its role in fulfilling the status quo, we do not intend to paint a static picture, for the moral economy of child mobility is in practice exceedingly dynamic. While children's movement may indeed support current conditions in many contexts, it can also represent a vehicle for both individual and collective ambition, as well as being a vector for personal and familial transformation. Migration to access work or schooling has been shown to signify an often-successful life choice with present and future social and economic benefits (Crivello, 2008; Howard, 2008).

That children's movement may embody such significant and potentially transformative features is evident from the way in which it has been deployed in many Young Lives sites in Ethiopia. Since the study gathered its first round of data in 2002, there has been unprecedented economic growth and infrastructural and service expansion in the country; this has been reflected in the lives and circumstances of the great majority of children in the sample. Most impressive has been the expansion in school enrolment. In Ethiopia, expectations concerning education are high and schooling has come to be seen as the major path towards a better future. So, since many rural communities do not have secondary schools, accessing education has emerged as one of the most important reasons why many children in the sample, especially boys, leave the natal home (Young Lives, 2009, p. 2; see also Abebe, 2008).

The movement of young people in Benin also has strong transformative connotations in many cases. 'Poverty' is nearly always and everywhere the immediate response to the question 'why do young people leave the village?' Nevertheless, deeper exploration generally reveals other motives, such as the quest for economic opportunity. When a group of young respondents in one village were asked, to their amusement, whether 'poverty' meant 'starvation', whether people remaining 'would go without food?' a resounding 'no' was the answer. In another conversation, a village chief and the friend who had joined him at this point smiled and explained, 'People don't die of hunger here. Even if you do nothing, you will be fed'. Similarly, Winston, the father of two adolescent migrants, declared, 'When there are no fish, people don't starve – it's not like that, people wouldn't let you starve – it's just that there's no money'. The same was also true of mixed group of 15 teenagers in Tenga village, all of whom explained that when they said 'ya', the Fon word for 'poverty', what they meant was 'no money, no jobs, no opportunity'.

Interviews with young Beninese migrants or aspiring migrants confirmed this picture. While it is undoubtedly the case that more boys than girls migrate independently in search of paid work in Benin, the understanding that migration can lead to individual opportunity and individual transition through access to cash is shared across the sexes. Thus, the teenagers in Tenga all declared that leaving was good because it gives you the chance to make money and become someone important. Likewise, youngsters in Atomè described how migrating is to be encouraged because it means you can go to where the money is and bring back riches. The same applied to boys who had already migrated for work in the artisanal quarries of Abeokuta in Nigeria. Though targeted by the governments and their partner agencies in Benin and Nigeria as epitomising the kind of child trafficking that needs to be stopped, this flow of adolescents is firmly part of individual and familial life strategies aimed at making money. The young migrants explained that the decision to work in the mines was a positive one, despite the challenges, since this was the only way of accessing the riches that would allow a better life for individual migrants and their families. 'If you are successful in Nigeria,' one young man explained, 'you can return with a motorbike, or put a roof on your father's house'.

Apart from the chance for economic gain, the movement of young people can also facilitate progression through the life course and the establishment of individuals as adults worthy of respect. In Benin, for instance, 'being considered' is a crucial goal—it means being respected, being a person of importance, having made good and being able to demonstrate this fact to others. Migrating away for work is very often viewed as an effective path to achieve this status, such that young people across several contexts referred to young migrant males who had returned with motorbikes, money or wives as illustrating successful outcomes. It can be the process of migration itself, rather than simply the successful outcome, which gives rise to such a transition. A local social worker who was deploring the repeated migration of a young man brought back by the authorities from a situation of 'trafficking', explained that this boy was so wedded to the idea of movement because 'it was through suffering elsewhere' that he could 'become a man'. Similarly, the repeated temporary migration to work summer jobs on farms that accompanies the onset of adolescence in Southern Benin, represents a vehicle for young boys to access and *keep*, their own money. Whereas working their fathers' farms may be an important familial contribution which they all value, temporarily migrating for wage labour, even when they remit a portion of their wages to their parents (as all claim they do), allows adolescent boys to begin to articulate their own independence, since they hold on to a share of what they earn.

That young people's movement, to marry, access school or work, or simply to become somebody can be a crucial economic and social strategy for boys and girls should by now be clear. We argue, though, that it is not simply a matter of individual advancement; intergenerational mutuality among kin implies that the fulfilment of migratory aspirations is as much about serving the wider group as about individual interests. Hence the young Beninese returnee from the Abeokuta mines in Nigeria cited roofing his father's house as one ambition, while others talked about remitting income. At the same time, parents, grandparents and other adults may make major sacrifices to enable the young to migrate for schooling, generally in the full expectation that the wider family will benefit from improved income and gain a foothold in an urban centre. In this sense, raised aspirations around the mobility of the young are at the same time transforming expectations of intergenerational mutuality among kin; no longer just one household resource among many others, young people are fast becoming the main locus of advancement of the kin group. Semira, in Ethiopia, is an example of this. Having lost her father to illness, her mother's recent descent into ill-health has convinced her she must leave the country to get a job and help her mother overcome poverty.

Raised aspirations can, however, be curtailed by immediate responsibilities. Feven's case exemplifies the dilemma many children confront in Ethiopia today. Her father has abandoned the family and while her sister migrated to the regional capital in search of a job, she also moved to go to school. However, when her mother fell ill, she had to leave school and return home, where she now undertakes all of the household chores, weeds the family's fields, collects firewood and works for pay in a government social protection programme and a local stone-crushing firm. Feven expressed great disappointment that the change in the family's circumstances had so undermined her ambitions. While many Ethiopian families support their children migrating to town to take advantage of new opportunities that have arisen with the expansion of the labour market and services, these same families are also under great pressure economically and are heavily reliant on their offspring to fulfil immediate labour needs. We will argue that this dilemma is, in essence, a product not just of localised moral economies, but more fundamentally of wider political-economic forces that bear down on the rural poor.

The Importance of Political Economy

This section places the brief vignettes above in their political-economic contexts and in so doing, questions the relevance and effectiveness of child trafficking and migration policy that is based on globalised norms that take little or no account of international, national and/or sub-national structural forces that bear down on poor families and their children. Although localised cultural values and economic circumstances undoubtedly inform children's movement in Benin and Ethiopia, mobility practices, be they wage-labour migration, or intra-familial relocation, depend on far more than local processes alone. While the local and indeed immediate contexts are fundamental, the decision and articulation of youth movement depend also on the wider, macro, structuring contexts which frame them. It is crucial to understand this in order to offer a comprehensive account that avoids the dominant pathologising of youth mobility that has so often been perpetuated by international policy actors and the wider child protection regime. In the remainder of this chapter, we highlight how decisions made at the level of the individual, family or community fundamentally also rely on, and interact with, the political-economic decisions and realities that form the super-structure around them.

Land and Education Policies

In Ethiopia, two nationally determined policies of importance for mobility decisions are those concerning education and land. That young people (and particularly young boys) in Ethiopia frequently migrate in order to access continued educational opportunities has already been established above; what we now contend is that this is no coincidence. Indeed, it depends in large part on active governmental investment decisions that in the past privileged the development of urban over rural education. Tafere and Camfield's (2009, p. 18) analysis of Young Lives' data demonstrates this clearly. They find that 'while 48 per cent of rural children have not achieved the correct age for grade, this only applies to 12 per cent of urban children', indicating a correlation between school attendance and the geographic distribution and quality of secondary schools. In explaining why this may be the case, they draw on an elder from Angar (where the secondary school may be a two-and-a-half-hour-walk away):

> The construction of schools in the community may reduce the risk of travelling long distances – this is especially good for younger children and girls, but the older children have to walk all the way and cross the forest to go to school to continue their education from grade 5 to 8. (ibid.)

The social and environmental dangers of long walks to school affect decisions as to whether or not particular children (in this case girls) should continue attending—and if so, how. Just as governmental choices as to where to build schools provide an imperative for *some* children to drop out, so we must assume that they inevitably provide an imperative for *some* children to move and migrate.

Similar dynamics have been at work in Ethiopia following the Land Law introduced by the Derg regime in 1975, which led to nationwide land nationalisation and redistribution under the principle of 'land to the tiller' (Clapham, 1988; Dessalegn, 1984). Morrissey (2012) explains that the country's land was shared out to each household according to household size and the private transfer of land was prohibited. When the Derg eventually fell in 1991, the new regime maintained the essence of this policy; land was still controlled by the state, with some smaller-scale redistributions from existing plots and previously communal tracts. Consequently, there was a divide between the older generation who maintained access to land and a disadvantaged landless youth, many of whom were forced to migrate. In such a context, the national policy provides a clear and tangible incentive for some young people to migrate. Thus, Morrissey contends that a 'youth bias' exists more broadly among Ethiopian migrants, as evidenced by those studied by Young Lives.

Cotton and Oranges

While it is clear that national policies have a significant impact on localised decision-making, one should not forget that both individual migratory choices *and* migrant-influencing national policy decisions are themselves significantly affected by wider, international political-economy dynamics. In Benin, this is the case with orange production and small-holder cotton farming.

Under the Kérékou Presidency, Benin was officially a Marxist-Leninist state that allied itself with Russia and China and espoused certain aspects of their centralised economic models. In 1974, Kérékou embarked on a campaign of nationalisation, purging the country of foreign capital and bringing all major industries under central control. Charley, the chief of Zelele village, and an employee of one of the nationalised companies—an Israeli-owned factory producing orange juice under the name of Sonafel— revealed its enormous effects.

Charley worked for Sonafel for 20 years. During the Sonafel period, he said, hundreds of hectares of the surrounding land were under orange cultivation, and farmers sold their produce to Sonafel for a good price. 'In those days, times were good. The Israeli developed a new crop of orange that was sweet and lovely, and farmers all around took cuttings and began to grow the same'. When the factory was nationalised, however, everything changed. After two or three years of decline, the factory and business were closed, people were laid off and farmers from across the region were forced to sell their oranges wholesale at extremely low prices. Charley reflected that: 'Before, people used to come from Nigeria, see how good things were, and not go back'. Now, by contrast, families cannot afford to send their children to school, and there is little prospect for youth employment: 'even the young from these villages must leave to Nigeria to find work'.

Cotton farmers in Benin's Zou region are documented as facing very similar problems. For much of the Twentieth Century, cotton was the most important cash crop in Benin, accounting for around 5% of GDP and up to 40% of the country's export receipts (OECD, 2005, p. 20).

Countless small-scale farms would compete in selling their cotton to national agricultural supply chains, who in turn would sell it on the international market (OXFAM, 2003, p. 20). Farmers and state agricultural agents alike argued during the course of research that when cotton 'works well, life is good. The country has money to spend, families have money to build, children go to school; we invest'.

However, in 2003, Benin and a group of neighbouring countries were forced to take a case to the World Trade Organisation's Appellate Body citing strong evidence that illegal US domestic cotton subsidies were depressing global cotton prices, damaging both West African national receipts and household economies. OXFAM (2003) concluded not only that US subsidies did lower international prices, but that they led to a '1–2% loss of gross domestic product' for some countries, including Benin. Scholars estimated that, in the Zou region alone, 'a 40% reduction in cotton prices results in a 15% decrease in per capita income and a 17-percentage point increase in the incidence of poverty' (Minot & Daniels, 2005, p. 17). Though the impact of the subsidies on the sector was thus established, diplomatic pressure at the World Trade Organisation and elsewhere ensured that the US escaped censure, that subsidies were maintained, and that cotton prices remained weak (Eagleton-Pierce, 2013). Cotton farmers explained that the collapse in prices led to a huge reduction in household income, an increase in family members entering the wage market and ultimately, many more migrating to Nigeria or elsewhere, with one respondent arguing that children '…wouldn't move at all if prices were still high. They'd all be in school'. The collapse of cotton earnings over the past 15 or so years is thus strongly correlated with an increase in the outward child mobility decried as child trafficking—and yet never, in formal policy-making circles, is such a link discussed.

Conclusion

We have argued that the dominant policy discourses surrounding child mobility and apparent 'child trafficking' fail to take into consideration the diverse socio-cultural and material conditions that are brought to bear in the extremely varied developmental trajectories of young humans throughout the world today. In so failing, policy ignores the ways in which different child rearing objectives and practices may 'prime' boys and girls in the early development of specific skills and behaviours that will be advantageous to them in their daily lives, both practically in terms of meeting their current and future needs, and socially and spiritually in terms of being morally valued. Hence, policy fails to consider the many ways in which children's independent migration can be constructive in supporting both individual and collective survival and personal development.

While children's departure is at times both unwilled and detrimental to their well-being, the migration of boys and girls does not necessarily involve exploitative intermediaries, the breakdown of familial ties or damage to individual prospects. Our research in Benin and Ethiopia concurs with a wide range of other studies which highlight the many constructive aspects of independent child migration for the young, and for their families and communities. We maintain that the movement of boys and girls needs to be understood in historical and economic-moral contexts in which childhoods were never fixed spatially within stable, nucleated family structures. When young people leave home, they are not leaving the supportive familial network that transcends that home, nor are they breaking ties central to their well-being. Far from physical departure leading to rupture, frequently children depart both within and because of those bonds, themselves more diffuse and less spatially constrained than is generally assumed by policymakers.

Generations and households are often interdependent, in Benin, Ethiopia and far beyond, learning involves important pro-social skills, care-giving is multiple, space is hierarchically related to wealth, and that which happens at the level of the individual depends quite intricately on decisions taken half-way across the world at the global head table. Life strategies therefore necessarily involve—and are indeed constituted by—navigating a path between all of the above. Migration is sometimes a key part of that path, such that policy-making that is divorced from this reality cannot expect to have the intended outcomes and may even, inadvertently, do harm, as various other chapters in this book suggest. Clearly therefore, if actors within the international child protection regime genuinely wish to support children effectively, their policies need to build on evidence concerning the multiplicity of economic and social forces that shape their movement.

REFERENCES

Abebe, T. (2008). Trapped between disparate worlds? The livelihoods, socialisation and school contexts of rural children in Ethiopia. *Childhoods Today, 2*(1), 1–29.

Abebe, T., & Kjørholt, A. T. (2009). Social actors and victims of exploitation: Working children in the cash economy of Ethiopia's South. *Childhood, 16*(2), 175–194.

Aitken, S. (2010). Not bad for a little migrant working kid. *Children's Goegraphies, 8*(4), 363–371.

Alber, E. (2003). Denying biological parenthood: Fosterage in Northern Benin. *Ethnos, 68*(4), 487–506.

Anderson, B. (2013). *Us and them: The dangerous politics of immigration control*. Oxford University Press.

Bales, K. (2005). *Understanding global slavery: A reader*. University of California Press.

Boonpala, P., & Kane, J. (2001). *Le Trafic des Enfants dans le Monde Problème et Réponses*. BIT.

Boyden, J. (2009). Risk and capability in the context of adversity: Children's contributions to household livelihoods in Ethiopia. *Children, Youth and Environments, 19*(2), 111–137.

Boyden, J., & Mann, G. (2005). Children's risk, resilience and coping in extreme situations. In M. Ungar (Ed.), *Pathways to resilience* (pp. 3–25). Sage.

Boyden, J., Pankhurst, A., & Tafere, Y. (2013). *Harmful traditional practices and child protection: Contested understandings and practices of female early marriage and female genital cutting in Ethiopia* (Working Paper 93). Young Lives.

Clapham, C. (1988). *Transformation and continuity in revolutionary Ethiopia*. Cambridge University Press.

Craig, G. (Ed.). (2010). *Child slavery now: A contemporary reader*. Policy Press.

Crivello, G. (2008). *'Becoming somebody': Youth transitions through education and migration—Evidence from Young Lives*. Young Lives.

Crivello, G., & Chuta, N. (2013). *I look for help from others when I can't do things on my own: Sources of support for orphaned and vulnerable children in Ethiopia* (Working Paper). Young Lives.

De Lange, A. (2007). Child labour migration and trafficking in rural Burkina Faso. *International Migration, 45*(2), 147–167.

Dercon, S. (2002). Income risk, coping strategies, and safety nets. *The World Bank Research Observer, 17*(2), 141–166.

Dessalegn, R. (1984). *Agrarian reform in Ethiopia*. Scandinavian Institute of African Studies.

Dobson, M. (2009). Unpacking children in migration research. *Children's Geographies*, 7(3), 355–360.
Dottridge, M., & GAATW. (2007). *Collateral damage: The impact of anti-trafficking measures on human rights around the world*. GAATW.
Eagleton-Pierce, M. (2013). *Symbolic power in the World Trade Organization*. Oxford University Press.
Goody, E. (1982). *Parenthood and social reproduction: Fostering and occupational roles in West Africa*. Cambridge University Press.
Hashim, I. M. (2003). *Child migration: Pathological or positive?* International Workshop on migration and poverty in West Africa. University of Sussex, UK.
Hashim, I. M., & Thorsen, D. (2011). *Child migration in Africa*. Zed Books.
Howard, N. (2008). *Independent child migration in Southern Benin: An ethnographic challenge to the "pathological" paradigm*. VDM Verlag & Co.
Howard, N. (2016). *Child trafficking, youth labour mobility, and the politics of protection*. Palgrave Macmillan.
Huijsmans, R. (2006). *Children, childhood and migration* (Working Papers Series No. 427). Institute of Social Studies.
Mann, G. (2001). *Networks of support: A literature review of care issues for separated children*. Save the Children Sweden.
Minot, N., & Daniels, L. (2005). Impact of global cotton markets on rural poverty in Benin. *Agricultural Economics*, 33, 453–466.
Morrissey, J. (2012). Contextualising links between mobility and environmental stress in northern Ethiopia. In K. Hastrup & K. F. Olwig (Eds.), *Climate change and human mobility: Global challenges to the social sciences* (pp. 110–146). Cambridge.
O'Connell Davidson, J. (2015). *Modern slavery: The margins of freedom*. Palgrave Macmillan.
O'Connell Davidson, J., & Farrow, C. (2007). *Child migration and the construction of vulnerability*. Save the Children Sweden.
OECD Sahel and West Africa Club Secretariat. (2005). *Economic and social importance of cotton production and trade in West Africa: Role of cotton in regional development, trade and livelihoods*. OECD.
OXFAM. (2003). *Cultivating poverty: The impact of US cotton subsidies on Africa*. OXFAM.
Punch, S. (2007). Negotiating migrant identities: Young people in Bolivia and Argentina. *Children's Geographies*, 5(1–2), 95–112.
Rogoff, B. (2003). *The cultural nature of human development*. Oxford University Press.
Tafere, Y., & Camfield, L. (2009). *Community understandings of children's transitions in Ethiopia: Possible implications for life course poverty* (Working Paper No. 41). Young Lives.

Thorsen, D. (2007). *"If only i get enough money for a bicycle!" A study of child migration against a backdrop of exploitation and trafficking in Burkina Faso* (Occasional Paper). University of Copenhagen.

Verhoef, H. (2005). A child has many mothers: Views of child fostering in Northwestern Cameroon. *Childhood, 12*(3), 369–390.

Weisner, T. S., & Gallimore, R. (1977). My brother's keeper: Child and sibling caretaking. *Current Anthropology, 18*, 169–190.

Whitehead, A., Hashim, I. M., & Iversen, V. (2007). *Child migration, child agency and intergenerational relations in Africa and South Asia* (Working Paper T24, Working Paper Series, Migration DRC). University of Sussex.

Young Lives. (2009). *Focus on children: Breaking the cycle of poverty, Young Lives conference report*. Young Lives.

CHAPTER 9

Child Protection in Palestine and Jordan: From Rights to Principles?

Jason Hart

Introduction

Over the last one hundred years child protection has become an important element of the work of the many humanitarian organisations that operate in settings of conflict and displacement around the globe. The strengthening of protection efforts has been bound up with the project of children's rights. In the wake of the devastation caused by the First World War, the League of Nations endorsed the Declaration of Children's Rights (1924). The 1924 Declaration was replaced in 1959 by the UN Declaration of the Rights of the Child which, in turn, has been superseded by the 1989 UN Convention on the Rights of the Child (UNCRC). This Convention—the most widely ratified of all UN legal instruments—has been invoked by many organisations as a basis and

---

J. Hart (✉)
Department of Social and Policy Sciences, University of Bath, Bath, UK
e-mail: jh462@bath.ac.uk

moral touchstone for their child protection efforts. Several of the 54 articles of the UNCRC relate explicitly to the rights of children caught up in armed conflict and political violence. Insistence on the *prevention of harm* through addressing root causes and on children's *right to be heard* in relation to all matters that affect them are key elements of a "rights-based" approach to child protection.

Yet, more than a quarter century after promulgation of the UNCRC, the safety of children caught up in situations of armed conflict and mass displacement remains as elusive as ever. At the time of writing the young are being subjected, systematically and en masse, to numerous and intense forms of violence in locations around the globe. This tragic reality raises questions about the efficacy of the child rights-based approach to protection in practice that the international child protection regime promotes.

Obligation to realise the rights articulated in the text of the UNCRC lies with States Parties. However, the mechanism for monitoring the efforts of governments to uphold these rights is weak. The UN Committee on the Rights of the Child—to which States Parties should submit reports every five years—lacks sanction for states that fail in their obligations even to the basic right of children to live in safety. Furthermore, the US is not a state party to the UNCRC, undermining efforts to strengthen commitment to norms surrounding the basic rights of children in settings of armed conflict.

Meanwhile, governments that have historically championed humanitarian activity are implicated in the killing and wounding of children in numerous conflict settings. Such harm has been direct, as occurred when Allied forces blockaded and then invaded Iraq, or through the sale of weaponry and provision of military expertise, as may be witnessed in Yemen. These activities co-exist with provision of aid from the same governments to many of the same locations. There is an evident disconnect between the statements of concern from Western governments about the safety of children and the pursuit of geopolitical and economic agendas to the benefit of their own elites.

Non-governmental humanitarian agencies (henceforth "NGHAs") that form part of the international child protection regime have generally embraced the notion that the young should be treated as subjects of rights rather than as passive objects of humanitarian pity. However, it is solely national governments that are signatories to the

UNCRC. NGHAs are not, from a legal perspective, accountable for their actions or inactions in relation to fulfilment of the articles of the Convention. While States Parties are thus subject to a weak and inadequate mechanism of accountability in respect of the UNCRC, NGHAs are subject to none at all. They may occasionally object to the double standards of donor governments, as evident in respect of Yemen,[1] but not in a manner that addresses the issue systemically entailing sustained, collective efforts.

In this chapter, I explore an alternative basis for NGHAs to be held accountable for their protection work in the context of armed conflict and political violence. The approach I consider shifts the focus from children's rights to core humanitarian principles. For the purposes of this discussion I employ the text of the *Code of Conduct for the International Red Cross and Red Crescent Movement and Non-Governmental Organisations (NGOs) in Disaster Relief* as the key reference point for those principles.[2] Formulated by a small number of humanitarian agencies and published in 1994, the *Code of Conduct* sought to articulate clear principles for humanitarian work globally. This Code incorporates—in somewhat amended form—principles established by the Red Cross more than a century earlier and crystallised in 1965. Signatories to the *Code of Conduct* now number in excess of 600 and include all of the major (Western-originating) international non-governmental organisations working in the humanitarian field, including Save the Children, the International Rescue Committee, Terre des Hommes, World Vision, War Child, and Plan, plus many national and locally-based NGOs.[3]

United Nations agencies are not part of this initiative. However, as Intergovernmental Organisations (IGOs), they are called upon in the text of the *Code of Conduct* (Annex III) to collaborate with NGOs on relief efforts in "a spirit of partnership" that entails respect for the "independence and impartiality" of agencies involved in humanitarian work. Moreover, UN agencies are obliged to act in accordance with the working principles of the UN General Assembly that are based on the four core humanitarian principles. Unsurprising, then, that the agency

---

[1] For example, see https://www.savethechildren.org.uk/news/media-centre/press-releases/statement-on-uk-arms-sales-to-saudi-arabia. Accessed 24 February 2020.

[2] https://www.icrc.org/eng/resources/documents/publication/p1067.htm.

[3] https://media.ifrc.org/ifrc/who-we-are/the-movement/code-of-conduct/signatories-to-the-code-of-conduct/.

most directly involved in child protection—UNICEF (2010)—states in its *Core Commitments for Children in Humanitarian Action* that it "is committed to applying humanitarian principles in its humanitarian action" (p. 6). However, while "humanity", "impartiality" and "neutrality" are mentioned explicitly, the fourth and last of these core principles—"independence"—is omitted (ibid.). The implications of this omission are considered below.

The text of the *Code of Conduct* makes explicit that it is voluntary and "self-policing". From that perspective its force may be even less than that of the UNCRC. The *Code of Conduct* has no equivalent requirements of its signatories and there is no body similar to the UN Committee on the Rights of the Child to monitor adherence. Nevertheless, as a professional code that so many agencies have endorsed, working in accordance with its principles carries important moral weight. A survey of over a hundred humanitarian professionals conducted in 2004 found high levels of support for the code and the widespread belief that it reflected "mainstream thinking…about what should constitute humanitarian aid" (Hilhorst, 2005, p. 354). Each of the ten individual articles of the code were deemed "useful in practice" by between 81% and 94% of respondents (ibid.). Evident failure to uphold these principles could have potential reputational consequences—a significant consideration in a crowded marketplace where agencies must compete for private and public funds. Furthermore, the first four principles articulated within the ten articles of the Code of Conduct— humanity, impartiality, neutrality and independence—are widely acknowledged and embraced even at the popular level. By contrast, the very notion of children's rights has been met with indifference, if not hostility, within many societies, including among citizens of the United States.[4]

In the ensuing text I seek to explore the potential of the *Code of Conduct* to serve as a framework for examining child protection work in settings of armed conflict and political violence. This will entail a principles-based analysis of the actions of NGHAs in addressing the situation of two specific groups of children. The first of these are Iraqi children displaced to Jordan and the second young Palestinians living under Israeli occupation. What does the framing of protection work in terms of the core principles of the *Code of Conduct* reveal about the shortcomings of

[4] See https://www.huffingtonpost.com/joe-lauria/why-wont-the-us-ratify-th_b_6195594.html?guccounter=1.

institutional efforts in practice with these two groups of children? Furthermore, how might the *Code of Conduct*, and the humanitarian principles generally, serve as the basis for evaluating the efforts of NGHAs towards realisation of children's basic rights and advocating for improvement? Before moving to that discussion, however, we should sketch out an understanding of the four principles at the heart of the *Code of Conduct*.

Core Principles: Humanity, Impartiality, Neutrality and Independence

In his discussion of humanitarian ethics, Hugo Slim (2015) draws a helpful distinction between humanity and impartiality, on the one hand, and neutrality and independence, on the other. The first couple he describes as the basis for "the universal ethical goal of humanitarian ethics as the preservation of every human person as a good in itself" (p. 65). In other words, humanity and impartiality indicate the "moral ends" of humanitarianism (ibid.). By contrast, neutrality and independence relate to humanitarian action: to the question of "how it is best done" (ibid.).

Taken together the principles of humanity and impartiality articulate the universal character of humanitarian endeavour. According to the text of the *Code of Conduct*, all of humanity inherently possesses the "right to receive humanitarian assistance" on the basis of need alone (Article 1). Article 2 asserts that "human suffering must be alleviated whenever it is found: life is as precious in one part of a country as another". The universality expressed in the Code resonates with the text of the UNCRC which indicates that the rights articulated in the Convention apply to "every human being below the age of eighteen years" (Article 1) and obligates States Parties to "respect and ensure the rights set forth in the present Convention to each child within their jurisdiction without discrimination of any kind" (Article 2). In the *Core Commitments* of UNICEF, "humanity" is explained as the principle that "all girls, boys, women and men of every age shall be treated humanely in all circumstances by saving lives and alleviating suffering, while ensuring respect for the individual" (ibid.). Thus a universal disposition is advanced as fundamental to the protection of children in settings of humanitarian emergency.

Unlike humanity and impartiality, the principle of neutrality has been subject to considerable debate and has been a cause of unease among scholars and practitioners alike. In *The Fundamental Principles of the*

Red Cross and Red Cross Movement (1965) neutrality is explained in the following terms:

> In order to enjoy the confidence of all, the Movement may not take sides in hostilities or engage at any time in controversies of a political, racial, religious or ideological nature.[5]

The *Code of Conduct* articulates a different view of neutrality: one that does not preclude the kind of engagement proscribed by the Red Cross and Red Crescent Movement three decades earlier. Here "neutrality" comes close to "impartiality" while "the right of non-governmental humanitarian agencies to espouse particular political or religious opinions" is upheld.

This reformulation of neutrality provides a principled basis for agencies to engage in "controversies" when the aim is strictly humanitarian. Here a distinction made by Antonio Donini (2012, p. 6) between "partisan politics" and "a politics of humanity" is instructive. As Slim (2015) comments:

> Partisan politics makes contributions towards a specific political outcome; the politics of humanity engages with political power only for a humanitarian goal. (p. 68)

Engagement in the "politics of humanity" is consistent with an approach to child protection (the prevailing one) that seeks to prevent harm and not just to respond with healing interventions once harm has occurred. Efforts to address root causes of children's suffering are key to moving from a needs-based to a rights-based approach (Cornwall & Nyamu-Musembi, 2004): a shift that may also entail moving from "purely technical solutions to socio-political action" (Gready, 2008, p. 743).

Just as realisation of the principle of humanity necessitates upholding the principle of impartiality, so neutrality requires independence. In other words, organisations require the independence to pursue of "politics of humanity" away from the pressures of donors with their particular political and economic agendas. The explanation of independence offered in the Red Cross and Red Crescent statement of principles differs somewhat

---

[5] https://www.icrc.org/en/doc/resources/documents/misc/fundamental-principles-commentary-010179.htm.

in its wording from that expressed in the *Code of Conduct*. However, they articulate the same basic concern to avoid co-option by government:

> The National Societies, while auxiliaries in the humanitarian services of their governments and subject to the laws of their respective countries, must always maintain their autonomy so that they may be able to act in accordance with the principles of the Movement. (*The Fundamental Principles of the Red Cross and Red Cross Movement* 1965)

> We shall endeavour not to act as instruments of government foreign policy. Non-governmental agencies are agencies which act independently from governments. (*The Code of Conduct for International Red Cross and Red Crescent Movement and NGOs in Disaster Relief* 1994)

In discussion of Palestinian children living under Israeli occupation I shall consider the shortcomings of child protection efforts by humanitarian organisations in relation to the failure to maintain independence from donor governments. As we shall see, lack of independence may have negative consequences for efforts to uphold the principle of "neutrality". Before that, however, I examine the situation of Iraqi refugee children in Jordan. This context yields important insights into the challenges to pursuing a universalistic approach required by the principles of "humanity" and "impartiality".

IRAQI REFUGEE CHILDREN IN JORDAN: A CASE OF INVISIBILITY

> The Iraqi refugees are not seen as anything anymore. Most of the humanitarian agencies are not looking, passively not looking. (Jordanian Aid worker, Amman, April 2014)

In 2014 Anna Kvittingen and I interviewed over fifty individuals working in government, NGHAs and UN agencies, most of them based in Amman (Hart & Kvittingen, 2016). This research took place over a three-month period. In addition, I spent time interacting with Iraqi families at social occasions and by volunteering as an English language teacher in an informal educational initiative run by an international NGHA in order to learn about the everyday lives and challenges faced by displaced Iraqis, especially children, living in Jordan.

Following the fall of Saddam Hussein in 2003 and in response to subsequent sectarian violence thousands of Iraqis fled their country, seeking immediate sanctuary in neighbouring nations. In Jordan they mostly found accommodation in urban centres, especially Amman. While the wealthy settled in elite neighbourhoods, the majority entered the private rental market in working-class areas of Amman, Zarqa and Irbid. Residency permits and access to formal employment have only been offered to Iraqis with financial resources to invest in local businesses or the skills to undertake specialised professional jobs for which there are insufficient Jordanian citizens with the requisite qualifications.

The status of those unable to gain residency is ambiguous. The Government of Jordan has not signed or ratified the 1951 UN Convention Relating to the Status of Refugees and does not offer formal asylum. UNHCR has been registering the Iraqis and providing a document attesting to their status as asylum seekers. However, this does not bring with it any privileges in terms of access to the labour market, while access to basic services is limited. We found very few reports about the situation of Iraqi refugee children and scant discussion by human rights bodies (for a rare and valuable contribution see Nelems, 2008).

Denied residency and the opportunity for legal employment, Jordan has served as a staging post on the path to resettlement. Several countries have run programmes to settle displaced Iraqis, most notably Australia, Canada, Sweden, Germany and the United States. At the perceived height of the Iraqi crisis—between 2007 and 2011—around 19,000 were resettled through UNHCR (UNHCR, 2013). After that period, however, the opportunity for resettlement diminished.

The Iraqis whose applications for resettlement were turned down and who remained in Jordan for lack of other options constituted one element of the displaced population as a whole. At the time of our fieldwork there were also thousands still awaiting review of their application either by UNHCR or by the country of potential resettlement. This process can take years. Meanwhile, savings expire, and relatives elsewhere struggle to sustain remittances. In addition, by 2014 cash assistance offered by agencies other than UNHCR had largely disappeared for all but new arrivals.

In a situation of dwindling resources and insufficient income it was inevitable that some sought employment in the informal economy, exposing them to exploitation from unscrupulous employers. According to anecdotal evidence, this included a growing number of Iraqi children who were engaging in some form of economic activity in order to assist their families, selling small items on the street, or working in petrol stations for example.

The Jordanian authorities were not directly responsible for inflicting harm on Iraqi refugee children. However, they were strongly implicated in what Kvittingen and I have described as a "network of disregard" (Hart & Kvittingen, 2016). In pursuit of their specific political agendas, Western donors and the Government of Jordan created a situation in which, directly and by extension, the rights of Iraqi children have been rendered a matter of contingency rather than principle.

Between roughly 2007 and 2011, considerable funding from Western donors supported programmes for Iraqi refugees in Jordan. By the time of our research in 2014, however, these funds had virtually dried up. The lion's share of financial and human resources made available by outside governments was going to the Syrians. For its part, the Government of Jordan obliged donors and NGHAs to ensure that 30% of monies was spent on Jordanians, Iraqis were not to be included in any programmes for which funds were given in the name of the Syrians.

While local staff members and those who had been in Jordan for a lengthy period were only too aware of the presence of Iraqi children (and of their Somali, Sudanese, Yemeni and Eritrean peers), the lack of funding combined with the immense task of responding to the Syrian refugees curtailed even discussion of their situation. Efforts were continuing to assist Iraqi children with particular needs, including the chronically ill and disabled, but this was largely on an ad hoc basis.

The lack of attention to young Iraqi refugees by donors and the organisations that they support constitutes a clear divergence from the core humanitarian principles of humanity and impartiality. Such divergence was illustrated by various regional and national plans being drawn up at the time of fieldwork in 2014. For example, a region-wide project focused on children—"No Lost Generation"—addressed only the situation of Syrian children. This initiative, supported by four international NGHAs, the governments of the US, Canada and the UK, and five UN agencies called upon the general public to provide support to organisations engaged in averting the risk that the future of Syrian children "could be lost forever" (Childrenofsyria.org, 2014, p. 12). The futures of Iraqi, Sudanese and other groups of displaced children living in equally dismal, if not worse, conditions were ignored in this initiative and not addressed by any comparable project.

For Western donors the priority is to ensure both the stability of the Jordanian regime amidst the turmoil in the region and the continuation of that country's function as a warehouse for refugees who might otherwise seek entry to their jurisdictions. In consequence we found no appetite to challenge the authorities over, for example, denying non-elite Iraqis access to the labour market or forbidding their inclusion in programmes of support to Syrians. These are measures that could have important beneficial consequences, enabling Iraqi parents to provide for their children and reducing the need for the young to enter the informal labour market. It might also reduce tension in the domestic realm where, as numerous experts reported to us, family discord and interpersonal violence had grown as a direct result of the stresses arising from many refugees' deepening poverty and chronic uncertainty about long-term solutions to their plight. In the words of an Iraqi father:

> What kind of fun do you think the children here have had? No fun, nothing, because they're at home and they're listening to us – the parents – struggling, fighting each other due to the lack of money, no source of income. (Amman, February 2014)

In 2014 it was notable that the US Government stood almost alone in its continued provision of funds for the support of Iraqi refugees and its ongoing programme of resettlement. Avoidance combined with high profile attention to the Syrian refugees characterised the British approach. Donor governments that had once been supportive had grown weary of providing aid and/or resettling Iraqi refugees and were similarly devoting themselves to the Syrians. As one Jordanian humanitarian worker remarked:

> We stopped supporting Iraqis simply because we didn't manage to get funds. The donors were pushing for an exit strategy for Iraqi programmes. We were requesting political pressure on governments to better react, but many donors said, "Syria is the priority now". The donors used the Syria crisis as the exit strategy for the Iraqi crisis. (Amman, February 2014)

By 2014 the incentives for the Jordanian government and Western donors to attend to Iraqi refugee children were minimal. The state of limbo to which they and their families were thereby consigned, entailed the prospect of steady pauperisation and the associated threats to their wellbeing and protection (Women's Refugee Commission, 2009). For humanitarian organisations, however, the move away from supporting Iraqi children and ensuring their equitable treatment raises a serious question about commitment to the principles of humanity and impartiality. This question was answered in a range of ways. Some of our interviewees working for UN agencies and NGHAs insisted that Iraqi children did not require particular support since their families were "middle-class" and lived in the wealthier neighbourhoods of Amman. It was certainly true that there were Iraqis whose wealth or skills had enabled them to access residency and regular employment. However, there were evidently thousands living in far more modest circumstances whose struggle to pay for basic necessities grew only more difficult with each passing year spent in limbo. Some humanitarian workers—notably those who had arrived relatively recently to work on the Syrian crisis—claimed to have little knowledge of other displaced populations. In any event, they were already overloaded with work relating to the needs of Syrian children. More senior and more experienced humanitarians appeared to accept the status quo, albeit regretfully, arguing that the lack of funding for the Iraqis put children from that country beyond their reach. Responding to our questions about the situation of displaced Iraqi children in Jordan one senior child protection worker remarked:

> Honestly speaking, I can't give specifics. Our interaction with the Iraqis has really gone down since the funding was cut two years ago. (Amman, March, 2014)

With notable exceptions, it was local organisations, some working on a voluntary basis, that appeared to offer most of the practical assistance to Iraqi refugee children and their families. This appeared to take two main forms. Firstly, as several told us, they endeavoured to bring up the need to act in an equitable manner towards all displaced children at every opportunity—including inter-agency co-ordination and planning meetings. Secondly, some staff worked quietly to obtain support for displaced children on the basis of need rather than nationality. To do so they used their personal networks across the various humanitarian organisations.

Efforts to advocate with the host government and foreign donors to offer sustained support to Iraqi children were not in evidence. This situation was not due to lack of concern among individual staff members but was the consequence of decision-making at senior levels not to engage or, at least, not to devote staff time and resources to such efforts.

The compromise of core humanitarian principles due to the vagaries of funding and the questionable justifications given for doing so are eloquently captured in the words of one interviewee—a long-standing Jordanian humanitarian worker:

> *Aid worker*: Both the Government and the NGOs believe that if [the Iraqis] managed for five years or more they should not need more assistance or it's more important to give it to new arrivals.
> *JH*: Is this true in your opinion?
> *Aid worker*: Under the circumstances and without funding, I will say "yes", but if I have no funding problems, I would say "no". (Amman, February 2014)

As some of our interviewees who had been working in Jordan for several years pointed out, the funding and support for the Iraqis began to wind down before the full onset of the Syrian crisis. In other words, the scale of the Syrian crisis was not the cause of decline in support for the Iraqis. While everyone was fully engaged in dealing with one population group the neglect of children of a different nationality was easily obscured. Neglect and discrimination were thus being camouflaged by extensive activity. Failure to fight for the resources to support Iraqi and other non-Syrian refugee children, brought into question agencies' commitment to the principles of humanity and impartiality at the heart of the *Code of Conduct* and UNICEF's *Core Commitments*.

PALESTINIAN CHILDREN UNDER OCCUPATION: THE POLITICS OF PREVENTION

> The problem is from the donors. They want us to ignore the problems and look at superficial wounds, superficial issues. That's what UNICEF is doing. (Palestinian Aid worker, Nablus, July 2009)

Discussion of the protection of Palestinian children living in the West Bank & East Jerusalem draws upon material from research conducted in 2009. Over a nine-month period Claudia Lo Forte and I explored institutional efforts to protect children at risk of occupation-related violence. We undertook roughly 120 interviews and focus groups with children, parents and a range of key informants working in local, international and UN humanitarian agencies and in governmental and multi-lateral donor organisations.

At the time of our research the number of Israeli Jewish settlers living in the West Bank and East Jerusalem was estimated at nearly 300,000 (Peace Now, 2009). This number had been reached through a programme of settlement building that began soon after Israel's victory in the Six-Day War of 1967. The transfer of a civilian population into land captured in war is in direct violation of Article 49 of the Fourth Geneva Convention (ICRC, n.d.). In the West Bank, the resident population has been concentrated and contained in areas sectioned off by fences, checkpoints and a permit regime. In several locations, attempts have been made by extremist settlers, aided by the Israeli authorities, to remove Palestinians altogether. In East Jerusalem a range of strategies has been employed to achieve expulsion of families from homes within the municipal boundaries.

Palestinian children living in areas particularly subject to Israeli settler and government efforts to occupy, colonise and expel have suffered systematically along with others in their communities. They have also been targeted explicitly *as children* with the aim of speeding up the exodus of their families from locations intended for settlement. This has happened, for example, in the South Hebron Hills and in the Old City of Hebron where children have been routinely attacked on their journey to and from school by extremist settlers determined to displace Palestinian families from their homes (Beinin, 2007; CPT & OD, 2010; OHCHR, 2012).

In addition, children have been arrested and imprisoned in large numbers. Over recent years, including at the time of our fieldwork, 500–700 children per year were being detained, often for months on end—a scale of detention that continues today (Defense for Children International—Palestine, 2016, 2020). Typically, this has been justified by the authorities on suspicion of stone throwing—a crime for which young settlers and ultra-orthodox Jews are treated in an incomparably gentler manner, imprisonment reserved for only the most extreme cases (Beinert,

2015; Kubovich, 2015). Several reports have highlighted the violations of international law entailed in the arrest, detention and punishment of Palestinian children (Defense for Children International—Palestine, 2016; House of Commons Library, 2016; UNICEF, 2013). These violations include practices that amount to torture, denial of access to parents and legal representatives, and extraction of confessions of guilt under severe duress.

Violations of children's basic rights take further forms. House demolitions (Levac & Levy, 2015), destruction of space intended for children's play and leisure (ICAHD, 2007), denial of family re-unification (B'tselem, 2006), obstructions to mobility preventing access to basic services (Vitullo et al., 2012), are among other harms commonly inflicted upon Palestinian children living in East Jerusalem and the West Bank. Such actions by the Israeli authorities had, by the time of our fieldwork, long since become routine.

The protection efforts routinely offered by the main UN and international agencies at the time of our fieldwork did not address these issues in a systematic manner. Moreover, the focus on prevention of violations was spasmodic. Our research revealed that the major part of protection work in this setting consisted of efforts intended to ease the impact of occupation-related violence or to help the healing process of children who have suffered harm. This work included a significant focus upon psychosocial programming. In addition, there were concerted efforts to develop a child protection system that would identify children "at risk" and refer them on to specialised services—pursuing a case management approach familiar in Europe and North America. This system was principally concerned with protecting children from the harm experienced in the community, school and domestic realms. The protection issues typically addressed in these domains were referred to as "internal" by NGHAs in contrast to the "external" issues related to violations by the Israeli authorities and settlers. A Palestinian staff member at an international child-focussed humanitarian agency characterised her organisation's interactions with Palestinian children in the following words:

> ...OK we know about the occupation but we do not talk about it, we know that you go through hell every day to come to our activities, but let's talk about how your father treats you and how your teacher treats you... (Ramallah, March 2009)

Efforts aimed at addressing the source of threat to children from the Israeli military and settlers were, by comparison, ad hoc campaigns devoid of strategy. They consisted of occasional reports on subjects such as house demolition, displacement and the use of administrative detention. These were generally not publicised widely. Advocating with visiting parliamentarians from the US, Western Europe or the EU was similarly low-key. The "lobbying, pleading, cajoling, and shaming" that Michael Barnett (2011, p. 41) associates with an approach to humanitarianism aimed at "addressing the root causes of suffering" (p. 39) were little in evidence.

The most systematic focus on Israeli violations that we encountered was in the form of the "Monitoring and Reporting Mechanism" (MRM). This was established in line with Resolution 1612 (2005) of the UN Security Council with the purpose of passing data to that body on violations against children in settings of political violence. As Lo Forte and I have observed, the creation of the MRM in the Occupied Palestinian Territories encouraged co-ordination among agencies and helped to systematise the collection of data (Hart & Lo Forte, 2010). However, in the estimation of our interviewees it had not delivered significant gains for child protection. For example, an international humanitarian worker observed:

> ...we have always felt that the mechanism [MRM] has very little impact for children on the ground. Even if the reports are of great quality, this has not been reflected in the situation facing Palestinian children. When action has been taken, it has been just to put 'bandages on the wound', instead of fighting the root causes of the problem. (Ramallah, April, 2009)

Several interviewees indicated that the lack of impact by the MRM may be partly attributable to the editing of reports in order to remove material deemed too sensitive politically. One Palestinian NGHA official, for example, stated:

> Unfortunately, the oPt MRM reports tend to get quite heavily edited in New York...The result is a somewhat watered down or sanitised version of the original. (Ramallah, August, 2009)

The pressure applied at the global level to prevent challenge to the Israeli government over its systematic harm to Palestinian children was demonstrated when, in June 2015, then UN Secretary-General Ban-Ki

Moon removed Israel from the list of states responsible for serious violations of international humanitarian law in respect of children. This was despite the recommendation from his Special Representative for Children and Armed Conflict—Leila Zerrougui—to include Israel together with Hamas. According to reports, the Secretary General had succumbed to pressure from the governments of the United States and Israel in making this change (*Guardian*, 2015; Human Rights Watch, 2015).

Independence Compromised

The lack of thoroughgoing efforts to prevent violations against Palestinian children by the Israeli authorities and settlers should be understood, in large measure, as a consequence of the lack of independence of humanitarian organisations from the governments and other bodies that fund and facilitate their work. Political pressure operating at the global level was also evident on the ground. Our interviews with staff in UN and international agencies working for child protection in the West Bank and East Jersualem revealed a common experience of such pressure to minimise public criticism of Israel. As indicated by the following comment from a former staff member at Save the Children, fear of loss of governmental funding was a major factor behind this pressure:

> Save the Children US didn't have the room to do anything independent (of government) if it wanted to support the numbers of staff dependent on government-funded operations…the message from Westport [Save the Children US HQ] was clearly 'no advocacy on Palestine publicly please'.

A former staff member at UNICEF East Jerusalem explained:

> We had more pressure on what we could say about violations of children's rights from New York [UNICEF HQ] than even from the Israeli government.

Reliant upon the financial and diplomatic support of governments and inter-governmental bodies such as the European Union, organisations working directly for the protection of children in settings of political violence were subject also to their agendas. As a region the Middle East has been the focus of intense geopolitical and economic interest since at least the early twentieth century—a focus that only grew with the discovery of oil. Governments in Washington, London and other Western capitals have been subject to the lobbying efforts of powerful corporations, including companies involved in the arms industry, whose pursuit of profit entails close collaboration with Israeli partners. In some cases, these companies work directly with Israeli weapons manufacturers—such as the collaboration between Thales UK and Israel's Elbit Systems (Hilary, 2011).

In the West Bank and East Jerusalem we can see with particular clarity the impact of political and economic considerations upon the manner in which the protection of children is pursued. At the time of our research a welfarist, response-oriented approach to child protection generally prevailed. This approach served a dual focus. On one hand it enabled humanitarian organisations to demonstrate both their concern for young Palestinians and their own industriousness through, for example, running activities and supporting psychosocial programming that might serve to reduce the stress experienced by children and their caregivers. On the other, such an approach obviated the need to confront the Israeli authorities over their violations. The aim was clear: "to help develop children's skills at coping with trauma" and to "teach them how to lead a normal life in abnormal conditions".[6] That is to say, assist children to survive—physically and psychologically—a status quo that entailed systematic violence and the abuse of basic rights.

In this context a more prevention focused approach to child protection would necessarily entail advocacy and thus risk confrontation with the Israeli government—something that Western donors were keen to avoid. Indeed, the very notion of child protection work that is centred on prevention was a sensitive subject for some of our interviewees working for governmental donors:

> *JH*: "It seems that for people themselves it's not just about responding when damage has been done in terms of, you know, psychosocial services. It's actually about preventing that damage from happening in the first place."
> *Interviewee*: "Well, that's a political agenda and one that I'm probably not best to go into with you here." (From interview with donor agency officer, Jerusalem, August 2009)

---

[6] http://ec.europa.eu/delegations/westbank/documents/eu_westbank/unrwa_en.pdf.

Child-focused humanitarian organisations seeking to fulfill their mandate to pursue a preventative (and rights-based) approach to protection would have had to counter pressure from donors, potentially putting their funding at risk. The evidence from the West Bank & East Jerusalem suggested that they were generally unwilling to do so. Occasional reports, the provision of information discreetly to global bodies, and some low-key diplomacy were the general shape of advocacy efforts. Independence from the agendas of major bilateral and multilateral donors was, in practice, largely foregone:

> I think if you were Palestinian you should say "thanks but no thanks". But unfortunately, we are guilty of having become very dependent, especially as NGOs, on international funding. And it's very hard to have income generating projects or whatever. So you're very dependent on what the foreigners think you should do. (Palestinian humanitarian worker, East Jerusalem, August 2009)

Negotiating Neutrality

Lack of independence has significant consequences for the way in which the principle of neutrality is negotiated. As noted earlier, this principle has generated particular debate and disagreement. The considerable difference in wording between the 1965 *Fundamental Principles of the Red Cross and Red Cross Movement* and the 1994 *Code of Conduct* indicates the complexity and divergence of thinking about this principle. The latter document offers greater latitude to humanitarian organisations to engage in public advocacy. It allows for agencies to "draw attention to humanitarian facts about the respect or violations of international humanitarian law" and to undertake "an advocacy of restraint in the conduct of armed conflict" (Slim, 2015, p. 69). Moreover, it is possible to make "specifically political comments and advocate for various forms of political intervention" (Slim, 2015, p. 70). The 1965 document articulates a far more restrictive view, reflecting the approach conventionally adopted by the Red Cross that has conventionally conflated neutrality and silence.

Careful consideration of the specific setting is vital in planning advocacy efforts that might secure the protection of children threatened by political violence. In East Jerusalem and the West Bank, however, we found that the space needed by humanitarian agencies to determine the best course of action had been severely reduced by the dictates of donors.

For many years, Western governments have argued that the best way to secure the safety of the Palestinians is through the "two-state solution". Were too much noise to be made about ongoing violations it would put at risk the hope for long-term peace, so the argument goes. Leaving aside questions about the viability of establishing a Palestinian state given the scale of land appropriation by Israel, this approach has led, ultimately, to humanitarian organisations sidestepping core humanitarian principles. It has also rendered the protection of Palestinian children contingent on a long-term political deal. In the meantime, they have been subjected systematically to physical attack and brutality, arrested and imprisoned in a manner that violates international law, denied access to basic services and to a normal family life. It is unthinkable that Western governments would urge forbearance if such suffering were to be inflicted upon their Israeli peers. The *Code of Conduct* in its formulation of the principle of neutrality requires NGHAs "not to tie the promise, delivery or distribution of assistance to the embracing or acceptance of a particular political or religious creed". Yet humanitarian agencies have been co-opted by Western donors for the two-state agenda that entails curtailment of actions that might prevent systematic harm to Palestinian children by the Israeli authorities. In the place of such efforts we found humanitarians busying themselves with technical solutions to immediate, local issues that minimised confrontation with the Israeli government and reduced the risk of upsetting donors:

> It's like someone who has cancer and all you are doing is treating the symptoms of that cancer but you're allowing the tumour, the cancerous growth, not only to remain there but to grow and grow. (International humanitarian worker, South Hebron Hills, May 2009)

> We focus on doing things right, rather than doing the right things. (International humanitarian worker, East Jerusalem, August 2009)

Conclusion

In this chapter, I have drawn upon my research with colleagues in two separate locations in order to demonstrate the use of humanitarian principles as a framework to analyse child protection efforts, including those pursued by actors comprising what this book understands as "the international child protection regime". In the case of Iraqi children in Jordan this approach reveals a failure to uphold the basic notion of universality expressed in terms of the principles of humanity and impartiality. The case of Palestinian children living under Israeli occupation in East Jerusalem and the West Bank provides acute illustration of NGHAs' inability to uphold the principles of independence and neutrality.

It should not be inferred from my account that it is non-adherence to these principles alone that each case illustrates. Further principles articulated in the *Code of Conduct* are also liable to be side-stepped when the four basic principles are not upheld. For example, the commitment to "hold ourselves accountable to those we seek to assist" (Article 9) is effectively meaningless in both cases, as indeed it is in many others, including those documented by other chapters in this volume. Accountability is denied when NGHAs ignore Palestinians' demands to challenge Israel over ongoing violations of the physical and moral integrity of their children. For displaced Iraqi children in Jordan the principle of accountability is a non-issue when agencies fail to acknowledge their existence and suffering in the first place.

Using a framework based upon the core humanitarian principles to identify and analyse the shortcomings of NGHAs in their child protection work is not complicated. Addressing these shortcomings is another matter. Accountability is essential. However, as the two cases indicate, accommodating to the political and economic agendas of major donors has been so central to humanitarian organisations' own survival that other lines of accountability are rendered tenuous. Such compromise seems hard to avoid in the humanitarian field as dominated, historically, by Western-originating NGHAs and UN agencies reliant on the funds of western governments. Many of these governments, in turn, are increasingly subject to, if not promoters of, right-wing populism and exclusionary nationalism that seeks to slash overseas aid and sidestep international law (Hopgood, 2019). The struggle to ensure that all children at risk from political violence and armed conflict are protected is therefore bound up with a larger struggle to build empathy transcending national borders.

There is a notable precedent for such effort in the establishment of the first NGHA focused particularly on the young—Save the Children. In the immediate aftermath of the First World War this organisation's founder, Eglantyne Jebb, sought to provoke popular concern in Britain for Austrian and German children suffering as a direct result of the

Allies' blockade of the defeated Axis powers. Jebb insisted that all children should be protected from the harms of war: a position entirely consistent with the core humanitarian principles of humanity and impartiality (Cabanes, 2014, p. 297). As she wrote in 1919: "Let us take this message, and live it out in practical action…with the saving of the children of Europe, irrespective of their nationality".[7] Her efforts to engender such a disposition across British society entailed direct challenge to the government: a demonstration of both independence and of "a politics of humanity" consistent with contemporary understanding of the principle of neutrality.

One hundred years after the establishment of Save the Children, fresh initiative to promote empathy towards the situation of children in settings of armed conflict and political violence around the globe is badly needed. Increasing popular awareness of the frequent sidestepping of principle in the conduct of child protection work by humanitarian organisations that form part of and prop up the wider child protection regime might be a useful element of such initiative, potentially provoking popular pressure for change. Yet, such pressure must be considerable if it is to counter that of major donors for whom the safety of children is of lesser import than the pursuit of immediate political and economic advantage. If such pressure can be created through concerted popular effort agencies mandated to keep children safe will be faced with a stark choice—either strive to act in full accordance with humanitarian principles or continue down the path of compromise and co-option.

REFERENCES

B'tselem. (2006). *Perpetual Limbo: Israel's Freeze on Unification of Palestinian Families in the Occupied Territories*. www.btselem.org/press_releases/200 60815. Accessed 3 June 2017.

Barnett, M. (2011). *Empire of humanity: A history of humanitarianism*. Cornell University Press.

Beinert, P. (2015, May 7). Violence doesn't erase the legitimacy of grievances in Baltimore, Tel Aviv or the West Bank. *Ha'aretz*. http://www.haaretz.com/opinion/1.655331. Accessed 15 July 2017.

Beinin, J. (2007). Letter from al-Tuwani. *MER244*. http://www.merip.org/mer/mer244/letter-altuwani. Accessed 12 May 2017.

---

[7] Press release by Eglantyne Jebb, 21 May 1919 cited by Cabanes (2014, p. 278).

Cabanes, B. (2014). Humanitarianism old and new: Eglantyne Jebb and children's rights. In *The Great War and the Origins of Humanitarianism, 1918–1924* (Studies in the Social and Cultural History of Modern Warfare, pp. 248–299). Cambridge University Press.

Campbell, K., Denov, M., Maclure, R., & Solomon, I. (2011). Introduction. In K. Campbell, M. Denov, & R. Maclure (Eds.), *Children's rights and international development: Lessons and challenges from the field*. Palgrave Macmillan.

Childrenofsyria.org. (2014). *No Lost Generation, Protecting the futures of children affected by the crisis in Syria: Strategic Overview.*

Cornwall, A., & Nyamu-Musembi, C. (2004). Putting the 'rights-based approach to development' into perspective. *Third World Quarterly, 25*(8), 1415–1438.

CPT & OD (Christian Peacemakers Team and Operation Dove). (2010). *The dangerous road to education: Palestinian students suffer under settler violence and military negligence*. www.cpt.org/files/palestine/shh-report_school_patrol_2009-10-the_dangerous_road_to_education.pdf. Accessed 16 May 2017.

CPWG (Child Protection Working Group). (2012). *Minimum Standards for Child Protection in Humanitarian Action*. CPWG. http://cpwg.net/wpcontent/uploads/2012/10/Minimum-standards-for-child-protection-in-humanitarian-action.pdf. Accessed 13 May 2001.

Defense for Children International—Palestine. (2016). *No Way to Treat a Child: Palestinian Children in the Israeli Military Detention System*. www.dci-palestine.org/no_way_to_treat_a_child_palestinian_children_in_the_israeli_military_detention_system. Accessed 16 February 2020.

Defense for Children International—Palestine. (2020). https://www.dci-palestine.org/military_detention_stats. Accessed 16 February 2020.

Donini, A. (2012). *The Golden Fleece: Manipulation and independence in humanitarian action*. Kumarian Press.

Gready, P. (2008). Rights-based approaches to development: What is the value-added? *Development in Practice, 18*(6), 735–747.

Guardian. (2015, March 17). UN officials accused of bowing to Israeli pressure over children's rights list.

Hart, J., & Kvittingen, A. V. (2016). Rights without borders? Learning from the institutional response to Iraqi refugee children in Jordan. *Children's Geographies, 14*(2), 217–231.

Hart, J., & Lo Forte, C. (2010). *The Protection of Palestinian Children from Political Violence: The role of the international community* (Forced Migration Policy Briefing No. 5). Refugee Studies Centre. https://researchportal.bath.ac.uk/en/publications/protecting-palestinian-children-from-political-violence-the-role. Accessed 10 September 2018.

Hilary, J. (2011). The security industry and the war industry. In A. Winstanley & F. Barat (Eds.), *Corporate complicity in Israel's occupation*. Pluto Press.

Hilhorst, D. (2005). Dead letter or living document? Ten years of the Code of Conduct for disaster relief. *Disasters, 29*(4), 351–369.

Hopgood, S. (2019). When the music stops: Humanitarianism in a post-liberal world order. *Journal of Humanitarian Affairs, 1*(1), 4–14.

House of Commons Library. (2016, January 4). *Child prisoners and detainees in the Occupied Palestinian Territories.* Debate Pack, UK Government. www.parliament.uk/commons-library. Accessed 3 June 2016.

Human Rights Watch. (2015, June 4). *UN: Ensure Integrity of Children's 'List of Shame'.* https://www.hrw.org/news/2015/06/04/un-ensure-integrity-childrens-list-shame. Accessed 1 May 2016.

ICAHD. (2007). *Municipality Tears down East Jerusalem Care Center for Disabled Children.* http://icahd.org/blog/2007/05/10/municipality-tears-down-east-jerusalem-care-center-for-disabled-children/

ICRC. (n.d.). *Convention (IV) relative to the Protection of Civilian Persons in Time of War. Geneva, 12 August 1949.* International Committee of the Red Cross. https://www.icrc.org/applic/ihl/ihl.nsf/7c4d08d9b287a42141256739003e636b/6756482d86146898c125641e004aa3c5. Accessed 1 June 2017.

Kubovich, Y. (2015, September 28). Jews throw stones too, but Arabs get harsher sentences. *Ha'aretz.* www.haaretz.com/news/israel/.premium-1.677685. Accessed 16 May 2017.

Levac, A., & Levy, G. (2015, August 29). Israel Leaves 80 Children at Mercy of August Sun. *Ha'aretz.* www.haaretz.com/weekend/twilight-zone/.premium-1.673301 Accessed 16 May 2017.

Nelems, M. (2008). *The Unity Circle Project: Experiences of Iraqi Children and Parents Living in Amman, Jordan.* International Institute for Child Rights & Development / Relief International / Save the Children / UNICEF.

OHCHR. (2012). *Report of the Special Rapporteur on the situation of human rights in the Palestinian territories occupied since 1967, Richard Falk.* OHCHR. http://www.ohchr.org/Documents/HRBodies/HRCouncil/RegularSession/Session20/A-HRC-20-32_en.pdf. Accessed 20 May 2016.

Peace Now. (2009, June). *West Bank Settlements—Facts and Figures.* http://peacenow.org.il/eng/node/297. Accessed 20 May 2017.

Slim, H. (2015). *Humanitarian ethics: A guide to the morality of aid in war and disaster.* Hurst & Company.

UNHCR. (2013). *2012 Statistical yearbook.* UNHCR.

UNICEF. (2010). *Core commitments for children in humanitarian action.* UNICEF.

UNICEF. (2013). *Children in Israeli Military Detention: Observations and Recommendations.* www.unicef.org/oPt/UNICEF_oPt_Children_in_Israeli_Military_Detention_Observations_and_Recommendations_-_6_March_2013.pdf. Accessed 3 June 2017.

Vitullo, A., Soboh, A., Oskarsson, J., Atatrah, T., Lafi, M., & Laurance, T. (2012, October 8). Barriers to the access to health services in the occupied Palestinian territory: A cohort study. *The Lancet* Special Issue. http://www.thelancet.com/pb/assets/raw/Lancet/abstracts/palestine/palestine2012-12.pdf. Accessed 3 June 2017.

Women's Refugee Commission. (2009). *Living in Limbo: Iraqi Young Women and Men in Jordan*. WRC.

Conclusion: Towards Politics and Participation

Neil Howard

At the heart of this book sit two simple critiques. On the one hand, that the international child protection regime tends to promote top-down, at times culturally imperialist modes of intervention, which act 'on' rather than 'with' people. On the other, that it does so in ways which are as depoliticised as they are depoliticising. Each of these critiques combines in an evaluation: that the international child protection regime often fails to achieve its goals and does so in part because of the way it goes about its business. This, in turn, leads to a postulate—that as things stand, it is arguably more a part of the problem than it is the solution.

In this, it is no different from many other regimes of social policymaking and is certainly reflective of trends that characterise both the social work and international development fields more broadly (of both

N. Howard (✉)
Department of Social and Policy Sciences, University of Bath, Bath, UK
e-mail: n.p.howard@bath.ac.uk

of which it is a part). Countless studies have documented the calamitous unintended consequences to which 'heroic developmentalism' has led (e.g. Escobar, 1994; Li, 2007), while others have put this observation in the historical context of modernity and its techno-rationalist modes of governance (Berman, 1982; Scott, 1998).

What are the specifics of this ongoing failure? This book has pointed to a number. First is the troubling lack of reflexivity on the part of many of the individuals and institutions operating within international child protection. To be reflexive is to embrace the relativity of one's standpoint, to question one's premises, and to take seriously the idea that all meaning is socially constructed. None of this is common to this field. Child protection actors are primed to universalise, to be suspicious of relativism, and to protect their normativity (Boyden, Postscript, this volume; Howard, 2016). In a sense, this reflects their valiant commitment to the well-being of *all* people, irrespective of wealth, status or background. It is also surely a by-product of the law, international or otherwise, which is always a blunt, universalising instrument. But this lack of reflexivity matters because the power imbalances between child protection actors and their would-be 'beneficiaries' are such that the former tend to impose their worldview and its behavioural imperatives on the latter. And at times, as a number of the contributions to this book have amply demonstrated, this can cause 'collateral damage' (cf. Dottridge and GAATW, 2007; see also Bourdillon et al., 2011), with lives made worse by misguided good intentions.

Related to this lack of reflexivity is what some call 'groupthink'. In this volume, Myers and Bourdillon (Chapter 4) argue that 'groupthink occurs when a group with a particular agenda makes irrational or problematic decisions because its members value harmony and coherence over accurate analysis and critical evaluation…'. Although it would be unfair to tar the entire field with this brush, there is no question, in our view, that many within it are hampered both by its echo-chamber nature and by the culture of closedness that borders on obstinacy in the face of dissenting information. The reality of institutional practice within this field, as in so many others, is that people interact mainly with their peers—those from the same or similar agencies who have been to the same schools and been trained in the same schools of thought. Added to this, institutional protocol ensures that agencies consult each other's work primarily and solicit each other's opinions first, with the consequence that bodies of misinformation are reproduced and recycled over and over again without anyone realising what they are missing. Worse still is the superiority-inflected defensiveness that tends to be a corollary. Inevitably, when you hear your views repeated back at you again and again by people you respect, you tend to assume that you are right and those who think differently are wrong. This manifests regularly within the child protection regime, blocking potentially productive channels for learning and growth. Often, however, that blockage is accompanied by *fear*. Across the 'social sector', among civil society, governmental and inter-governmental bodies pursuing goals other than profit, these are challenging times, for neoliberalism has not been kind to progressive agendas (Dauvergne & LeBaron, 2014) and in the age of Covid things are arguably getting worse. Agencies are therefore everywhere on the defensive and this makes them highly resistant to even legitimate critique.

This points to a major design flaw in the system—it suffers from a structural lack of meaningful feedback loops. Within systems theory, feedback loops provide an ongoing flow of information that helps the system to self-regulate by correcting imbalances and returning things to optimal functioning (cf. Burns & Worsley, 2015; Ramalingam, 2013 for how systems thinking can apply to development). I recall clearly meeting a good-natured and high-ranking US official who was genuinely shocked at the stories I shared of policy-gone-wrong in relation to child labour. 'I had absolutely no idea', she said, 'because there is nothing in place to make sure we hear of things like this'. Nor was she aware of the evidence of working children's movements like those documented in Chapter 3 by Jessica Taft. Similarly, although most major agencies do regularly sponsor research, few if any mechanisms exist to ensure that what they do is fundamentally evidence-based or that corrective measures can be taken when the evidence suggests that things are not working. Likewise, while formal researcher/practitioner exchanges are becoming more common, very rarely do those who pull the levers of power within the child protection regime substantively engage with those affected by their policy or project decisions, and nowhere do 'beneficiaries' have a direct line to those designing interventions on their behalf.

All of this is of course compounded by the fact that accountability in this field ultimately travels in one direction—upwards. As Jason Hart's chapter so clearly and painfully demonstrates (Chapter 9), donors set the agenda. Although some agree that participation matters and others really do wish to see policy addressing the structures that (mis)shape our world, the bottom line in child protection is the same as almost anywhere in national or international policy-making—priorities are set in the service of interests that go well beyond the well-being of poor children and their communities (see also Okyere, Chapter 2 and McMullin, Chapter 6, this volume). Philanthropic actors have their 'generous' identities to promote. Ministers want to be re-elected and know that doing so means appealing to their publics and avoiding alienating the powerful. The same is true of high-ranking officials within the firmament of international and inter-governmental child rights organisations like UNICEF or the ILO. This is why so few are willing to rock the boat by calling for structural, system-altering steps like the decentralisation of aid budgets, bottom-up project design, or for concerted radical action on existential threats such as climate change; it is also why no one decries systemic forces like capitalism or white supremacy as those we need to tackle, in which we are all complicit, and which have differential effects based on our positionality and our power.

* * *

Yet within these critical observations there lie a number of important caveats and acknowledgements. The first is simple and still bears repeating: most people who work in this field really do care. They invest their time, their energy and very often their emotions to make life better for those whose difficulties motivate their compassion. This is no small matter. And too often, the critical writing on the child protection regime—as is often the case with critical writing more generally—misses it entirely. Indeed, in its urgency to show people what is 'wrong' with what is happening, the critical literature at times forgets that its targets are themselves also *people* as well as systems and institutions. Misinterpreting mistakes for malevolence, it casts protection actors and their institutions as the real 'baddies' in the story, rather than as would-be allies who are caught between the rock of wanting to help and the hard place of not knowing how, not believing it is possible, or simply not being able to because of structural forces beyond their control.

This relates to our second point. In truth, many within this field recognise the limitations of what they do, the simplistic paradigms they perpetuate, the band-aid nature of their interventions, and at times their outright futility (very rarely, however, does this stretch to acknowledgement of actual harm done). But the question they understandably ask is, 'What alternatives do we have? If the whole system is broken, it is beyond our power to change it. So, aren't we better off accepting our limitations, navigating the structures, and using our jobs to at least channel some resources to where they are needed?' This is a reasonable question to ask and in the end it is empirical. We simply do not know for sure whether children and their communities will be better served by confronting the failures and hypocrisies of the system head-on or by working surreptitiously inside it.

Tough questions over what to do sit at the very heart of the work of the international child protection regime (Kiconco's, McMullin's and Montgomery's chapters in this volume, 5, 6 and 7, respectively, raise this point starkly). This is also an important acknowledgement, for it speaks to the difficulty that many face, both in the day-to-day and in terms of their strategic planning. It is simply not easy to make trade-off calls between poor and marginalised populations over who is more 'deserving' of limited resources. Nor is it uncomplicated to decide whether to prioritise pragmatic responses to lived difficulties in the present or long-term advocacy for large-scale change in the future which may alienate necessary allies in the present. Similarly challenging is making judgement calls when the 'right' thing to do shifts depending on one's (normative) standpoint. This is easily illustrated when it comes to children's labour and migration. Okyere's chapter (Chapter 2) and that by myself and Jo Boyden (Chapter 8) both demonstrate that some children are so poor and have such limited options that they have to work or migrate, even in difficult conditions which may cause them short- and long-term harm. But for them *not* to do so would likely cause them further harm; not only would it see them going hungry, but it may harm them psychologically by preventing them from contributing to the survival of their families. To complicate matters further, although these children recognise that their work is physically difficult or their migration hard, some may enjoy it and experience little distress from engaging with it. Yet for advocates committed to a world where all children matter and work and migration should be 'adult-only', to accept that these children work or migrate is to tacitly condone the injustice of their having to do so, as well as to imperil the ideals contained in international conventions saying they must not. There are no easy solutions.

* * *

So what, then, is to be done? For researchers and practitioners who have the luxury of taking critical distance, an important step is to reflect on how we deliver our message 'upwards' to those within the regime who we wish to change. Condemnation, insults and accusations will almost always trigger an emotional shut-down on the part of those we are trying to reach. Likewise, simply telling people that they are wrong. This is because openness to feedback typically requires *trust*. And the building of trust requires genuine, non-judgemental connection, which is founded on mutual understanding of each other's (good) intentions (Rosenberg, 1999).

The editors of this book have seen the power of this first-hand. Within the community of actors working on child labour, conflict has been the order of the day for the past few decades. Institutions such as the ILO maintain that children's rights can best be advanced by promoting Minimum Age legislation, while researchers, child-centred NGOs and working children's movements all know that such legislation often leads to perverse unintended consequences (see Chapters 2–4 and 8 in this volume). Although not a simple disagreement, the pattern of communication around it has led each side to accuse the other of 'not getting it' and of bad faith. In 2017, we were part of a team that sought to broker a détente between them in the hope that better relations might at least shift things in a more positive direction. This involved bringing representatives of all sides together using Convergent Facilitation, which is a process that supports people to build trust and mutual understanding by identifying the underlying shared goals hidden within their seemingly irreconcilable viewpoints (Kashtan, 2016, 2020).[1] It is no exaggeration to say that the process can be transformative—in our case it led to the establishment of collaborative working groups to think through how to overcome systemic failures around child labour without threatening the integrity of the child protection regime itself. Although this breakthrough has been insufficient to trigger a fundamental overhaul of the system, it has led to a number of important initiatives, which themselves have system-altering potential. For example, one group comprising donors,

---

[1] Convergent Facilitation works by listing the core positions that people hold, in particular those which are a source of conflict with others. Then, as a group, people are encouraged to dig 'inside' these in order to identify other non-controversial positions that both capture the essence of the original position and are worded in terms agreeable to everyone.

critical NGOs and academics is presently running a large-scale trial of an alternative approach to addressing child labour, working in bottom-up fashion using participatory action research and unconditional cash transfers and seeking to scale findings through high-level political advocacy. The creation of trust is therefore a vital step in fostering openness on the part of child protection actors to receive feedback *and* attempts on the part of critics to deliver that feedback with care; in turn, this can open previously closed doors.

But this example is not simply about how one communicates. It also points to the need for *strategic* engagement on the part of those wishing to change the way that the international child protection regime works. Evidently, it is not enough just to document its problems and then assume that the information will automatically lead to change. Systems are complex and power structures deeply entrenched. Change will therefore require the hard work of identifying leverage points and applying coordinated pressure to them. This, in turn, will require careful analysis and collective organisation (Green, 2016). Who occupies key nodal positions within particular structures and how can they be influenced? Which alliances need to be made across constituencies to affect a change in core narratives? What public campaigns can delegitimise current approaches and promote alternatives? Which alternatives can be built and how can they be nurtured and shared? Can feedback loops be created to alter the information flow within the system? What of new agreements around system *purpose*—is the point of the regime simply to advance issue-based responses to particular ills or to promote child well-being *in general*? With time dedicated to thinking through such difficult questions, academics in particular are well-placed to collaborate with progressive practitioners in strategic forms of advocacy around them.

However, it is just as vital that progressive energy be channelled horizontally and 'downwards', in solidarity with those who are typically acted on by the child protection regime—namely children and their communities, particularly in the Global South. Attempting to persuade those in positions of power to change will never be enough; it is essential to support resistance, to build counter-power, and to nurture alternatives. On the first two points, the task is relatively clear: for anyone who can, decry the failings of the regime as loudly and widely as possible, while celebrating and supporting the efforts of ordinary people to refuse and resist (for example, in the ways that Okyere notes in Chapter 2). In this, as ever, getting organised is important. Working children, their associations and their allies provide a powerful example of how and why. Jessica Taft's chapter in this volume (Chapter 3) shows that these associations can be sources of mutual support, learning, skills development, emotional growth and, in the end, political pressure. Manfred Liebel is perhaps their most celebrated scribe and he has documented at length the ways in which, in South America, their pressure has led certain governments to turn away from the abolitionist anti-child work stance of the ILO and towards legislation protective of child workers (Liebel, 2012; see also Hanson & Niewenhuys, 2012). In our view, it is vital to support such initiatives and we are heartened that even certain major NGOs have adopted heterodox positions in doing so (with *Terre des Hommes* the most notable and successful example). Much more needs to be done in this vein to support those who resist and to co-build their counter-power.

Most pressingly, of course, these efforts need to target the climate crisis, in the face of which millions of children around the world have begun regularly taking to the streets. Climate change is *the* existential threat we all face and day-by-day it becomes more apparent and urgent that we all mobilise in response to it. In this, the child protection regime is no different. Climate chaos, perhaps more than anything, is a child rights and child protection issue, manifesting intergenerational injustice in the starkest of ways and calling on everybody to recognise that the seeds of inaction today will be reaped as a bitter harvest by our children and their children in the tomorrows to come. It is vital therefore that the child protection regime respond; indeed, it should arguably be dedicating considerable portions of its not insignificant resources to doing so already, primarily in solidarity with the marching children, as *colaboradores*, in the mould of those documented in Chapter 3. If the regime tarries in making this decision, then for those of us keen to shift it in more progressive directions, the task is clear: get behind the children who are taking matters into their own hands in the streets and support those heterodox institutions already building their counter-power and growing their resistance.

This relates to our third point—nurturing alternatives. These are important not only for their own sake but also for their potential as seeds of large-scale change. Danny Burns and Stuart Worsley explain how in their important application of complexity theory to development studies and social change. Claiming that the old 'Logframe model' of development misunderstands the intricacy of the social world (in that it wrongly assumes that change happens in cause-effect fashion, with the selection of the right 'inputs' being followed automatically by the right change 'outputs'), they argue instead for using the concept of 'attractors':

> Attractors are an important concept in complexity theory. They explain the ways in which social relationships shift from one equilibrium point to another. In complexity theory the social landscape is made up of ideas or positions or activities around which people and activity are centred. [These can be understood as] 'stable and coherent patterns of thought and behaviour'. (2015, p. 27)

Attractors work by pulling people towards new ideas, positions and activities, forming the nucleus of a new equilibrium that eventually replaces the old. In their complexity-inspired model of change, Burns and Worsley (2015) see the nurturing of successful alternatives to the hegemonic way of doing things in terms of building these attractors. In their view, the key to sustainable large-scale change is to build these attractors in ways that embed participation, learning and ownership, and then to nurture them with strategically cultivated networks of support. In terms of the child protection regime, we can understand this less as building the new on the ashes of the old and more as building the new alongside and with a view to replacing the old, once its obsolescence has clearly been demonstrated.

* * *

Ultimately, as the subtitle of this book suggests, we believe that international child protection has to become more political and more participatory if it is to more regularly benefit poor and marginalised children and their communities. In this final word I will underline why. Needless to say, scholars as well as practitioners can and should take steps in this direction. When the stakes are so high, neutrality is not an option.

Participation matters for practical and ethical reasons. In practical terms, the key issue is that no matter how well intentioned we are, we are unlikely to be able to understand the nuances of another's circumstances sufficiently well to be able to build appropriate interventions without them. Effectiveness therefore demands that interventions be developed collaboratively, with the meaningful participation of beneficiaries. This also matters for sustainability, since we know from psychological research that people are more likely to be satisfied and take ownership of decisions that affect them if they are included in the process of making them.

Yet the ethics of this are even more compelling. As we know, most development work and most social policy, including child protection, happens in top-down fashion. And at times, the consequences of this can be tragic—'collateral damage' is the term that many of our colleagues use, and, as this book has shown, many of us have stories of interventions gone wrong as a result of the distance between their architects and their targets. The avoidance of harm therefore requires us to adopt more participatory approaches. As, indeed, does a commitment to equality. At the heart of the push for child participation is the commitment to children's social personhood, to their citizenship, and thus to their right to be consulted and included in all matters concerning them, as the CRC articulates so forcefully. In the inimitable words of indigenous Australian activist, Lilla Watson, 'If you have come to help me then you are wasting your time, but if you have come because your liberation is bound up with mine, then let us work together'. This, in the end, is where participation marks the difference between charity and solidarity.

Solidarity requires us to get political. Although mainstream child protection and wider child rights discourse explains the problems that children face as consequences of abstract concepts such as poverty or culture, the reality is that all social issues (including climate breakdown or the manifold injustices and inequities made stark by the ongoing Covid crisis) are ultimately human-made and result from political decisions over the distribution of rights and resources. This has been made repeatedly clear throughout this book. And changing this reality means changing the rules of the global game to ensure that everyone everywhere possesses the necessary minimum to live flourishing lives in sustainable ways. Plenty of our practitioner colleagues know this. The problem however is that political and funding constraints often prevent them from speaking out about it. In the words of Nina, a senior UN employee that I interviewed in 2011: 'Stories about…political-economic injustice simply don't sell. It's suffering that sells…. You have to be sexy to raise money, and [things like] trafficking or slavery are sexy'. This results in political narratives that simplify complex patterns of causality and avoid the inconvenient truths about power and its concentration. To achieve the Sustainable Development Goals and more broadly push our world towards greater equity and social justice, we will require something very different indeed. And this requires of practitioners and institutions within the child protection field to be bold, to put themselves on the line, and to speak truth to power. It is time to get political.

REFERENCES

Berman, M. (1982). *All that is solid melts into air: The experience of modernity.* Verso Books.
Bourdillon, M., Levison, D., Myers, W., & White, B. (2011). *Rights and wrongs of children's work.* Rutgers University Press.
Burns, D., & Worsley, S. (2015). *Navigating complexity in international development: Facilitating sustainable change at scale.* Practical Action Publishing.
Dauvergne, P., & LeBaron, G. (2014). *Protest Inc.: The corporatization of activism.* Polity Press.
Dottridge, M., and The Global Alliance Against Trafficking in Women (GAATW). (2007). *Collateral damage: The impact of anti-trafficking measures on human rights around the world.* GAATW.
Escobar, A. (1994). *Encountering development: The making and unmaking of the third world.* Princeton University Press.
Green, D. (2016). *How change happens.* OXFAM and Oxford University Press.
Hanson, K., & Niewenhuys, O. (2012). Introduction. In K. Hanson & O. Niewenhuys (Eds.), *Reconceptualizing children's rights in international development: Living rights, social justice, translations* (pp. 225–249). Cambridge University Press.
Howard, N. (2016). *Child trafficking, youth labour mobility, and the politics of protection.* Palgrave Macmillan.
Kashtan, M. (2016). A blueprint for collaborative lawmaking. *Interdisciplinary Journal of Partnership Studies, 3*(1), 1–17.
Kashtan, M. (2020). *The highest common denominator: Using convergent facilitation to reach breakthrough collaborative decisions.* The Fearless Heart Publications.
Li, T. (2007). *The will to improve: Governmentality, development, and the practice of politics.* Duke University Press.
Liebel, M. (2012). Do children have a right to work? Working children's movements in the struggle for social justice. In K. Hanson & O. Niewenhuys (Eds.), *Reconceptualizing children's rights in international development: Living rights, social justice, translations* (pp. 225–249). Cambridge University Press.
Ramalingam, B. (2013). *Aid on the edge of Chaos.* Oxford University Press.
Rosenberg, M. (1999). *Nonviolent communication: A language of life.* Puddledancer Press.
Scott, J. C. (1998). *Seeing like a State: How certain schemes to improve the human condition have failed.* Yale University Press.

Postscript: What Is Wrong with International Child Protection and What Changes Are Needed?

Jo Boyden

BACKGROUND

This chapter draws, in part, on my experience as a researcher who has studied a range of child protection issues in a number of countries, as well as the literature I have reviewed in order to inform and help guide that research. It also reflects findings from Young Lives, a multidisciplinary mixed-methods longitudinal study of child poverty that I led from 2005 to 2019. Young Lives has been recording the experiences, perspectives and outcomes of 12,000 boys and girls in Ethiopia, India, Peru and Vietnam for over 15 years. The study sample comprises equal numbers of boys and girls from over 80 rural and urban locations and is diverse in terms of household economic status and social determinants

---

J. Boyden (✉)
Department of International Development, University of Oxford, Oxford, UK
e-mail: jo.boyden@qeh.ox.ac.uk

© The Author(s), under exclusive license to Springer Nature Switzerland AG 2022
N. Howard and S. Okyere (eds.), *International Child Protection*, Palgrave Studies on Children and Development,
https://doi.org/10.1007/978-3-030-78763-9_11

such as ethnicity, maternal language, religion and caste. This makes it possible to compare the varied experiences, trajectories and outcomes of different groups of children in the four countries, while also examining between-country differences. The research employs an ecological life-course framework, which tracks the many changing influences on children's well-being and development as they transition from early childhood, through middle childhood to early adulthood. These influences range from macro factors operating at community and school levels, to those that are more proximal, and function at household, parental and individual child levels. They include exposure to extreme weather events, changes in policy and terms of trade, parental education, service access, family crises, aspirations and decision-making and many other factors besides.

Research and monitoring by Young Lives and many other sources shows that there have been remarkable advances in children's survival, development and well-being in the last three decades, even in some of the world's poorest countries. Particularly striking has been the progress in infant and under-5 survival, which reflects unexpectedly high levels of economic growth and associated investment in infrastructure, water and sanitation, as well as improved health and nutrition. Access to primary schooling has also risen at impressive rates and attendance is now near universal in the majority of countries, while enrolment at the secondary level is increasing steadily. Though at one time girls generally lagged behind boys in school access, their attendance rates have often climbed faster than those of boys, so that gender parity has now been achieved in numerous locations, especially at the primary level. The spread of education has resulted in a dramatic upsurge in literacy and numeracy among boys and girls, producing a generation that is not just healthier, but also far better informed and with far higher social aspirations than previous generations.

These developments owe much to the momentum generated around the UN Convention on the Rights of the Child (CRC) and Millennium Development Goals (MDGs). Highlighting for the first time the numerous challenges children face globally, the CRC in particular has led to a substantial increase in child-focused policies and programmes at international, national and sub-national levels across rich and poor countries alike. It embodies several novel features that provide important foundations for the international child protection regime. In this sense, the CRC holds much promise in terms of safeguarding children against risk. Most significant is the integration of child protection with rights to provision and participation. This holistic view provides a basis for multi-sectoral and multi-level interventions in which the young may potentially have a significant role. The treaty identifies numerous circumstances that represent a risk to children, from the most immediate personal jeopardies experienced through familial abuse and neglect, to major macro-level violations associated with armed violence, forced migration and other structural forces. In doing so, it vastly expands the range of policy and intervention beyond the bounds of earlier approaches that were largely confined to health, education and social welfare. Its uniquely child-centred standpoint also requires that children's perspectives and best interests be a primary consideration in all decisions affecting them, allowing for protection systems that are not just responsive to and respectful of the young but also fully grounded in their lived realities.

The international child protection regime draws heavily on the conceptualisation of children, childhood and children's rights embodied in the CRC. However, in doing so it brings to light some of the contradictions at the heart of the treaty. Overall, protection practice lays greater emphasis on children as passive victims of circumstances beyond their control and thus objects of intervention—than participants in their own protection, or in other words, subjects of rights. This tendency has much to do with the historical origins of the field and of the CRC itself. While the treaty was intended to offer a universal framework, it is in reality an artefact of a particular Euro-American historical-cultural view, the treaty drafting having been led by lawyers and advocates based in the Global North. Today, as Hart's chapter most painfully demonstrates (Chapter 9), most of the funding and power in international child protection remains concentrated in international organisations headquartered in the North, their field operations in low- and middle-income countries staffed by expatriates and local elites who largely concur with its Euro-American ideals. Likewise, most of the evidence on child development, the kinds of risks children experience, the protective mechanisms they access and the developmental and well-being outcomes of risk exposure draws on research with children in the North (Bornstein et al., 2012). As a result, Euro-American understandings, objectives and standards consistently prevail in child protection systems globally—shaping what is considered a threat to children, what is understood to protect them and which safeguarding structures and processes should be laid down for the young in situations of adversity.

As has been argued throughout this book, in the Euro-American way of thinking that undergirds the child protection regime, children are inherently needy and vulnerable and must strive to achieve the competencies expected of them as adults. Thus, childhood is taken to be an extended period of dependence and socialisation into adulthood during which the institutions of family and school provide nurture, care and guidance. These ideas provide the primary justification for a separate human rights treaty tailored to meet children's specific needs. At the same time, the advance of global capitalism and white-collar employment has led to certain outcomes for children being valued more highly than are others and individual autonomy, competitiveness in, and adaptation to the modern market economy taking precedence over collective responsibility and mutuality (Hart & Boyden, 2018). Increasingly, 'human capital formation' (literacy, numeracy and other cognitive competencies and personality traits such as grit or perseverance of effort and motivation to achieving long-term objectives) takes priority over the learning of everyday practical and pro-social skills. As these values have spread, so children have become progressively more contained in schools and excluded from the routines of community life and the workplace. In turn, as children have disengaged from the trials and tribulations of the everyday, they have become ever more reliant on the family and organs of state to defend them against risk.

Given the perception of children as vulnerably dependent, many regard keeping them away from peril as the only moral stance. Thus, preventative interventions focus on eliminating specific social practices and/or situations deemed exploitative, abusive or otherwise harmful to the young. Intervention modalities include a combination of legal measures prohibiting such practices and circumstances, sanctions against perpetrators, employed as both deterrent and penalty, and advocacy campaigns aimed at alerting the public to the dangers and changing attitudes and behaviour. Remedies include the rescue of children trapped in dangerous situations such as war zones or trafficking rings, and rehabilitation measures in support of victims, for example, psychosocial support and catch-up schooling. A smaller though important proportion of initiatives employ a very different approach, which centres on children's empowerment, collective organisation and self-help.

Conceptual and Implementation Limitations of Child Protection

Notwithstanding the many positive features of the CRC, international child protection policies and interventions have a chequered history. This is despite the accumulation of experience in child protection going back to at least the fifteenth century and the establishment of the Ospedale degli Innocenti (Hospital of the Innocents) for abandoned and orphaned children in Florence, Italy. Indeed, reflecting on their engagement with the field over many years, Michael Bourdillon and William Myers (2012 and Chapter 4 in this volume) contend that it has seriously failed children, repeatedly doing them more harm than good.

There are a number of reasons for these shortcomings. Possibly most important are the enormous challenges involved. The sorry state of current policy and practice has, in part at least, to do with the multi-faceted nature and sheer scale and complexity of risks to children the field contends with and the fact that these risks are present in all settings and at all societal levels, from the most proximate to the most distant. When it comes to interpersonal practices like abuse, violence and exploitation, these are far less amenable to intervention than are the areas of life addressed by sectors such as education and health (although we are seeing the limitations of many health systems in the response to the ongoing Coronavirus pandemic). One reason for this is that activities and behaviours that deviate from local norms about what is acceptable for and what is harmful to the young are often hidden from public view, to prevent discovery, and this greatly hampers detection. On the other hand, customary codes of belief and practice commonly reinforce and replicate deep-seated power structures, so that change efforts come up against strong personal and collective interests and risk disrupting children's social worlds. But often the greater problem is that the underlying drivers of risk have their origins in macro-level structures and processes that are thought to be beyond the remit of the child protection regime, which, as has been argued in this book, tends to concern itself technically and somewhat a-politically with symptoms rather than causes.

However, shortcomings in policy and practice do not simply derive from the challenging nature of risk, since the field is also cluttered with conceptual and practical weaknesses. In terms of application, child protection involves diverse disciplines and arenas of expertise—including the developmental sciences, social work, law, sociology, paediatrics, psychology, neuroscience and anthropology—this resulting in widely divergent epistemological paradigms, which creates confusion and even contestation in the application to practice. One example of this is the clash between international agencies involved in supporting the 100,000 or so orphaned and abandoned children found languishing in state orphanages in Romania following the fall of President Nicolae Ceauşescu. Whereas some agencies favoured specialised professional intervention, on the grounds that the children were living in inhumane conditions and had suffered significant psychological, emotional, social and physical harm, others backed community options as being more sustainable and culturally appropriate and more likely to secure children's reintegration into society. Thus, while some agencies strove to improve the orphanages through staff capacity building, infrastructure development and the like, others were intent on closing them down and establishing alternative care in local communities, while others still promoted inter-country adoption as the best solution. Serious disagreement among practitioners over the most appropriate form of care for children separated from their families continues to this day.

The CRC awards equal weight to children's political-economic and civil rights and their socio-cultural rights in all respects. Yet organisations involved in the international child protection regime are generally extremely reluctant to tackle the political-economic dimensions of risk, particularly when it involves confronting political actors over their protection failings. This is complicated by the fact that adherence to the CRC has awarded the state a central role as the chief duty bearer in child protection. The institutional arrangements provided by the CRC imply a high degree of self-regulation by States Parties. The Committee on the Rights of the Child is charged with holding them to account, by regularly monitoring their performance and offering guidance in implementation. However, even though the Committee has the power to investigate, rebuke and call for sanctions against governments that commit infractions, it lacks the means to enforce compliance. Meanwhile, UNICEF's role as custodian of children's political-economic and civil rights is to a significant extent compromised by the fact that, as a bilateral organisation, it is required to partner with government.

In this sense, the CRC holds true to an established Euro-American tradition whereby the organs of the state—social welfare institutions, courts of law, administrative and legislative bodies—have primacy over all other bodies and institutions in the care and protection of children who cannot rely on functional family and community structures. However, automatic resort to state bodies somewhat goes against the evidence that government policies and programmes have often themselves been sources of harm. Indeed, over the centuries a significant proportion of Euro-American state systems that were set up seemingly to care for children were founded on openly racist or misogynist norms that were abusive towards their young charges. Examples include the forced removal by the government in Australia of children of mixed descent from Aboriginal communities and families and their placement in church-run missions, and in the UK the forced removal and adoption of children of unmarried mothers. And the UK's Independent Inquiry into Child Sexual Abuse established to examine how the country's institutions handled their duty of care to protect children from sexual abuse has been in perpetual disarray since its creation in 2014. Continued breaches against children cared for by state and religious institutions have led to the development of a new community of practice devoted to investigating claims of violations against children and securing reparation (Sköld & Swain, 2015). Similarly, in fragile or authoritarian states and in countries engaged in civil or international conflicts children are regularly forcibly detained, recruited into the military, attacked and even executed by organs of the state, as McMullin's contribution here, Chapter 6, attests.

Beyond the more visible and flagrant violations are the numerous 'everyday' injustices governments either allow or actively perpetuate, particularly by failing to prevent or tackle social exclusion and inequality. The distribution of risk across population groups and locations is seldom a matter of chance and in practically all societies certain groups of children are affected far more consistently than are others, whether due to socio-cultural or political-economic factors or the interaction of the two. These children tend to experience multiple intersecting disadvantages owing to their minority social status—for example their gender or sexual orientation, or because they belong to a minority ethnic, religious, or language group, or a low caste—and live in households and communities that are poor, lacking quality services and located in marginal geographic regions. Social exclusion acts together with, exacerbates and is exacerbated by poverty and inequality, greatly limiting the options open to children and their families, in terms of livelihoods, supportive social networks, institutional access and the like. This, in turn, renders children more susceptible to exploitation, abuse and other harmful circumstances and practices.

Paradoxically given the primacy awarded to the state under the CRC, in the three decades since the treaty was adopted the strengthening of neoliberal governance across many parts of the globe has debilitated already weak systems of protection. There has been a progressive consolidation of wealth and power in the hands of elites, depressed wage growth among the majority, informalisation of labour markets and substantial public spending cuts, much of which has taken place even in the context of economic growth (Hart & Boyden, 2018). These trends have led to mounting disparities between more privileged and poorer populations and increasing need for child protection, both at a time when the public sector is less well-resourced and less able to respond. Sustaining government services with diminishing budgets has often come at the cost of access and quality for children from the poorest and least powerful sections of the population. In some countries, services have been increasingly marketised as the public sector has retreated, so that significant portions of early childhood development, education and health care provision has been privatised, further intensifying disparities between children based on wealth.

Partly as a consequence of public sector retreat and also as a corollary to the disregard of the political-economic origins of risk, neoliberal governance has overseen the reconfiguring of children from a population for which the nation or society bears a collective responsibility to mere individuals who are the concern of their families (Hart & Boyden, 2018). This trend is consistent with a rising tendency to responsibilise citizens as both the primary perpetrators of risk to children and their primary protectors, which in turn allows a growing emphasis on the pathological behaviours of individuals and perceived harms of societal practices to the neglect of inequitable or repressive political regimes (cf. also Hart, Chapter 9, this volume). At the same time, the modality of child protection has begun to shift away from service provision towards attitudinal and behavioural change and the identification and punishment of perpetrators. In other words, in recent decades the thrust of child protection internationally has been twofold: a strong focus on the social-cultural drivers of risk and on eliminating traditional practices such as child and forced marriage and female circumcision; and attention to risks more proximal to the child, such as familial abuse and neglect, while ignoring those with more distant roots.

When addressing the socio-cultural origins of risk, policymakers, practitioners and child advocates have had to balance the commitment to universal applicability that lies at the heart of the CRC and the values and norms that prevail in specific contexts. This is far from easy. Social and cultural change involves judgements about what is harmful to, and what is good for, children. In the event, while some agencies, policies and measures certainly do work with local ideas, institutions and processes, many hold on to the Euro-American conception of the child, giving little credence to alternative beliefs. This accounts for the common focus on eliminating patriarchal norms and practices that are customary in many cultural contexts, together with the related assumption prevailing in many circles that girls have a greater need of protection than do boys. Thus the emphasis on children's (or girls') empowerment as the vehicle for overcoming adversity and realising modern ideals of individual autonomy and individual rights. Although the Euro-American way of thinking and the institutional and social practices this perpetuates within the international child protection regime may appear both reasonable and appropriate to practitioners, its unquestioning application in contexts where ideas about childhood and conditions for children are very different, and the frequent failure to engage with local cultural logics, means that law enforcement, social work and other agents commonly find themselves in opposition to children, their families and communities. Moreover, cultural change efforts may jeopardise other rights, such as those connected with children's right to freedom of thought, belief, language and religion and the protection and preservation of identity.

The bias resulting from implementing the Euro-American way of thinking can be so pervasive that advocates and practitioners sometimes fail to recognise when this leads to implementation shortcomings. An example repeatedly discussed in this book is the conviction that work is an intrinsic threat to children's development and well-being, whereas school education—as a fundamental right—is invariably beneficial. Until recently, unquestioning faith in schooling in international circles led to a lack of acknowledgement of the extremely poor quality of many education systems or the threats to children posed by hostile school environments in which corporal punishment and bullying are normalised. It is only in the last few years that practitioners and policymakers have finally come to accept that there is a learning crisis across the majority of low- and middle-income countries. On the other hand, when children under a specified age are excluded from work, this can intensify household poverty and fracture intergenerational interdependence. Also, while facilitating children's education is frequently one of the objectives of prohibiting child work, in circumstances of poverty, school attendance may not be a realistic alternative. Boys and girls removed from one job may have no choice but to seek employment elsewhere. This commonly entails shifting into enterprises that are more difficult to scrutinise, a circumstance that can significantly heighten vulnerability to physical hazard and exploitation by unscrupulous employers. Above all, punitive approaches to children's work fail to recognise the developmental value it often involves, for example, the building of important life skills. Euro-American ideas about children's work proved particularly difficult for African governments to accommodate. Thus, the 1990 African Charter on the Rights and Welfare of the Child has a rather different vision, since it assigns children responsibilities as well as rights.

When it applies to child protection, social and cultural change also involves intervening in important affective relationships, frequently with unknown outcomes. It may of course be that these relationships are the main source of threat to children. But more often than not they are the first line of defence. Though many child protection practitioners and advocates are committed to operating in partnership with families, communities and children, they generally work from the premise that 'outsiders', social workers, psychologists and other professionals, have greater insight into risk concerns and expertise around children's well-being and development. Such assumptions often fail to take account of the extent to which children's risk exposure and risk responses are mediated and/or moderated by the social relations, institutions and processes in which their lives are embedded, as Vanessa Pupavac (2001) highlights:

> The impulse for the institutionalisation of children's rights is the vulnerability and incapacity of children. Inherent in children's rights is the need for advocacy on behalf of the child.... The overall impact of children's rights is to empower outside professionals to represent the interests of the child, displacing the child's family as advocates of the child's interests. (p. 100)

Thus, separating children from danger by allowing professionals to assume responsibility for their care can dismantle intricate and vital systems of social support.

What Should Be Done?

The problems described above stem primarily from the fact that the people and processes articulating, interpreting and applying rights and policies intended to protect children are unaccountable for the results of their decisions in children's lives. They get away even with policies shown to harm children because there is nobody and no mechanism in place to flag and stop them. Therefore, the top priority action must be to hold all child rights and protection policies accountable for their outcomes for children. This requires that all policies be evidence-based; that decisions about how to intervene in the lives of children be decentralised to a level where local context can be taken into consideration; and that children old enough to speak and understand, as well as their families and communities, have ample chance to participate in decisions about their protection. All three are necessary; let us consider them in order.

Make Policy Evidence-Based

Recognition of the complexity, diversity and interactions of risks confronted by children makes it imperative to understand what is being dealt with before intervening. But the many child protection systems now in place do not understand very much. As described above, international child rights and protection instruments are largely devised and phrased as statements of agreed-to norms, these representing values held by the negotiators. Being values-based, they make little effort to understand even the most important facts shaping the realities of children whose lives they impact. Experience shows that a purely rules-based system based only on the values of the powerful tends towards abuses of power that afflict the powerless. The only corrective is to ensure that rules based on values are monitored and held accountable for their consequences in the lives of children; in the abstract language of ethics, a currently deontological system needs to be made more consequentialist. This entails understanding children's rights not as ends merely to be complied with, but as instruments serving the end purpose of survival and flourishing, against which their articulation, interpretation and application must be measured, judged and modified as necessary.

All child protection policies should be based both on prior empirical research establishing through clear evidence the need for such policies and on evaluative research revealing to what extent their implementation has met that need. There should be no such thing as a child protection policy that is not accountable, through systematically collected evidence, for both its need and its consequences for the children it affects. Recent advances in the development of child well-being indicators, longitudinal study methods and data management and analysis now make it possible to monitor the physical, mental and social development of children, individually or in sample groups, from infancy through adolescence to ensure that they survive and thrive, catching and correcting many problems as they arise and before they become serious threats.

Empower Families and Communities as the First Line of Child Protection, and Provide a Supportive Economic and Social Environment for Them

Since families are the first and most dependable line of protection for most children, child protection policy should as a high priority seek to ensure they are able and equipped to fulfil that responsibility. UNCRC Article 27 calls on States Parties to 'take appropriate measures to assist parents and others responsible for the child...and shall in case of need provide material assistance and support programmes'. Recent research, including from Young Lives, strongly suggests that economic and social policies and services designed to support families, rather than just focusing on children, effectively and efficiently support the well-being of children. Such programmes are most effective when decisions are decentralised to address the specifics of local contexts, allowing families to decide how resources are best spent to meet their particular situation and needs. Moving away from the current public policy and programme emphasis on remedial interventions directly in the lives of children and towards a more sustainable social and economic environment suggests a complete revamp of the architecture of child protection. It begins by tackling the social, political and economic conditions of risk, which, as described above, are in much of the world generated at least in part by gross political, economic, social and cultural inequality and injustice. The state, which is supposedly responsible for ensuring that children's survival and development needs are met, is in much of the world itself an important source of children's risk. A logical first step is to reduce the child risk conditions actually caused by the state. That includes reducing entrenched inequalities and establishing democratic governance that facilitates the representation and participation of families and communities directly responsible as the first line of protection of their children.

Fashioning an enabling environment for children implies a different approach to the understanding of risk and the governance of child protection than now predominates. While it remains necessary to attend to threats proximal to the child, it is equally necessary to recognise the global dimensions of risk and the interdependence of sub-national, national and international responses to it. Increasingly, children's well-being and protection rely on activities, decisions, events and institutions situated well beyond national borders. At the same time, national and sub-national actors lack the power to secure children's interests without recourse to supra-national forces and resources. For example, conditions of international trade in much of the Global South systematically disadvantage small-scale producers and manual workers to the extent that they are unable on their own to provide their children with even rudimentary opportunities and resources. In such cases, intervening in unfair terms of trade would in the long-run benefit children and reduce their risk much more than providing welfare and other compensatory services to the poor and their children. Many hope that the much celebrated Sustainable Development Goals (SDGs), with their 169 concrete targets and 232 progress indicators, will provide a solid step in the direction of a more just and sustainable world economy that will eventually benefit children. However, it must also be recognised that each of the last three UN Secretaries-General has repeatedly called attention to the growing climate emergency as the greatest collective crisis ever faced by humanity and the greatest threat to the survival and well-being of its children. Despite ample and repeated warnings, the world's political and economic system lags badly in addressing this growing emergency, and none of even the advanced countries are, as of this writing, meeting their promised greenhouse gas emissions goals, let alone surpassing them as would be necessary to hold expected global warming to under the maximum catastrophe threshold of 2 °C.

In essence, the older half of the world's population is maintaining its comfort and prosperity by condemning the younger half to a badly degraded planet and future prospects. Also, at the time of this writing, a growing world movement of fearful children and youth is protesting in the streets to pressure recalcitrant governments to take even the minimum necessary action to protect their lives and future. The good faith of governments in protecting children could not be more questionable than it is at this moment. The children, families and communities of the poorest and most threatened parts of the globe appear, at least so far, to be pretty much on their own. Despite positive hopes for the SDGs and eventually saving the world from the worst ravages of climate collapse, a dose of hard realism is very much in order.

Make Children Agents of Their Own Lives

Risk cannot be definitively abolished, and the young cannot be inoculated against peril through rescue, rehabilitation or any other type of outside intervention. Thus, children's interests are better served when they are able, and in fact encouraged, to participate in their own protection. There are two important reasons for this. First, there is evidence that learning how to recognise, manage and overcome risk can itself be developmental, building resilience (Rutter, 2012), whereas shying away from danger does not necessarily reduce vulnerability. If risk is an inevitable part of life, then accountability to children requires building their resilience to deal with it. Beyond developing their individual confidence and self-efficacy, building resilience may well include developing children's collective organisation and advocacy, much in the way that Jessica Taft argues in Chapter 3. Second, involving young people in their own protection can also significantly improve intervention effectiveness since boys and girls commonly bring unique insights and resources to bear on both their problems and the solutions to them. However, creating an enabling environment for children implies a far greater onus on states, civil society and the private sector to ensure that they are fully accountable to children. In addition to building meaningful partnerships between children and adults and the state, opening up accessible channels of communication with children and youth and taking account of their perspectives enhances children's knowledge and awareness of issues relevant to their protection. It also guarantees that they can access systems of referral and heightens their ability to contribute actively to the effectiveness of protection systems. That said, such channels must be appropriate to children's means, age, gender, culture and interests, be tailored to their needs and circumstances, and be available through technologies and in locations and times that maximise the access of all, especially the most disadvantaged.

As indicated above, the world's children and youth, faced by increasing economic and climate threats (not to mention the ongoing Coronavirus pandemic and the miserable way that is being managed in much of the world), and disillusioned by the paralysis of their elders in protecting them, are now stepping forward to take their future into their own hands. The old systems and notions of child protection are failing them, and now they must, at early ages, become agents of their own lives, protecting their own interests and futures and those of their children to come. In so doing they are demonstrating their capacity for self-organisation, advocacy and leadership in pursuit of personal and collective objectives. That said, the question remains as to whether adults and adult institutions are prepared to accept the legitimacy of children's role in advocating on their own behalf, in particular in the context of climate emergency. What will be the judgement of powerful adults concerning children's competence and participatory rights as citizens and political subjects with their own generational interests to defend? Will they accept the burgeoning movement of the young to press their own interests and agenda? In a bid to be taken seriously as citizens, the initiative is now with children and youth, but we have yet to see the response from adults. Will they permit the young to act as agents of their own protection, or will they move to suppress the attempt, perhaps even with the heavy hand of violence? If States Parties will not be accountable to children and youth, even to save their lives and futures in the face of the greatest crisis humanity has ever faced, will they let the young be accountable to themselves, and perhaps to the rest of humanity in the attempt to save it? For its part, the international child protection regime faces a stark choice—continue to be part of the problem or stand in solidarity with children towards the solution.

References

Bornstein, M. H., Britto, P. R., Nonoyama-Tarumi, Y., Ota, Y., Petrovic, O., & Putnick, D. L. (2012). Child development in developing countries. *Child Development*, 83(1), 16–31.

Hart, J., & Boyden, J. (2018). Childhood (re)materialized: Bringing political economy into the field. In S. Spyrou, S. Rosen, & D. Cook, D. (Eds.), *Reimagining childhood studies*. Bloomsbury Academic.

Myers, W., & Bourdillon, M. (2012). Introduction: Development, children, and protection. *Development in Practice*, 22(4), 437–447.

Pupavac, V. (2001). Misanthropy without borders: The international children's rights regime. *Disasters*, 25, 95–112.

Rutter, M. (2012). Resilience as a dynamic concept. *Development and Psychopathology*, 24, 335–344.

Sköld, J., & Swain, S. (Eds.). (2015). *Apologies and the legacy of abuse of children in care*. Palgrave Macmillan.
UNICEF. (n.d.). *UNICEF Data: Monitoring the situation of children and women*. https://data.unicef.org/children-sustainable-development-goals
United Nations. (2015). *Transforming our world: The 2030 Agenda for Sustainable Development*. https://sustainabledevelopment.un.org/post2015/transformingourworld

Index

A
abandon, 176, 180
abducted, 13, 134
abductions, 104
abolition, 7, 220
abusing, 160
academia, 170
academics, 8, 98
acceded, 174
accelerated, 23
access, 202
accountability, 18, 20, 191
accusations, 218
Acholi, 113
Acholiland, 103
activist, 161
actors, 4, 216
address, 197
ad hoc, 197
adolescents, 11
adoption, 231
adult-child, 73
adulthood, 11, 116

adultism, 68
advancement, 179
adventure, 136
adverse, 3, 174
adversity, 174
advocacy, 59, 86, 131, 206
Aegean Sea, 17
affect, 89
affection, 158
affective commitment, 176
affluent, 8
Afghanistan, 8, 16
African, 139
African Studies, 30
age, 7
age-appropriate behaviour, 11
age-based hierarchies, 68
agency, 11, 78, 168, 171
age-normativity, 11
age-relatedness, 12
aggressors, 101
agriculture, 16, 85
aid, 17, 137, 190

à-la-carte, 14
alcohol, 158
alien, 158
alienating, 216
Allied forces, 190
alternative, 4
Amazon, 59
ambulant scratch-card, 174
American military, 152
amidst, 116
ammunition, 134
amplify, 67
Andes, 59
anecdotal, 160, 197
Angola, 123, 132
animals, 106
anthropology, 169, 170, 230
anti-capitalist, 69
anti-developmental, 14
anti-migration, 168
anti-mining, 70
anti-movement, 170
antisocial, 38
antithesis, 94
apolitical, 18
application, 196
apprenticeships, 43
appropriate, 125
appropriateness, 11
aptitude, 92
architecture, 4, 123
armed conflicts, 6
armed forces, 121, 122
armed groups, 18
arms, 205
arrest, 154, 201
articles, 192
articulate, 172
articulation, 171
artisanal gold mining, 16
Asia, 151
aspirations, 179

assistance, 13, 138, 196
associates, 134
assumption, 39, 169
asylum seekers, 2, 17, 196
attachment, 170, 171
attack, 201
attitudes, 5
Australia, 17, 151, 196
authoritarianism, 23
authoritative, 175
authorities, 80
autonomy, 11
avaricious, 170
awareness-raising, 149
Ayacucho, 63

B
Baan Nua, 155
baby, 173
backward, 14
backwardness, 93
baddies, 216
bail, 151
band-aid, 216
Bangkok, 153
Bangladesh, 12
banning, 43
beggars, 152
behavioural imperatives, 214
Belgium, 151
beliefs, 5
beneficiaries, 81, 124, 138, 215
Benin, 12
best interests, 81
betrothal, 172
bilateral, 125
binaries, 152
biodiversity, 69
biological, 10, 177
biological mothers, 173
birth, 175

blacksmith, 174
blanket ban, 50
blueprint, 159
Bolivia, 21
bonds, 170, 171
border control, 2
borders, 208
bottom-up, 23, 216
Bourdillon, Michael, 20
boycott, 95
Boyden, J., 12
Brazil, 5
breaking, 171, 184
bred resentment, 113
bridewealth, 109
bright academic future, 175
broker, 114, 218
brothel, 149
brutality, 207
Burmese, 154
Burmese border, 153
Burundi, 139
bush mentality/behaviour, 108
business, 8, 95, 122, 196
business as usual, 3
Butterfly Trust, 80

C
Cajamarca, 70
cajoling, 203
calendar, 12
Cambodia, 160
campaigns, 16, 148
camps, 17
Canada, 196
capable, 73
Cape Town, 130
capita, 183
capital, 182
capitalism, 216
capitalist relations, 153

capital-poor, 173
CAR, 126
care, 6, 169
career, 91
caregivers, 173
care-giving, 171, 184
carpentry, 80
cartels, 17
cash payments, 134
cash transfers, 96
cassiterite, 30
causal, 16
causes, 3
caveats, 216
central, 170, 172, 182
Centro de Culturas Indígenas del Perú (Chirapaq), 63
change, 169
cheap, 79, 154
checkpoints, 201
chequered, 229
child, 1
child-centred, 96
child domestic work, 19
childhood, 1, 2
childhood-centric instruments, 2
childhood studies, 12
child labour abolitionist, 3
child labour exploitation, 1
child labour politics, 62
child marriage, 13
child migrants, 2, 16
Child Pornography and Trafficking of Children for Sexual Purposes, 149
child prostitution, 147
child protection, 5
child protection practices, 3
child-rearing, 171
children's rights, 2
children's suffering, 71
Children and Armed Conflict, 131

244 INDEX

child rights, 2, 3
child rights violations, 2
child saving, 52
child sex tourism, 20
child slaves, 15
child soldiers, 121
Child Soldiers International, 122
child trafficking, 1, 7
child upbringing norms, 19
China, 5
Chinese migrants, 152
Chomsky, Noam, 29
chores, 180
chronically, 11, 134, 197
circumscribed, 133
citizenship, 69, 155
civilian, 122, 201
civilising, 19
claimants, 133
clean, 176
clients, 149
climate emergency, 23
cloaked, 159
coercion, 31, 38, 170
coercive, 136, 151
cognitive, 97
coherence, 214
colaboración, 65
colaboradores. *See* collaborators
collaborators, 98
collateral, 214
colonise, 201
combatants, 104, 133
combatting child trafficking, 17
commanders, 104
Committee on the Rights of the Child, 6
communalism, 69
communal tracts, 181
communication styles, 62
community, 9, 12, 16, 171
compassion, 97, 216

compatible, 96
compensation, 36
competence, 10, 78, 90, 92
complementary, 96
complex, 174
complicate, 12
comply, 19
compromised, 204
computer, 80
concentrated, 201
condemnation, 218
condone, 152, 217
confinement, 2
conflation, 169
conflict, 122, 189
conformity, 93
conjugal, 13, 104
consent, 174
consequences, 93
conservative, 12
construction, 12, 181
constructive, 171
consultants, 87
consultation, 123, 140
contained, 201
contemporary, 86, 167
contemporary importance, 169
contextual, 170
contours, 125
controversies, 194
Convention No. 182, 7
Convention on the Rights of the Child, 6
conventions, 7, 13
Convergent Facilitation, 218
conviction, 121, 128
cooks, 130
corollary, 232
corporal punishment, 130
corporations, 205
corpus of knowledge, 4
corrugated, 155

corrupting, 39
Côte d'Ivoire, 126, 173
Cotonou, 173
cotton, 182
counter-intuitive, 162
counterproductive, 20, 86, 159
countries, 17
course, 178
court, 151
crafts, 80
crimes, 138
criminalisation, 13, 121
criminals, 101, 106
crises, 92
crisis, 172, 173
critical, 159
critical distance, 218
critical thinking, 97
criticising, 113
critiques, 8, 168
crop, 182
cross-cultural contexts, 83
culpability, 138
culpable, 135
culture, 11, 90, 214
curative, 82
currency revenue, 152
custodian, 230
customarily owned, 115
customary, 171
customers, 160

D
dangerous, 15, 79, 138
dangerous chemicals, 31
daughters, 173
debilitating injury, 97
debt bonded, 156
debt regime, 69
debt relief, 53
decade, 173

decentralisation, 216
deception, 170
decision-makers, 57
Declaration of the Rights of the
  Child, 6, 189
declarations, 7
deconstruction, 136
decries, 216
decriminalise, 60
decry, 219
default defined, 170
defensive, 215
definition, 9
degrade, 69
de-legitimise, 219
deleterious, 169
deliberate, 152
delinquent, 72, 80
demobilisation, 123, 125
Democratic Republic of the Congo
  (DRC), 30, 123, 126
demolitions, 202
denial, 202
departure, 170, 173
dependence, 15, 133
depoliticises, 53
depressing, 183
descriptive statistics, 89
design, 215, 216
desirability, 125
destigmatise, 60
destitution, 16, 173
detained, 201
détente, 218
deterrence, 122
deterrent, 131
detrimental, 20, 78, 170, 184
devalue, 158
development, 1, 4, 152
develop value, 175
deviance, 48
devil's advocate, 88

diagnosis, 83, 159
dichotomy, 137, 139
dictates, 14
diffusion, 171
dignity, 59, 154
diplomatic, 183, 204
dirty minerals, 30
disability, 6, 197
disadvantage, 81
disarmament, 123
disastrous, 15
discarded, 159
disciplines, 170
disconnect, 190
discord, 198
discounts, 171
discourse, 137
discredited, 14
discrimination, 200
discursive, 168
discursive monopoly, 124
disease, 97
disempowering, 9
disenfranchised, 20
disjunctures, 3
displaced, 18, 192, 196
displacement, 16, 189
disposable, 39, 45
dispossession, 36
disruptive, 135, 174
dissenting, 214
dissociated, 11
distress, 217
divergence, 197
diverse, 12, 137
diversity, 169, 173
divorce, 173
doctrines, 89
document, 196, 206
documentary film, 30
dollar, 172
domestic, 174

domestic economies, 169
dominant, 3, 137
dominates, 106, 208
donor, 20, 191
dragging, 150
drought, 172
drug cartel, 16
duration, 125
duress, 202
dwindling, 172
dysfunction, 87

E
earn-and-learn, 78
East Jerusalem, 201
echo-chamber, 214
ecological, 226
economic, 13, 80, 161
economic justice, 84
economic reforms, 16
economy of makeshifts, 40
Ecumenical Council on Third World Tourism (ECTWT), 149
education, 2, 8, 43
effects, 96
egalitarian relationship, 58
elaborate, 106
electricity, 156
elimination, 7, 45
elite, 134
El Movimiento de Adolescentes y Niños Trabajadores Hijos de Obreros Cristianos (Movement of Working Children and Adolescents, Children of Christian Workers), 59
El Salvador, 16
Embassy, 151
emotional, 97
emotional shut-down, 218
empathy, 97

empirical, 171
empirical data, 171
empirical material, 23
employment, 7
empower, 96
encompass, 170
encumbered, 172
End Child Prostitution, 149
End Child Prostitution in Asian Tourism (ECPAT), 149
energy, 36
engage, 215
enlistment, 131
enrolment, 177
enterprises, 60
entitled, 138
entitlement, 2
environment, 11, 171
environmental hazards, 37
environmentalism, 63
equilibrium, 221
equitable, 58
equity, 69
Eritrea, 16
Eritrean, 197
errant, 175
erratic, 161
escape, 130
ethics, 93, 95, 154, 193
Ethiopia, 15, 22
ethnocentric, 9, 92
ethnography, 32
Euro-American, 228
Europe, 17, 161
European model, 84
European Union, 204
evaluation, 3, 8
evidence, 175
evidence-based, 235
evil spirits, 106
exclude, 13
exclusion, 58

ex-combatants, 123
exercise choice, 173
exigencies, 176
existence, 11
expansion, 177
expel, 201
experiences, 3
expertise, 80, 86
explicitly, 152
exploit, 170
exploitation, 6, 23
exploitative, 170
export, 182
extend, 172
extended kin group, 172
extra-parental, 171
extra-territorial legislation, 151
extremist, 201

F
facade, 19
facilitation, 62
factories, 152
failure, 3, 12, 168, 173, 183
fairness, 97
faith organisations, 8
familial death, 172
family, 6
family dynamics, 62
famine, 16
farming, 36
fearful, 106
feasibility, 125
feedback, 215
feminist, 72
fences, 201
fictionalised, 150
fields, 79, 180
fieldwork, 201
filial, 148, 157
finance, 8, 160, 196

findings, 173
firewood, 176
First World War, 189
fish stock, 172
flaws, 159
flexibility, 14
flourish, 175
food, 176
foothold, 179
force, 13, 31, 38, 180, 231
forced conscription, 16
forced marriage, 104
forced pregnancy, 104
forced separation, 2
forced wives, 13
forcibly, 173
foreign, 149
foreigners, 147
foreign folk devil, 149
formula, 11
fosterage, 171
Foucault, Michel, 4
Foundation for Women, 150
foundations, 6
fragility, 18
framework, 208
framing, 192
France, 151
freedom, 97
Free the Slaves (FTS), 31
Free Trade Area of the Americas, 69
Freirean pedagogy, 59
Frenchman, 151
fuel, 175
functionalist, 30
fundable, 72
fundamental, 218
fundamental rights, 6
funding, 5, 71, 200
futility, 216
future, 96

G

gambling, 158
gatekeeping, 137
Gay-Straight Alliances, 72
GDP, 182
gender, 42
gender bias, 62
generation, 174, 175
Geneva Declaration of the Rights of the Child, 85
Geneva Migration Group, 168
genital mutilation, 19
geographic distribution, 181
geography, 169
geopolitical, 190, 204
Germany, 151, 196
Ghana, 16, 31, 37
Ghanaian, 16
girls, 13
global, 172, 180, 184
Global Alliance against Child Labour, 31
Global Commission on International Migration, 167
globalised middle-class, 11
global leaders, 2
Global North, 8, 16
global poverty, 71
Global South, 8, 139
gold, 30, 36
good-natured, 215
governments, 178
grandparents, 173
greedy, 149
gross, 154
ground, 204
groupthink, 87
growth, 177
growth in love, 97
guardianship, 171
Guatemala, 16
guidance, 175

guilty, 151
guns, 134

H
hairdressing, 161
Hamas, 204
happiness, 92
hard life, 79
hardship, 36
harmony, 214
harvest failure, 172
hated, 176
haunted, 106
hawking, 40
hazardous work, 3
head-on, 217
head porterage, 40
healing, 202
healthcare, 2, 8, 43
healthy, 15, 169
heart, 217
heartless, 149
heavily structured, 171
hegemonic, 4, 159
herd, 90, 176
heritage, 69
heroic, 214
hierarchies, 92, 184
High-level Dialogue on International Migration and Development, 167
high-ranking, 215
hindrance, 171
hip hop activists, 72
historical, 11, 16, 169
historical material, 23
HIV, 149
holistic, 12
home(s), 16, 173
homelessness, 19
homogenous, 14
Honduras, 16
honourable, 159
hostility(ies), 126, 138, 192
hours, 84
households, 171–173
houses, 158
housing, 8
humane, 2
humanitarianism, 1, 2, 4, 58, 191
humanity, 154
human maturity, 10
human rights law, 94
Human Rights Watch, 122
human smuggling, 17
human trafficking, 17
hunger, 6
hurts, 77
husband, 173
hypocrisies, 217

I
ideology, 194
ignore, 94
illegal, 156
illegal immigrants, 154
illegal work, 3
illegitimacy, 106
illegitimises, 11
illiteracy, 6
illness, 173
illusion, 80
ILO Conventions 138 and 182, 5
ILO Forced Labour Convention (No. 29), 33
immaturity, 11, 39
impartiality, 18, 193, 199
imperative, 172
imperialism, 19
impinging, 171
implement, 17
impoverished rural areas, 91
impoverishment, 18

250 INDEX

impressionable, 169
imprisoned, 201
imprisonment, 151, 160, 201
improve, 12
impute, 170
inaction, 191
inadequate mechanism, 191
inalienable, 154
inappropriate, 14
income, 52
income-generating, 96
incomparably gentler, 201
incompetent, 38, 81
inconvenient, 153
independence, 168, 171, 195
Independent Inquiry into Child Sexual Abuse, 231
India, 5, 22
indigenous, 63, 153
indigenous systems, 13
individualising, 53
indivisible, 154
industrial, 84
industrialisation, 152
industrial undertaking, 85
industrious, 92
industriousness, 205
inequality, 16, 52
inevitably, 170
infantilisation, 11
infantilise, 122
infected, 162
infirm, 175
inflicting, 197
influence, 5, 19, 57, 219
informal, 155, 195
infrastructure, 86, 177, 226
inherently needy, 228
inhumane immigration detention, 2
inimical, 12
initiative, 195
injurious, 16, 79, 169

injustice, 217
innocence, 135
innovative, 3
insecure, 16, 135
institutionalisation, 153, 193
institutions, 20
insufficient, 218
insufficient Jordanian, 196
insults, 218
integrate, 13
integrity, 218
intention, 159, 170
interconnectedness, 176
intercultural, 69
interdependence, 69, 184
intergenerational, 22
intermediaries, 135
international, 77
International Bill of Rights, 82
international child protection regime, 1, 3
international child rights conventions, 3
International Criminal Court (ICC), 121
international development, 2, 12
internationalism, 23
International Labour Organisation (ILO), 1, 6
International Monetary Fund (IMF), 16
International Organization for Migration, 168
international standards, 94
interpersonal, 229
interpersonal violence, 2
interpretations, 5
interpretivist, 35
interrogating, 171
intervention, 5, 16, 94, 168, 216
intra-familial, 175
intra-household dynamics, 171

invest, 196
investment, 181
involuntary, 137, 168, 174
Iraq, 16, 18, 190, 192
irrational, 214
irreconcilable, 218
irresolvable, 159
irresponsible, 30
Israel, 18, 204
Israeli occupation, 18

J
jail, 154
Jewish, 201
Jordan, 18
journalistic, 149
judge, 170
judgement(s), 93, 173
jurisdiction, 139, 198
jurists, 131
justice, 13, 71
justifications, 171
juvenile, 72

K
Kenyasi, 36
killing, 190
kinship, 176
kinship-group, 174

L
labour, 7
labour-oriented, 81, 84
labour shortages, 172
lacunae, 148
lake, 172
land, 36
land appropriation, 207
language structure, 2
language teacher, 195

Latin America, 59
lawless, 38
laws, 168
lawyers, 64
lazy, 175
League of Nations, 85, 189
Leftist, 69
legal age, 151
legal imperative, 94
legislation, 2, 5, 8, 63, 220
leisure, 202
leverage, 71
liberal democracies, 17
liberation theology, 59
Liberia, 123, 126
life, 43
life phases, 11
life skills, 97
life strategies, 184
Lima, 63
limbo, 199
limitations, 217
limiting, 15
literacy, 97
literature, 161
livelihood, 85
lobby, 57
local, 180
localising, 53
lodging, 176
London, 205
longitudinal, 22
long-term, 91
Lord's Resistance Army (LRA), 13, 103
Lubanga, 131

M
mainstream, 135
makeshift, 155
male, 174

male combatants, 13
malevolence, 80, 216
Mali, 126
maligned, 14
malnutrition, 16
maltreatment, 39
mandates, 133
marginalised, 62, 140
market, 61, 196
marriage, 13, 172
material, 81, 174–176
maternal, 173
maturation, 12
maturity, 11, 175
maximum, 10
media, 137
medical, 162, 176
medical injury, 48
Mediterranean Sea, 17, 168
melodrama, 20
menial, 161
mental, 10, 97
mentally unsound, 106
messengers, 130
Middle East, 204
migrated unaccompanied, 91
migration, 37, 155, 169, 174
military, 37, 126, 190
militia, 132
Millennium Development Goals (MDGs), 8, 226
miners, 37
minimize, 204
minimum, 10
minimum age, 86
Minimum Age Convention, 1
mining, 30
ministry, 79
minors, 12
MINUSCA, 126
misanthropic, 22

mischievous, 135
misguide, 163
mission, 79
mistreating, 176
mixed, 231
mobile, 172
mobility, 15, 57
modalities, 4
model, 68
modernisation, 153
modern slavery, 19
modest, 199
molesting, 151
monetised, 152
money, 18, 158
monitor, 6
monitoring, 83
month, 173
MONUSCO, 126
moral, 93, 176
moral economy, 15, 171
moralistic, 12
morality, 93, 137, 152
moral judgements, 48
morals, 39
moral touchstone, 190
motherhood, 112
motivate, 216
motorbikes, 158
motorcycle mechanics, 80
movement, 57, 168, 169, 215
Movimiento Nacional de Niños, Niñas y Adolescentes Organizados del Perú (MNNATSOP), 22, 58, 63
Mozambique, 123, 133
multi-country, 12
multidisciplinary, 22
multinational corporations, 5
municipal boundaries, 201
murders, 108
mutuality, 174–176

N

Myanmar, 16
Myers, William, 20
mythology, 150

naked, 151
narrative, 137, 170
natal, 177
national, 4, 77
nationalism, 181, 208
nationality, 155
national laws, 94
nation-state, 168
natural disasters, 6
navigating, 217
needs-based, 194
negative, 109
neighbouring, 153
neo-abolitionist, 31, 34, 53
neo-colonialism, 159
(neo)liberal, 9
neoliberal capitalism, 69
neuroscience, 230
neutral(ity), 18, 71, 192, 206
Newmont Ghana Gold Limited (NGGL), 36
New Zealand, 151
NGOs, 5, 86
Niños y Adolescentes Trabajadores (NATs), 59
#niunamenos, 70
nodal, 219
non-combatant, 138
non-compliance, 17
non-discrimination, 2
non-dogmatic programming, 23
non-exploitative, 82
non-hierarchical relationship, 58
non-implementation, 17
non-judgemental connection, 218
non-kin, 173
non-nuclear, 171
non-nuclear nature, 171
non-state, 127
non-Western, 155
normalising, 30
normativity, 214
North America, 17
Norway, 151
notorious, 103
nuance, 50, 91
nurture, 176
nutrition, 8, 226

O

obligation, 190, 197
obstacle, 87
obstinacy, 214
obstructions, 202
occupation, 192
occupy, 201
offences, 80
offered, 196
official, 215
oil, 205
older sisters, 173
one-size-fits-all, 14
openness, 218
opposed, 174
oppressive, 2, 12, 30
opprobrium, 157
optimal, 215
Optional Protocol, 124
Optional Protocol on the Sale of Children, Child Prostitution and Child Pornography, 33
2000 Optional Protocol to the CRC on the Involvement of Children in Armed Conflict, 124
orange production, 182
organisations, 197
organised groups, 21, 152

254 INDEX

orphanages, 230
orphaned, 172
orthodox, 12
othering, 138
outcomes, 3, 77, 93
overloaded, 199
overnight, 156
overseas, 152, 208
oversimplify, 19
ownership, 34

P
paediatrics, 229
paid, 178
paid work, 7
Palermo Protocol, 7, 170. *See also* Protocol to Prevent, Suppress and Punish Trafficking in Persons, Especially Women and Children
Palestinians, 18, 192
palliative, 140
paradigms, 15, 168
paradox, 122
Paris, 30
Paris Principles, 124
participatory, 43, 219
passive, 190, 195
passport, 151
paternal, 173
paternalistic, 12
pathologise, 122, 139, 180
patrilineal, 104
patronising, 136
Pattaya, 153
pauperisation, 199
payment, 79, 84
peacebuilding, 133
peaceful, 135, 140
pejorative, 95
penalising, 122
penalties, 151

perfect victim, 148
permit, 201
perpetrators, 101, 136, 158
perpetuate, 231
persecution, 16
perspectives, 139
Peru, 22
pervasive, 93
pessimistic, 170
petition, 133, 151
petrol, 197
Phuket, 150, 153
physical, 10, 156
physical neglect, 176
physiological injury, 48
piece-work, 79
pimps, 150
pioneer, 169
pirates, 132
pity, 190
placement, 174
play, 79, 202
plots, 137
polemic, 18
police, 37
policies, 2, 169
policymakers, 98
policy-making, 12
political, 18, 171, 219
political activism, 72
political discussion, 62
political structure, 2
politicized, 58, 71
polluted, 106
poorly remunerated, 172
popular thinking, 95
population, 153, 172
pornography, 18
porters, 130
positive, 159
post-conflict, 102
Postscript, 22

INDEX   255

post-war, 121, 133
potential, 6
potential physical injury, 48
power, 5
powerful, 216
practical, 154
practical policy, 98
practices, 4
practitioners, 98
precarious, 177
precipitated, 172
preclude, 194
preferences, 173
pregnant, 173
premature, 138
premises, 214
press, 150
pressure, 136, 204
preventative, 82
pre-war, 135
primary, 174
principles, 2, 17
private rental, 196
privilege, 20, 181, 196
pro-active, 173
problematic, 214
proclamations, 61
procurers, 150, 160
productive, 215
professional code, 192
prognosis, 162
programmes, 58
progress, 93
progression, 171
progressive social change, 22
prohibit, 38, 170
promises, 3
promulgation, 190
proper guardians, 19
property, 36
property rights, 34
proscribing, 171

prosecution, 101, 136, 138, 151, 160
prostitution, 16, 42, 149
protagonismo, 65
protection, 2
protective domestic sphere, 170
protocols, 7
Protocol to Prevent, Suppress and Punish Trafficking in Persons, Especially Women and Children, 5
provide, 198
provisions, 17
psychology, 90, 160
psycho-social level, 92
pubescent, 172
punishment, 202
pupils, 79

Q
qualitative, 89
qualitative methods, 169
quality, 181
quarries, 178
Quechua, 63
queer, 72

R
racism, 72, 194
radical, 3, 216
radical actions, 3
raids, 150
Ranong, 154
raped, 149
ratification, 17
rationale, 171
rationalisations, 163
rationalised, 135
reactive, 173
realities, 171
reaped, 220
reciprocity, 161, 176

recovery, 125
recruitment, 121, 131, 133
Red Cross, 206
redemption, 149
redistribution, 52, 181
reducible, 11
reducing, 198
reflexivity, 214
refugee camps, 2
refugees, 2, 197
regime, 181, 198
regulations, 7, 69, 84
rehabilitation, 137, 149
reintegration, 13, 121
related, 175
relatives, 173, 196
relativism, 214
relief programmes, 96
religious, 194
relocation, 174, 175
remedy, 83
remittances, 157
remitted income, 172
remitting, 175
remitting income, 179
removing, 81
remuneration, 42, 89
reparations, 53
repayment, 157
reports, 206
representatives, 22
reputational consequences, 192
requisite, 196
re-recruitment, 121
rescue, 18, 149
research, 169
reservations, 17
resettlement, 196
residency permits, 196
resolution, 139
resonates, 193
resource, 18, 137, 173, 179

resource extraction, 68
respect, 97
respectable, 161
respondents, 172
responsibilities, 11
restorative, 18
restrictive, 89
retreat, 23
return, 173
returnee, 174, 179
reuniting, 116
revenge, 136
review, 196
rhetoric, 159
riches, 178
rights, 197
rights activists, 5
rights-based, 194
rights-bearers, 10
right-wing populism, 208
risk, 72, 169
robotics, 23
Romania, 230
romantic, 9, 85
Rome Statute, 124
roof, 178
roofing, 179
root, 176
root causes, 194
rubbish, 156
rupture, 176
rural, 181

S
safeguard, 6, 8, 43
Sahara Desert, 17
sale of children, 18
sanction, 96, 157
sanctuary, 196
saved, 147
savings expire, 196

saviourism, 19
scale, 219
scavenging, 156
scholars, 124, 170
scholarships, 162
schooling, 46, 175
scientific discourses, 4
scouts, 130
scrap, 155
sea, 85
search, 172
secondary, 177
Secretary General, 204
sectarian, 196
secure, 135
securitisation, 122, 133, 140
security, 135, 136
Security Council Resolutions, 126
seekers, 196
self-awareness, 97
self-employed, 41
self-esteem, 91, 92
self-policing, 192
self-regulation, 97
self-sufficiency, 175
sensationalist, 19
senseless, 108
sensitise, 168
sensitive, 38
sensitivity, 13
sentence, 151
service expansion, 177
servicing, 149
severing familial ties, 170
sex, 10
sex industry, 148
sexual acts, 157
sexually, 156
sexual slavery, 20
sexual slaves, 31
sexual violence, 39
sexy, 222

shape, 174
shock, 215
shortcomings, 192
side-lined, 153
Sierra Leone, 123
silence, 206
simplistic, 216
simplistic victim-perpetrators, 163
skepticism, 138
skills, 175
skills training, 43
slave owners, 34
1926 Slavery Convention, 33
sleep, 79
slums, 153
smaller-scale, 181
small-scale gold mining, 36
smugglers, 17
social, 175
social age, 12
social change, 58
socialisation, 64, 175
socially constructed, 91
socially marginalised, 152
social movements, 5
social norms, 10
social policy, 1, 2
social problems, 1
social protection, 180
social scientists, 87
social structures, 97
social work, 2
societies, 116
socio-cultural, 6
socio-culturally mediated, 171
socio-economic, 36, 116
sociology, 64, 169
socio-political, 4, 194
soldiers, 122
solidarity, 13, 18, 97, 138, 222
Somalia, 8, 197
south, 172

258 INDEX

South Africa, 139
South Sudan, 126
spatial, 15, 170
specialised, 196
special needs, 138
special treatment, 138
spies, 130
spirituality, 41
sponsor, 215
standards, 81
starkest, 220
state, 10
States Parties, 94
stigma, 13, 115
stigmatisation, 12, 92, 106
Stockholm Declaration and Agenda for Action, 153
stone-crushing, 180
strategy, 122, 153, 219
street vendors, 60
structural adjustment, 16
structural forces, 180
structural violence, 2
stubborn, 108
studious, 175
stupid, 108
subject, 190
sub-region, 103
sub-Saharan Africa, 8, 122
subsidies, 79, 183
subsistence, 36, 172
Sudan, 16
Sudan-Darfur, 126
Sudanese, 197
suffer, 201
suffering, 137, 179, 194
summer, 179
superiority, 81
superstition, 41
1957 Supplementary Convention on the Abolition of Slavery, the Slave Trade, and Institutions and Practices Similar to Slavery, 33
supply chains, 95
supplying, 175
supportive, 184
surreptitiously, 217
survey, 192
survival, 6, 135, 217
survival dependent, 172
suspicion, 201
suspicious, 214
sustain, 80, 196
sustainability, 135, 221
Sustainable Development Goals (SDGs), 7
sustenance, 96
Sweden, 151, 196
sympathies, 160
Syria, 16, 200
systematizing, 30
systemic failures, 218

T

taboo, 42
target, 2, 201
taxed, 152
tea, 78
teachers, 64
technical solutions, 194
technology, 23
teenagerhood, 116
teenagers, 173
telecommunications, 36
television, 158
tend, 175
terror, 104
terrorised, 149
Thai, 149
Thailand, 148
The Child Soldiers World Index, 122
The Hague, 122

theoretical material, 23
third-party, 41
third wave, 72
threats, 199
Time to Talk, 12
tokenistic, 19
top-down dictates, 19
torture, 202
torturous, 2
tourist sending countries, 151
trade-offs, 122
Trades unions, 90
traditionally, 12
traffic fumes, 91
trafficking, 1, 17
training, 15
transformation, 169
transformative, 69, 177, 218
transient, 153
transmitted diseases, 162
traumatised, 138, 149
Treaty of Versailles, 6
trends, 173
trickery, 31, 38
tropes, 135
trust, 218
truth, 4
turmoil, 198

U
Uganda, 101
Ugandan civil war, 13
UK, 151
ultra-orthodox Jews, 201
unacceptable work, 95
unambiguous emotional, 176
UNAMID, 126
uncertainty, 169
unconditional, 219
uncontrollable, 108
1989 UN Convention on the Rights of the Child (UNCRC), 189

UN Convention on Transnational Organised Crime, 170
UN Convention Relating to the Status of Refugees, 196
UN Conventions, 1
UN Declaration of the Rights of the Child, 189
underage, 133, 154
underground, 45
underlying, 16
undermining, 190
Understanding Children's Work (UCW), 89
undesirables, 152, 159
undignified, 52
undocumented labourers, 153
uneasy, 163
unemployment, 52
unenforceable, 123
unethical, 94
unexpected hardship, 173
unfree, 41
UN General Assembly, 6
UN Global Compact for Migration, 168
unhappy, 173
UNICEF, 6, 80
unifying clans, 109
unions, 22
United Nations, 124
United Nations Convention on the Rights of the Child, 1
United States, 72, 196
universal, 71
universalise, 214
universalistic, 195
universal primary school, 8
unjust, 16
unmarried, 231
UNMIL, 126
UNMISS, 126
UNOCI, 126

unorthodox, 115
unpopular, 162
unprotected, 135
unquestionably, 12
unrealisable, 159
unsafe, 106
UN Security Council, 126
unsound mind, 108
unsuitable, 14, 170
un-willed, 169, 184
upper age, 10
urbanisation, 152

V

vacuum, 163
validity, 174
valid knowledge, 4
veterans, 133
victim, 158, 168
victimisation, 39, 137
victory, 79
Vietnam, 22
vignettes, 171, 180
village, 168
villagers, 172
violations, 18, 95, 168, 205, 207
violence, 8, 38
violent, 138
vocal, 64
voices, 47
volatile, 138
volunteering, 195
volunteers, 136
vulnerability, 15, 115, 122

W

wage migration, 152
wages, 84
Walk Free Foundation, 31
war-making, 122, 138

Washington, 205
water, 175
weak, 191
weaknesses, 3, 20
wealth, 5
wealthy, 196
weapon, 134
weaponry, 190
weather, 226
wedlock, 109
weeds, 180
weight, 192
well-being, 3
West, 161
West Bank, 201
Western, 205
Western societies, 5
wicked, 152
widespread assumption, 169
widow, 176
wilfully, 156
women, 37
women's groups, 66
work, 2
work-free, 15
working, 173
working children, 21
working-class, 59
working conditions, 84
workload, 176
workshops, 62
World Bank, 36
World Congress against the
    Commercial Sexual Exploitation,
    153
world leaders, 3
Worst Forms of Child Labour
    Convention, 1
Worst Forms of Child Labour
    Recommendation (No. 190), 7
wounding, 190

wrong, 163
WWII, 85

Y
Yemen, 190
Yerbateros, 62
young, 169

Young Lives, 12
young persons, 7
youngsters, 178

Z
Zimbabwe, 78
Zou Department, 169

Printed in the United States
by Baker & Taylor Publisher Services